228

Standard & Poor's 401(k) Planning Guide

Standard & Poor's 401(k) Planning Guide

Alan J. Miller

McGraw-Hill, Inc.
New York   San Francisco   Washington, D.C.   Auckland   Bogotá
Caracas   Lisbon   London   Madrid   Mexico City   Milan
Montreal   New Delhi   San Juan   Singapore
Sydney   Tokyo   Toronto

Library of Congress Cataloging-in-Publication Data

Miller, Alan J. (Alan Jay).
    Standard & Poor's 401(k) planning guide : every employee's guide
to making 401(k) decisions / Alan J. Miller.
        p.   cm.
    Includes index.
    ISBN 0-07-042196-X—ISBN 0-07-042197-8 (pbk.)
    1. 401(k) plans.   2. Pension trusts—United States—Investments.
3. Old age pensions—United States—Finance.   4. Individual
retirement accounts—United States—Finance.   I. Title.   II. Title:
Standard and Poor's 401(k) planning guide.
HD7105.45.U6M55   1995
332.024'01—dc20   94-40808
                                                        CIP

1 2 3 4 5 6 7 8 9 0   DOC/DOC   9 0 9 8 7 6 5 4 (PBK)
1 2 3 4 5 6 7 8 9 0   DOC/DOC   9 0 9 8 7 6 5 4 (HC)

ISBN 0-07-042197-8 (PBK)
ISBN 0-07-042196-X (HC)

*The sponsoring editor for this book was David Conti, the editing supervisor was
Virginia Carroll, and the production supervisor was Pamela Pelton. It was set in
Palatino by North Market Street Graphics.*

Printed and bound by R. R. Donnelley & Sons Company.

McGraw-Hill books are available at special quantity discounts to use as
premiums and sales promotions, or for use in corporate training programs.
For more information, please write to the Director of Special Sales,
McGraw-Hill, Inc., 11 West 19th Street, New York, NY 10011. Or contact
your local bookstore.

This publication is designed to provide accurate and authoritative information in regard to the subject matter covered. It is sold with the understanding that the publisher is not engaged in rendering legal, accounting, or
other professional service. If legal advice or other expert assistance is
required, the services of a competent professional person should be sought.
        *—from a declaration of principles jointly adopted by a committee
           of the American Bar Association and a committee of publishers*

Contents

Introduction

401(k) plans are the fastest growing employee benefit in the United States. At last count, approximately 17,500,000 workers were participating in some 210,000 plans—more than a sixfold increase over the level of participation less than a decade ago. According to Access Research, assets in these plans totaled $475 billion at the end of 1993, up from $105 billion in 1985.

Approximately $50 billion is contributed to 401(k) plans annually with assets in such plans accounting for between one-fourth and one-third of total personal savings. Indeed, the 401(k) plans of many families represent more than half of their total net worth.

More than 95 percent of large employers currently offer 401(k) plans to their employees, and approximately 72 percent of those eligible to participate do so (according to Hewitt Associates, an employee benefits consulting firm). Moreover, it is not only highly paid workers who participate in 401(k) plans: half of all families with annual incomes below $10,000 also enroll when offered the opportunity.

With so large a percentage of national personal savings committed to 401(k) plans, with so many companies providing them, and with so many workers participating, one might expect the average participant in a 401(k) plan to be knowledgeable about this subject. And yet, quite the opposite is true. According to a survey of 401(k) plan participants conducted by New York Life Insurance Company and the Gallup Organization, nearly two-thirds of all participants don't understand what is meant by *tax-deferred saving,* a concept intrinsic to retirement planning and 401(k) plans. About three-quarters don't know what *compounding* means,

1

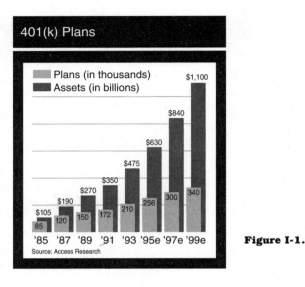

Figure I-1.

although that is equally important in understanding retirement planning and 401(k) plans. In a nationwide survey of 1000 401(k) plan participants, The Frank Russell Company discovered that the average assets in those participants' 401(k) plans had been allocated to produce a real rate of return of only 3 percent, although a reasonably balanced asset mix with limited risk would have produced a return of as much as 5 percent.

We are writing this book to provide you with a basic understanding of how 401(k) plans fit into your retirement planning. To that end, we will discuss concepts such as life-cycle investing, the relationships between risk and reward, the magic of compounding, the benefits of tax deferrability, asset allocation, security selection, and performance measurement. We will explain not only what 401(k) plans are and how they differ from other retirement plans but also what you should know about them in order to get the most out of any plan in which you already are (or are considering) investing.

But are you the sort of person who might really benefit from reading this book? You certainly are if you fall into any of the following three categories:

1. *If you're already in a 401(k) plan.*   If you already are a participant in a 401(k) plan (or a similar 403(b) plan) but are concerned that you might not be getting the most out of it, then this book has been written with you in mind.

    If you're not sure, for instance, whether you allocated the funds in your 401(k) account most appropriately in stocks, bonds, cash equivalents, GICs, or other alternatives, we'll provide you with the guidance you'll need to make that decision intelligently. Or if you are confident that your funds have been allocated appropriately but don't know whether those responsible for managing your funds have been doing a good job, we'll show you how to determine that too.

Maybe you've been considering switching some of your funds from a more aggressive to a more conservative asset class because you're now approaching retirement age. Or maybe you've been thinking about doing just the opposite because you're convinced that the stock market is on the verge of taking off. But do making changes of either sort make sense? Those also are among the issues we'll discuss.

Or perhaps you want to find out if there's some way you could get money out of your 401(k) plan even before retirement in order to finance the purchase of a house or pay medical bills or send your daughter to law school. Or maybe your retirement date is imminent and you're not sure what to do with the money in your plan when that day comes.

Or maybe . . . .

But all this presupposes that you're *already* a plan participant. Maybe you're not, and are *considering* becoming one. In that event, this book also would be of use to you.

2. *If you're thinking about joining a 401(k) plan.* You may not be a participant in a 401(k) plan because you are not yet eligible to join one or because your company only began offering one recently. You may be thinking of enrolling but may be reluctant to cut your take-home pay in order to participate. This book will help you to make that decision.

Perhaps your company has been offering a 401(k) plan and you've been eligible to enroll for a while, but until recently you didn't think it made sense for you personally. You may have thought that you were too young to be planning for your retirement. Or you may have felt that you weren't earning enough to afford it. But now that you're getting older, or you just got that raise, or your company modified its plan to include a "match" of the money you invest, you ought to take a fresh look.

3. *If your company doesn't offer a 401(k) plan.* You may not be a participant in your company's 401(k) plan simply because your company has not offered you one. But you may have heard a lot about them and you may have been wondering whether you should mention 401(k) plans to your boss. You may remember having read that a 401(k) plan could be a good deal for employers and employees alike, so maybe your boss would go for it and it would benefit you too. Who knows: you might have discovered a rare free lunch for both of you.

Indeed, maybe you're even on your company's or union's negotiating committee. If so, you may want to bring this up at your next meeting.

Of course, even if you don't fall into any one of these three categories, this book still could be very valuable to you. If you are, for instance, a business or economics student specializing in the area of pension plan investment, this book may merit a place in your permanent reference library. And if you're a plan sponsor or an employer considering becoming a plan sponsor, this book could provide much of the information you'll need to make reasoned decisions in this area.

Before addressing what you may learn from this book, consider the following expressions you may have heard:

"Money is the root of all evil."

"Consistency is the hobgoblin of little minds."

"The only thing worse than dying young is outliving your money."

"Don't expect to rely on social security benefits in your old age; it won't be enough."

"It's never too early to plan for your retirement."

Platitudes? Absolutely. Cliches? Without a doubt. Truisms? Well . . . only partially.

What the *New Testament* actually says is not that "Money is the root of all evil," but, rather, that "*The love of* money is the root of all evil," which is quite a different sentiment.

And Emerson didn't just say that "Consistency is the hobgoblin of little minds." Rather, he said "*A foolish* consistency is the hobgoblin of little minds," which again is something quite different from the truncated version.

Similarly, expanded versions of the three "retirement" maxims we quoted might better read as follows:

"The only thing worse than dying young is outliving your money, *but with a little common sense, self-discipline, and advance planning, that needn't happen to you.*"

"You won't be able to rely on social security benefits to provide you with a comfortable retirement, *but there's no reason you should have to.*"

"It's never too early to plan for your retirement, *but if you haven't started yet and you're still gainfully employed, it's probably not too late, either.*"

And that brings us back to the basic purpose of this book: to teach you enough about retirement planning and 401(k) plans to help ensure that you *won't* outlive your money, that you *won't* have to depend on social security, and that you *will* be able to make the most of your financial planning opportunities.

To accomplish that goal, we hope to provide you with practical financial and retirement planning guidance to enable you to live better in your golden years without making undue sacrifices or accepting excessive risks in the years preceding your retirement. In doing so, we will discuss the similarities and differences between financial planning and retirement planning. We will help you to learn how to budget your expenses, both before and after retirement. We'll show you how to forecast your future needs. We'll provide you with a minicourse in personal finance. We'll discuss the impact of inflation on retirement planning. And we'll explain the roles (and limitations) of social security, traditional pension and profit-sharing plans, and different asset classes in retirement planning programs.

Most importantly, however, we will provide you with the necessary information about 401(k) plans to make your plan the centerpiece of your own retirement plan since for many people, 401(k) plans can provide the basic framework upon which to structure a complete and effective retirement program. To that end, we will address the following very specific issues:

- What are financial planning and retirement planning all about? What do they have in common and how do they differ? And how do 401(k) plans fit into both kinds of programs?

- What actually are 401(k) plans? How do they differ from other retirement programs such as IRAs, Keoghs, SEPs, and traditional company pension and profit-sharing plans?

- What are the advantages inherent in 401(k) plan investing? What are the disadvantages?

- If you are like most Americans, why should you probably invest in the 401(k) plan offered you at work?

- If you do decide to invest in a 401(k) plan, how much would you be allowed to contribute? Are there any circumstances under which you could contribute any more or less than that and, if you could, should you?

- What would it mean to you if your employer offered to make matching contributions to your plan?

- Once money that you contributed yourself to a 401(k) plan is in your account, can you be assured of eventually getting it all back, no matter what? Must you wait until you retire to get it or is there any way to get it out earlier if you really need it? If you can get it out earlier, would you lose anything by doing so?

- What about funds in your account that your employer may have contributed in matching grants? Would the same rules apply to those funds or is there any way your boss could take that money back? What does it mean if you're told that you have to get "vested" first?

- What, if any, are your employer's responsibilities and obligations to you in regard to your 401(k) plan? What kind of information do you have a right to expect your employer to communicate to you regarding the plan?

- Who bears the risk of a possible decline in the value of your account: you, your employer, your investment managers, some government agency, or someone else entirely? If the value of the assets in your 401(k) account decline because of adverse market conditions or poor investment decisions, can you sue your boss or will the government make up the difference or are you just plain out of luck?

- If you're given a number of different choices as to how you can invest your 401(k) funds, how can you decide what to do? When should you invest in stocks, when in bonds, and when in GICs? Or should you diversify your investments by putting a little in each asset class? If so, how should you decide how much to put in each?

- When should you consider altering the investment choices you originally made? Should you only make such shifts when your own personal circumstances dictate it? Should you also consider making shifts in light of changing market conditions? Or should you just continually and automatically move your assets to those managers who achieved the highest recent absolute performances?

- How can you tell whether the managers entrusted with your funds are doing a good job? Would calculating their absolute performance returns be sufficient? Or should you make some adjustment for the different levels of risk they incurred?

- Finally, if you're close to retirement, what should you arrange to do with your 401(k) plan assets after you stop working? Can you just leave them where they are and draw them down as needed? Should you withdraw them all at once in their entirety? Or should you roll them over into another tax-advantaged account?

These, then, are some of the major issues relating to 401(k) plans and their place in overall financial and retirement planning that we will be discussing. First, let's consider what we mean by financial and retirement planning.

1
Financial Planning, Retirement Planning, and Inflation

The Concept of Financial Planning

In the very broadest sense, *financial planning* means the consideration and evaluation of the consequences of financial choices on your overall life and the rearrangement of your financial affairs in light of those considerations. In that sense, it includes the myriad of financial and economic decisions that confront you every day, ranging from purchasing insurance to refinancing a home mortgage, from deciding whether or not to change jobs to deciding whether to lease or buy a new automobile, and from budgeting for the cost of a new birth or adoption to arranging for the financing of your children's college educations.

In a narrower (but much more common) sense, however, financial planning refers strictly to the design of an investment program for the purpose of achieving one or more specific financial goals, such as the creation of a college fund for children or grandchildren, the purchase of a home, or the establishment of a retirement nest egg. In other words, it refers to the structuring of a plan to enable you to earn enough from your investments to create a fund sufficient to fulfill many, if not all, of your financial goals.

The Concept of Retirement Planning

The concept of financial planning subsumes retirement planning. By that we mean that financial planning may be engaged in for a number of reasons, only one of which may be to accumulate sufficient assets to provide for one's own retirement. Specifically *retirement planning* is financial planning to provide adequate funds to live comfortably in one's retirement years.

In general, it makes sense to establish different funds for different purposes, i.e., one for the accumulation of capital with which to buy a house (a home purchase fund), a second for the accumulation of assets with which to provide for your children's schooling (an education fund), and a third to provide for your own retirement (a retirement fund). The reason that you are better off doing that than simply establishing one fund for multiple purposes is that different objectives imply different time horizons and different tax considerations that imply different priorities regarding safety, liquidity, inflation protection, and diversification. And that, in turn, suggests the desirability of employing a variety of different asset classes (or the same asset classes but in different combinations) in different funds.

You may, for instance, expect that you will need to withdraw the money in a home purchase fund all at once within three to five years in order to make a down payment on a house, but the precise timing of that withdrawal may be very uncertain, depending on when you actually find your dream house or when your first child is born. Consequently, if you already have most of the money you think you'll need for a down payment or if you expect to earn that money over the next few years, you might invest the assets of this fund primarily in highly liquid short-term fixed income securities. By doing so, you could feel confident that the money you would require would be there when you needed it, even if the economy was in recession or the stock market was in decline at the time.

To be sure, in emphasizing liquidity and safety above all else, you might have had to sacrifice some inflation protection and potential return, but it would have been worth it if you planned to buy a home in only a few years and didn't want to take the chance of coming up empty-handed. And since your time horizon was relatively short (only three to five years), inflation protection would not have been a paramount concern.

The money in an education fund, however, may not be needed for 15 or 20 years, only then to be withdrawn over a fixed period of, for instance, 4 or 6 years, with the specific years in which the withdrawals would be made well known in advance. An education fund would have less need for liquidity and a greater requirement for inflation protection. Thus, it might better be invested in a combination of common stocks and zero coupon bonds with laddered maturities, which would ensure that some monies would become available over a predetermined number of years (from the zero coupon bonds), while some inflation protection against the rising costs of college tuition would be provided by the common stock component.

Finally, money in a retirement fund may not be needed for 30 or 40 years or even longer, only then to be withdrawn over an extended but indefinite period up to a possible 20 years or more. For such a fund, *inflation protection would be a very high priority and liquidity a minor concern,* at least in the early years (which would be just the opposite of the home purchase fund), suggesting the relative attractiveness of common stocks as funding vehicles. Over the years, you might expect to change the asset mix in this fund, reducing equity exposure and increasing the percentage of assets committed to fixed income securities, as the passage of time acted to foreshorten your investment horizon.

Under the tax laws, retirement funds also can be structured with important advantages not generally available to such other pools of capital as home purchase funds or education funds. This would be another valid reason to separate the assets in a retirement fund from the monies in other funds.

Inflation Considerations in Retirement Planning

One of the major factors affecting retirement planning is inflation, both *before* retirement and, *even more importantly, during* the retirement years themselves. Here's why.

1. The Preretirement Effect of Inflation

As a rough rule of thumb, you might reasonably expect to spend in each of your retirement years about 70 to 80 percent as much as you would have spent annually if you still had been employed. The precise amount will vary from individual to individual, of course, depending on your health and the extent to which you may choose to modify your lifestyle, but the 70 to 80 percent rule has proved to be a workable one. If you would like to attempt to come up with more precise figures for yourself, however, you can do so by using the budget worksheet in Table 1-1.

Table 1-1. Calculating Your Living Costs

	Current monthly living costs	Estimated monthly living costs at retirement	Inflation-adjusted estimated monthly living costs at retirement
Housing			
Utilities			
Maintenance			
Food			
Clothing			
Consumer goods			
Entertainment			
Transportation			
Laundry			
Medical care			
Insurance			
Reading material			
Debt payments			
Vacation, travel			
Continuing education			
Personal care			
Contributions			
Hobbies, sports			
Taxes			
Investments			
Savings			
Miscellaneous			
Total monthly			
Total annually			

Completing this worksheet will not be an easy task, and the further away you are from retirement, the more difficult it will be for two reasons. First, the younger you are, the harder it will be for you to estimate your future needs. While you realize, of course, that you are bound to change in the years ahead, you can't really know what form those changes will take. Will you develop new interests or give up some that you now have? Will your health deteriorate? Will you decide to sell your house and move into a smaller apartment? Or will you move into a new community altogether where expenses are much higher (or much lower) than those where you presently reside? Will you choose to travel extensively or not to travel at all? Only time will tell.

Second, even if you had all those answers, what will all of that cost two or three decades from now? Will the inflation rate average 2, 4, or 6 percent annually between now and then? If you're 45 years old now, 20 years away from retirement, and expect to spend $30,000 (in today's dollars) in your first year of retirement, the difference between a 2 percent inflation rate and a 4 percent rate will mean the difference between spending $44,578 and spending $65,736. And at a 6 percent inflation rate, you'd be spending $96,216 in that first retirement year alone.

If you do attempt to forecast your future retirement needs with some precision, however, rather than simply relying on the 70 to 80 percent guideline, you should do it in three stages (corresponding to the last three columns in Table 1-1).

First, determine what you're spending today. Here you'll find that some of the numbers are quite precise, others are reasonable averages, and still others are only rough approximations. For instance, you probably know your monthly rent or maintenance costs or mortgage payments to the penny, and you have a good idea of the average amount of your monthly telephone or electric bills. But when it comes to most other things, such as medical care, entertainment, contributions, or clothing, the chances are that what you spend in any specific month is not necessarily typical of what you spend on average over an entire year. So for these things, you'll have to go back over the past year, add up everything you spent, and divide by 12.

Once you've done that, make sure that the expenses you incurred during the past year really were typical of what you're currently spending. For instance, if you just enrolled in two adult education courses at the local college and you expect to continue your education by taking more courses in the future but you took no courses last year, then you'll have to increase your "Continuing education" expense estimate to reflect that change. Or, if you suffered a serious illness and incurred very substantial medical expenses last year, but you have fully recovered so that that expense is now behind you and is unlikely to recur, you should reduce your "Medical care" estimate accordingly.

Now post those numbers in the column headed "Current monthly living costs" and you'll see what you presently are spending (which, you may discover, really is significantly more, or less, than you thought). That completes step 1. But that's the easy part.

Next try to estimate what you'll be spending when you begin your retirement, assuming no inflation between now and then. For instance, if you expect to continue to reside where you presently are living, you might assume no change in your cost of housing, maintenance, or utilities. On the other hand, if you plan to relocate, you might project a very large change up or down.

You also might assume declines in your taxes, transportation, laundry, and clothing expenses, once you stop working, since your income will be reduced and you no longer will have to commute to and from work daily in appropriate work attire. On the other hand, you probably should assume increases in your medical care and insurance expenses, which are an almost inevitable consequence of the aging process. Insofar as most of your other expenses (such as entertainment, vacation, travel, continuing education, reading material, hobbies, and sports) are concerned, only you will be able to decide whether they're likely to go up or down. That will depend on the particular lifestyle you expect to lead in retirement. Post these numbers in the next column headed "Estimated monthly living costs at retirement." That completes step 2.

Step 3 is adjusting for inflation. Historically, the average annual inflation rate in the postwar United States has been between 4 and 5 percent, although in some years, it's been close to zero and in others it's been in double digits. Since no one knows for sure what it will be over the next several decades, you might just want to assume that it will average 4 or 5 percent during the years between now and your own retirement.

If you're really optimistic, however, that we are at last coming to grips with our budget deficit and national health-care problems, you might want to use a lower figure of, say, 3 percent. Or if you are pessimistic that the quadrupling of the national debt during the Reagan-Bush years, double-digit inflation in medical care costs, and a reintroduction of tax and spend policies under the Clinton administration are harbingers of higher future inflation rates, you might want to use a more pessimistic assumption of, say, 6 percent. In either case, it is a good idea to look at a range of assumptions in order to gauge your sensitivity to inflation.

In the end, of course, you can use any number you like, whether lower than 3 percent or higher than 6 percent or anywhere in between, say 3.8, 4.5, or 5.3 percent, and you may compound that rate over the precise number of years remaining between now and your own retirement, whether 17, 22, 33, or whatever. That would give you the precise inflation adjustment factor to use in your own specific case, but it would involve some detailed calculations on your part.

If you're willing to settle for some reasonable approximations instead, you can use (or modify) the factors in Table 1-2, which we have calculated on the basis of assumed inflation rates of 3, 4, 5, 6, and 7 percent for periods of 5, 10, 15, 20, 25, 30, 35, 40, and 45 years. Simply select the rows in which the numbers of years come closest to the actual number of years between now and your own retirement and the columns in which the assumed inflation rates come closest to your own estimate. Then select a factor that appears reasonable within the range where those rows and columns intersect.

For instance, suppose you are 50 years old, you expect to retire in 15 years at age 65, and your best guess is that the inflation rate will average 4 percent annually over the next 15 years. Where the "15 Years to retirement" row and the "4% Inflation rate" column intersect, the inflation adjustment factor is 1.80 so that's the number you would use.

If, however, you think that the inflation rate will average 5 percent, the inflation adjustment factor would be 2.08 (where the "15 Years to retirement" row and the "5% Inflation rate" column intersect). And if you think the inflation rate will be 4.5 percent, you would split the difference and use an inflation adjustment factor midway between the two—1.94.

Similarly, if you are 55 years old, expect to retire in 10 years, and think that the inflation rate will average 4 percent over the next 10 years, you'd use the inflation adjustment factor of 1.48 (which appears where the "10 Years to retirement" row and the "4% Inflation rate" column intersect). If you think the inflation rate will average 5 percent, you would use the inflation adjustment factor of 1.63. And if you think the inflation rate will be 4.5 percent, you would split the difference between 1.48 and 1.63 and use a factor of 1.55.

Finally, if you are 52 years old with 13 years to work before you retire, and you think the inflation rate will average 4 percent, you'd use an inflation adjustment factor of about 1.65 (approximately midway between the 1.48 and the 1.80 which appear where the "10 Years to retirement" and the "15 Years to retirement" rows intersect the "4% Inflation rate" column). If

Table 1-2. Expense Adjustment Factors for the First Year of Retirement

Years to retirement	Inflation rate				
	3%	4%	5%	6%	7%
5	1.16	1.22	1.28	1.34	1.40
10	1.34	1.48	1.63	1.79	1.97
15	1.56	1.80	2.08	2.40	2.76
20	1.81	2.19	2.65	3.21	3.87
25	2.09	2.67	3.39	4.29	5.43
30	2.43	3.24	4.32	5.74	7.61
35	2.81	3.95	5.52	7.69	10.68
40	3.26	4.80	7.04	10.29	14.97
45	3.78	5.84	8.99	13.76	21.00

you think the inflation rate will average 5 percent, you would use an inflation adjustment factor of about 1.85 (approximately midway between the
1.63 and the 2.08 which appear where the "10 Years to retirement" and the
"15 Years to retirement" rows intersect the "5% Inflation rate" column).
And if you think the inflation rate will average 4.5 percent, you would use
an inflation adjustment factor of about 1.70, which is midway between the
1.55 you would have used at 4 percent and the 1.85 you would have used
at 5 percent.

Now multiply the numbers that you entered in the column headed
"Estimated monthly living costs at retirement" in Table 1-1 by the "inflation adjustment factor" you've computed and post those adjusted figures
in the last column headed "Inflation-adjusted estimated monthly living
costs at retirement." This is what you might reasonably expect to spend in
just your *first* year of retirement.

Let's see how this all might work out in just a few hypothetical cases.
Suppose you are now spending $40,000 annually but you estimate that
you can reduce that to $30,000 (in today's dollars) in your first year of
retirement. Assuming that you now are between 20 and 60 years of age
and that average annual inflation between now and your retirement will
be between 4 and 5 percent, here's what you actually might expect to
spend in your first year of retirement. See Table 1-3.

If you're 50 years old today and the annual inflation rate averages 4 percent between now and your retirement 15 years hence, you may expect to
spend $54,000 in your first year of retirement. If you're now 45 and the
annual inflation rate averages 5 percent between now and your retirement
20 years from now, you can anticipate spending $79,500 in that first year.

Table 1-3. Projected Annual Expenses ($) Assuming 4% and 5%
Inflation Rates

			4% Inflation rate		5% Inflation rate	
Age	Years to retirement	Current expenses	Adjustment factor	Retirement expenses	Adjustment factor	Retirement expenses
20	45	$30,000	5.84	$175,200	8.99	$269,700
25	40	30,000	4.80	144,000	7.04	211,200
30	35	30,000	3.95	118,500	5.52	165,600
35	30	30,000	3.24	97,200	4.32	129,600
40	25	30,000	2.67	80,100	3.39	101,700
45	20	30,000	2.19	65,700	2.65	79,500
50	15	30,000	1.80	54,000	2.08	62,400
55	10	30,000	1.48	44,400	1.63	48,900
60	5	30,000	1.22	36,600	1.28	38,400

And if you're now 35 and the inflation rate averages 5 percent annually between now and your retirement 30 years hence, you may expect to spend $129,600 in that first year. And that's just the *first year!*

2. The Impact of Inflation on Fixed Retirement Incomes

We have seen how great an impact inflation can have on living expenses in the years before retirement. If, for example, you estimate that it will cost you $30,000 (in today's dollars) to maintain the standard of living you desire in your first year of retirement, if your retirement is 10 years away, and if the average annual rate of inflation between now and then will be 4 percent, then the amount you will need in nominal dollars in just that first year alone will be $44,400. If retirement is 20 years away and the average annual inflation rate turns out to be 5 percent, the amount you will need will be $79,500.

But that's only the beginning. Inflation doesn't stop the moment you retire and, in fact, in some ways it actually worsens. No, the overall price level doesn't somehow know when you stop working and begin to rise at a more rapid rate than it had. But some components of your living expenses, such as medical care and insurance, have tended to rise faster than the overall price level, and those sectors are likely to become an increasing percentage of your total costs as you age.

In Table 1-4, we calculated how your living costs may rise between now and retirement and on into the years following retirement, assuming that (1) you presently are "spending your age," i.e., you are spending $1000 for each year of your age, (2) in your first year of retirement, you will reduce your expenses to 75 percent of whatever you had spent in your last year of employment, and (3) inflation will average 4 percent annually over the entire period. In Table 1-5, we assumed a 4 percent average annual inflation rate prior to your retirement and a 5 percent average annual rate therafter.

Inflation during your working years is a concern, but not an overriding one, since the chances are that your income will increase more or less in line with the inflation rate. If prices are rising at 4 percent annually, you probably are receiving annual salary increases of at least that much (at least until you're close to retirement).

To be sure, it may be momentarily unsettling to realize that if you're now 35 years old and *spending* $35,000 annually and if the inflation rate averages 4 percent annually over the next 30 years, you'll be spending $113,400 in the last year of your employment without having raised your standard of living at all. But by the same token, if you're now *earning* $40,000 per year and your salary also grows by just 4 percent a year, your income in that final year will be $129,600.

Table 1-4. Estimated Annual Living Expenses ($) at Five-Year Intervals During Retirement (Assuming 4% Annual Inflation)

	Age								
	20	25	30	35	40	45	50	55	60
Present expenses	$ 20,000	$ 25,000	$ 30,000	$ 35,000	$ 40,000	$ 45,000	$ 50,000	$ 55,000	$ 60,000
Years to retirement	45	40	35	30	25	20	15	10	5
Expenses in last year preretirement	116,800	120,000	118,500	113,400	106,800	98,550	90,000	81,400	73,200
Expenses in first year of retirement	87,600	90,000	88,875	85,050	80,100	73,912	67,500	61,050	54,900
Expenses in fifth year of retirement	106,872	109,800	108,428	103,761	97,722	90,173	82,350	74,481	66,978
Expenses in 10th year of retirement	129,648	133,200	131,535	125,874	118,548	109,390	99,900	90,354	81,252
Expenses in 15th year of retirement	157,680	162,000	159,975	153,090	144,180	133,042	121,500	109,890	98,820
Expenses in 20th year of retirement	191,844	197,100	194,636	186,260	175,419	161,868	147,825	133,700	120,231
Expenses in 25th year of retirement	233,892	240,300	237,296	227,084	213,867	197,346	180,225	163,004	146,583

Table 1-5. Estimated Annual Living Expenses ($) at Five-Year Intervals During Retirement (Assuming 4% Annual Inflation Before Retirement and 5% Thereafter)

	Age								
	20	25	30	35	40	45	50	55	60
Present expenses	$ 20,000	$ 25,000	$ 30,000	$ 35,000	$ 40,000	$ 45,000	$ 50,000	$ 55,000	$ 60,000
Years to retirement	45	40	35	30	25	20	15	10	5
Expenses in last year preretirement	116,800	120,000	118,500	113,400	106,800	98,550	90,000	81,400	73,200
Expenses in first year of retirement	87,600	90,000	88,875	85,050	80,100	73,912	67,500	61,050	54,900
Expenses in fifth year of retirement	112,128	115,200	113,760	108,864	102,528	94,608	86,400	78,144	70,272
Expenses in 10th year of retirement	142,788	146,700	144,866	138,632	130,563	120,477	110,025	99,511	89,487
Expenses in 15th year of retirement	182,208	187,200	184,860	176,904	166,608	153,738	140,400	126,984	114,192
Expenses in 20th year of retirement	232,140	238,500	235,519	225,383	212,265	195,868	178,875	161,782	145,485
Expenses in 25th year of retirement	296,964	305,100	301,286	288,320	271,539	250,563	228,825	206,960	186,111

Once you retire, however, the impact of inflation upon your financial condition will change in kind, not only in degree. No longer will price increases likely be offset, or more than offset, by increases in earnings. Once you're living on a fixed income, you'll discover that price increases in retirement have a much more potent sting than they did during your working years.

In retirement, your income is likely to consist of some combination of social security payments, pension benefits, and income from the investments in your retirement fund (including your 401(k) plan). While social security payments are currently pegged to the rate of inflation, your pension benefits probably won't be. And, depending on how high a return you require from your investments to make up the probable shortfall between your expenses and what you receive in social security and pension benefits and how high a return you actually realize on those investments, the value of your retirement fund may or may not fluctuate in line with the rate of inflation.

The Limitations of Social Security

By this time, you probably are aware that you simply won't be able to rely on social security alone to provide you with a comfortable retirement. But the point is important enough that it bears repeating.

To be sure, the annual cost of living increases included in social security benefits are a big plus. In effect, as the law now stands, it means that the social security payments that you will receive in the first year of your retirement will increase annually in line with the rate of inflation during all of the subsequent years of your retirement. And that means that if your social security payments were enough to provide for you comfortably in that first year, they probably would continue to be enough to provide for you comfortably throughout the remainder of your retirement.

But there's the rub. Social security alone never was intended to provide recipients with enough for a comfortable retirement; it was designed only as a safety net to keep recipients from the poorhouse, as a result of which payments in that year almost surely *won't* be enough for you to live on comfortably. In fact, had you been fully qualified and retired in 1993 at age 65, having earned $20,000 in your last year of employment, your 1993 social security payments only would have replaced $8,988, or approximately 45 percent, of your last year's preretirement income.

Moreover, the more you earned before you retired, the worse it would have been (relatively speaking). If you earned $40,000, for example, social security would have replaced only $12,768, or 32 percent, of your preretirement income, and if you earned $57,600, it only would have replaced $13,536, or 23.5 percent. And that $13,536 is where your benefits as an individual would have been capped in 1993, which means that if you retired in that year with preretirement earnings of $70,000 or $90,000 or $120,000, it wouldn't have mattered: $13,536 is all you would have gotten. As a result, in those instances, your social security benefits would have amounted only to 19 percent (of $70,000), 15 percent (of $90,000), or 11 percent (of $120,000).

If you retired at age 65 and collected benefits both for yourself and your spouse (also aged 65 and previously unemployed), your combined benefits might have been increased by as much as 50 percent. In that event, if your preretirement income were $20,000 in 1992, your social security benefits in 1993 might have been as much as $13,476, or 67 percent of that income. If your preretirement income were $40,000, your combined benefits might have been as much as $19,152, or 48 percent of your former income. And if your preretirement income were $57,600, your combined social security benefits in that first year might have been as much as $20,304, replacing only 35 percent of your income.

Again, however, note that the percentage of your income replaced by combined social security benefits still would have declined as your former income rose. And, again, your benefits would have been capped at a former income level of $57,600 so that, in 1993, the maximum combined benefit you and your spouse would have received would have remained at $20,304, even if your preretirement income had been $70,000, $90,000, $120,000, or even more. That means that with preretirement income of $70,000, even *combined* social security benefits would have replaced only 29 percent of your income; with a former income of $90,000, combined social security benefits would have replaced 23 percent; and relative to an income of $120,000, combined social security benefits would have replaced only 17 percent.

Of course, if your spouse had been employed, he or she also could collect social security benefits upon retirement, based on his or her own work history. Those benefits, together with your own, could add up to more than the combined benefits you might otherwise claim for yourself and a previously unemployed spouse. But the relatively low percentages of former income being replaced for an individual still would apply.

A few other points regarding social security benefits deserve mention:

1. Although the normal retirement age for receiving social security benefits currently is 65, you may begin receiving benefits as early as age 62. In that event, however, the amount you would receive would permanently be reduced by 20 percent.

2. Beginning in the year 2000, if you were born after the year 1937, the earliest dates at which you will be able to begin receiving social security

benefits will be increased. Eventually, normal retirement age (the age at which full benefits will be payable) will be 67, rather than 65, and reduced benefits won't be payable before age 64.

3. If you work after you retire and are between the ages of 62 and 64, your social security benefits will be reduced by $1 for every $2 you earn over $7680 (in 1993). If you are between 65 and 69, your benefits will be reduced by $1 for every $3 you earn over $10,560. After you reach age 70, your social security benefits will not be affected by your income.

4. Under the tax law passed in 1993, up to 85 percent of social security benefits may be taxable, depending on the amount of "provisional income" you receive from other sources. *Provisional income* is defined as the sum of adjusted gross income, tax exempt income, certain foreign source income, and half of your social security benefits. Taxes become payable when this provisional income exceeds $34,000 for an individual or $44,000 for a couple.

You can get a precise estimate of your future social security benefits by visiting your nearest social security office or calling 800-772-1213 (toll free) and requesting Form SSA-7004 (Personal Earnings and Benefits Estimate Statement). Within about six weeks after you complete and return that form, you should receive a yearly breakdown of salary credited to you since 1950 and an estimate of the benefits you will receive when you retire. If you are 60 years old or older, the Social Security Administration will provide you with an estimate of those benefits over the telephone. Any estimate would be subject to future tax law and social security changes.

The Limitations of Pensions

Unless you are one of the really fortunate few, you won't be able to bank on a pension to provide you with the funds you'll need for a comfortable retirement either, even in conjunction with your social security benefits, for four reasons.

1. To begin with, you may not receive any pension at all, either because you never worked for any one company long enough to have earned vested benefits or because the company or companies you did work for just didn't provide pensions for their employees.

2. Even if you do receive a pension, however, you'll probably discover that the amount you get will be but a small fraction of what you had been earning in your working years.

3. Many companies, both large and small, have underfunded their pension plans substantially. Even when these plans are insured by the United States Government's Pension Benefit Guaranty Corporation, *such underfunding can result in "insured" workers losing up to half the amounts due them under their present plans.*

4. Finally, and perhaps most importantly, even if you do receive a pension of meaningful size in the first year of your retirement, your pension is unlikely to be indexed to the rate of inflation. Consequently, over time, it will satisfy a smaller and smaller percentage of your retirement needs.

Putting It All Together

Suppose, for example, that in the first year of your retirement you require an income of $60,000 and that you receive $20,000 in social security payments and $20,000 in pension benefits. Suppose that you also have accumulated a retirement fund (including your 401(k) plan) of $250,000 which you've conservatively invested in a combination of high-quality dividend-paying common stocks and fixed income securities to generate a total return of 8 percent annually. In that event, your retirement funds would throw off another $20,000 in that first year. So it would seem that you'd be home free: with $20,000 from social security, $20,000 in pension benefits, and $20,000 in income from your retirement fund, you would have the $60,000 you require.

But now suppose that inflation is running at 5 percent annually so that next year you need $63,000 (1.05 × $60,000) just to maintain the same standard of living. You receive $21,000 from social security (1.05 × $20,000) since social security benefits are pegged to the inflation rate, and another $20,000 in pension benefits, which are not pegged to inflation. Your investment fund throws off another $20,000 (8 percent of $250,000), but now you're coming up short. You receive $21,000 from social security, $20,000 from your pension, and $20,000 in income from your retirement fund, for a total of $61,000—but you need $63,000. So you dip into the principal of your retirement fund for the other $2000.

In the third year, your expenses rise to $66,150 (1.05 × $63,000), you receive $22,050 from social security (1.05 × $21,000) and you get $20,000 from your pension. Since the value of your retirement fund has been reduced to $248,000 (you withdrew $2000 last year, remember), an 8 percent return on that slightly reduced principal generates income of $19,840, rather than $20,000.

So now you're $4260 short. With $22,050 in social security payments, $20,000 in pension benefits, and a $19,840 return on your investments, your

Table 1-6. The Impact of Inflation on an Inadequately Funded Retirement Plan ($ Except as Otherwise Indicated)

Year	Annual expenses	Annual social security payments	Annual pension benefits	Annual Investment return at 8%	Total of social security pension and Inv. Ret.	Starting Value of Retire. Fund	Withdrawal From Retirement Fund	Ending Value of Retire. Fund
1	$ 60,000	$20,000	$20,000	$20,000	$60,000	$250,000	$ 0	$250,000
2	63,000	21,000	20,000	20,000	61,000	250,000	(2,000)	248,000
3	66,150	22,050	20,000	19,840	61,890	248,000	(4,260)	243,740
4	69,457	23,152	20,000	19,499	62,652	243,740	(6,806)	236,934
5	72,930	24,310	20,000	18,955	63,265	236,934	(9,666)	227,269
6	76,577	25,526	20,000	18,181	63,707	227,269	(12,870)	214,399
7	80,406	26,802	20,000	17,152	63,954	214,399	(16,452)	197,947
8	84,426	28,142	20,000	15,836	63,978	197,947	(20,448)	177,499
9	88,647	29,549	20,000	14,200	63,749	177,499	(24,898)	152,600
10	93,080	31,027	20,000	12,208	63,235	152,600	(29,845)	122,755
11	97,734	32,578	20,000	9,820	62,398	122,755	(35,335)	87,420
12	102,620	34,207	20,000	6,994	61,200	87,420	(41,420)	46,000
13	105,597	35,917	20,000	3,680	59,597	46,000	(46,000)	46,000
14	57,713	37,713	20,000	0	57,713	0	0	0
15	59,599	39,599	20,000	0	59,599	0	0	0
16	61,579	41,579	20,000	0	61,579	0	0	0

total income amounted to $61,890. But you required $66,150. So you dip into the principal of your retirement fund again, this time to the tune of $4,260. And now the value of your retirement fund has been reduced to $243,740.

Now it might seem that you could go on like this indefinitely, just withdrawing a few thousand dollars in principal annually from your retirement fund. After all, the fund started out with one-quarter million dollars and is generating an 8 percent annual return in the face of 5 percent inflation, so what's a few thousand dollars a year?

Unfortunately, much more than you might think. In Table 1-6, we have calculated what would happen if you were to continue along this course for *just 16 years* and in Figure 1-1, we have depicted these consequences graphically. After less than 13 years of 5 percent annual inflation, 8 percent returns on your investments, and withdrawals from your retirement fund to make up the difference between your expenses and the total income you received from social security, pension benefits, and the return on your investments, your investment fund would have been totally depleted!

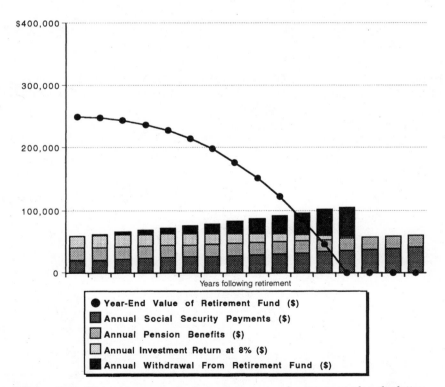

Figure 1-1. Rising expenses, declining income, and retirement plan depletion.

In your first year of retirement, social security provided 33.3 percent of your needs ($20,000 out of $60,000); in your 11th year, since social security payments are indexed to inflation, it continued to provide 33.3 percent of your requirements ($32,578 out of $97,734). In your first year, your pension also provided 33.3 percent of your needs ($20,000 out of $60,000); but in the 11th year, since your pension benefits were *not* indexed to inflation, those benefits provided only 20.5 percent of your requirements ($20,000 out of $97,734).

In your first year, the earnings on your retirement investment fund provided the remaining 33.3 percent of your needs ($20,000 of the $60,000); but in your 11th year, because of the substantial depletion of the fund, the nonindexation of your pension, and the inflationary increase in your requirements, it provided only 12.5 percent. Finally, in your first year, you did not have to touch the principal of your retirement fund at all; in the 11th year, however, you had to withdraw $35,335 to come up with the remaining 30.5 percent of funds that you required.

In your 13th year of retirement, you would have had to begin to reduce your standard of living in order to make ends meet, and in your 14th year, you either would have had to return to work (at age 79), you would have had to go into debt (but to whom?), you would have had to apply for charity or state aid, or you would have had to slash your standard of living by nearly half. And every year after that, your standard of living would continue to decline a little more because the increase in your social security payments and your fixed pension benefits wouldn't be sufficient to keep you abreast of inflation (unless you somehow managed to come up with some other outside income).

2

What Are 401(k) Plans and How Do They Differ from 403(b)s, IRAs, Keoghs, and SEPs?

Recapping the Bad News

First, let's summarize just how serious your retirement situation may be:

1. When you retire, you may anticipate spending 70 to 80 percent as much as you spent while you were still employed if your goal is to maintain a comparable standard of living. If you decide to travel extensively or relocate to a more expensive retirement community, you could wind up spending even more.

2. Because of inflation, your expenses will continue to rise, year in and year out, throughout your retirement, even if your standard of living doesn't improve. Indeed, if you retire at age 65, require $50,000 to live the way you want to in your first year of retirement, and inflation averages just 4 percent annually after that, you'll need $74,000 in the 10th year of your retirement when you turn 75 and $109,500 in the 20th year of your retirement when you turn 85. If inflation averages 5 percent annually, you'll need $81,500 at age 75 and $132,500 at age 85.

3. Social security probably won't provide you with more than 45 percent of your prior income and, more likely, much less than that. The higher your income, the smaller the percentage that social security will replace.

4. You may not receive a pension and, even if you do, it probably won't amount to very much compared to what you've been earning. Moreover, your pension (if you are entitled to receive one) may not be quite as secure as you thought it was if your company turns out to have been one of the many that underfunded their pension plan liabilities. Additionally, your pension plan, even if relatively generous and secure, probably is not indexed to inflation, so that it will provide for a diminishing percentage of your total expenses with the passage of time.

What should you do? You would appear to have only three real choices:

1. You may choose to delay your retirement as long as possible. If you keep working, for instance, to age 75 rather than 65, you will have 10 more years in which to accumulate capital for your ultimate retirement and 10 fewer years in retirement in which to spend the income generated by that capital or the capital itself.

2. You may plan to reduce your standard of living sharply in retirement, not by cutting your expenses to 70 to 80 percent of what you spent in your preretirement years but, for example, to as little as 40 to 50 percent.

3. You may seek to create as large a retirement fund as possible in the years before you retire in order to supplement what you will receive from social security and pension payments and to offset the potential ravages of inflation.

Now you may opt for (1) or (2) above if you like and, in some cases, that may be necessary. But if (3) is at all possible, that certainly appears to be the most desirable option. So let's see how you might go about doing just that.

An Alphabet Soup of Retirement Plans

There is a myriad of different kinds of retirement plans in the United States, and 401(k) plans are just one of the many. The best known plans, of course, are the social security system and those defined benefit pension plans provided by your union, your employer, or both. But, as already discussed, even in combination, social security payments and your company or union pension benefits probably won't provide you with enough to see you comfortably through your retirement years.

In order to achieve the goal of a comfortable retirement, therefore, you'll almost surely have to supplement what you receive from social security and your company or union pension with funds accumulated during your preretirement years. But there are lots of different ways in which supplementary tax-deferred retirement accounts may be established: not only through 401(k)s, but also through 403(b)s, Individual Retirement Accounts (IRAs), Keogh plans, or Simplified Employee Pension (SEPs) plans. You may choose to set up any one or, ideally, even more than one of these.

What makes 401(k) plans so special? Several things, ranging from their tax deferral features to the amounts you would be allowed to contribute, from employer matching grants to loan provisions, from the convenience of automatic payroll deductions to professional management, and many, many more. So let's examine just what 401(k) plans are and some of the ways in which they differ from 403(b)s, IRAs, Keoghs, SEPs, and other qualified and nonqualified defined benefit and defined contribution retirement plans. See Table 2-1.

What Are 401(k) Plans?

401(k) plans are qualified defined contribution retirement plans that contain a *cash-or-deferred arrangement* (CODA). We will first explain what these terms mean in normal everyday language.

A *retirement plan* is any plan maintained by an employer, an employee organization (such as a union), or both that is designed to provide employees with retirement income and that allows employees to defer receipt of income until the end of their employment or even later.

Defined contribution means that the amount of contributions, but not of benefits, is preestablished, with the ultimate amount of benefits depending on both the amounts contributed and the rate of return realized on the plan's assets. To that extent, the *risk* of a defined contribution benefit plan is borne by the employee, not the employer: if investment returns are poor, the employee's ultimate benefits will be low, and the employee will have no recourse to his or her employer who, in turn, will have no obligation to supplement those benefits.

Conversely, a *defined benefit* plan is one in which a predetermined amount will be paid to retirees; here, contributions are not preestablished since the amounts that will have to be contributed will vary depending on the returns realized on investments. In these plans, risk is borne by employers, not employees: if investment returns are too low to fund the

Table 2-1. Comparison of 401(k), 403(b), IRA, SEP, and Keogh Plans

Type of plan	Who is eligible?	Maximum annual contribution	Permissible investments	Is borrowing permitted?
401(k)	Employees of public and private companies that have adopted such plans. Individuals are eligible to enroll within 12 months of beginning employment.	Individuals may contribute a maximum of $9240 in 1994. Annual limit is adjusted for inflation each year. Employers may match individual contributions but total combined contributions may not exceed the lesser of $30,000 or 25% of employee's compensation.	Varies according to individual plans. Choices limited to those offered by the plan.	Allowed by law, but availability depends on individual plans. If borrowing is allowed by a particular plan, amounts borrowed are subject to a number of restrictions, including a maximum of 50% of your vested interest up to $50,000.
403(b)	Employees of certain tax-exempt organizations, including churches, schools, state and local governments.	Individuals may contribute maximum of $9500 in 1994.	Varies according to individual plans. Choices limited to those offered by the plan.	Allowed by law, but availability depends on individual plans. If borrowing is allowed by a particular plan, amounts borrowed are subject to a number of restrictions, including a maximum of 50% of your vested interest up to $50,000.
IRA	Anyone under age 70½ who receives compensation.	100% of compensation up to $2000 a year ($2250 if married to a non-working spouse).	Most types of assets usually considered as investments, except life insurance, works of art, antiques, gems, stamps, coins, metal, rugs, alcoholic beverages, or any other tangible personal property.	No.
SEP	Employees of unincorporated businesses or self-employed individuals, provided a plan has been adopted.	The lesser of $30,000 or 15% of employee's compensation annually.	Same as above.	No.
Keogh	Self-employed individuals with earned income doing business as sole proprietors or partners.	The lesser of $22,500 or 25% of earned income annually.	Same as corporate benefit plans.	Yes, but not to owner-employees (sole proprietors or partners with greater than 10% ownership of partnership).

Employer match?	Minimum requirement for withdrawals or distributions	Tax considerations
Often, but not universally offered.	Attainment of age 59½; death, disability, retirement, or other termination of service; hardship; plan termination (under certain conditions). Withdrawals or distributions not meeting one of these requirements are subject to tax penalties.	• Under certain circumstances, distributions may be eligible for 5- and 10-year income averaging. • Individual contributions may be made from pretax income, thereby lowering your taxable income. • Penalties for early withdrawal.
Often, but not universally offered.	Attainment of age 59½; death, disability, retirement, or other termination of service; hardship; plan termination (under certain conditions). Withdrawals or distributions not meeting one of these requirements are subject to tax penalties.	• Distributions *not* eligible for 5- and 10-year income averaging. • Individual contributions may be made from pretax income, thereby lowering your taxable income. • Penalties for early withdrawal.
NA	Attainment of age 59½, death, disability, or if payments are part of a series of substantially equal periodic payments over life expectancy of the owner (or joint life expectancy of owner and designated beneficiary).	• Distributions taxed as ordinary income when made. • Not eligible for 5- or 10-year averaging. • Contributions are made from after-tax income, but under certain circumstances may be tax-deductible. • Tax deductibility of contributions is subject to severe restrictions. • Penalties for early withdrawal.
Yes, by definition.	Same as IRA above.	Same as IRA.
NA	Attainment of age 59½, death, disability, or retirement.	• Distributions taxed as ordinary income. • Eligible for 5- and 10-year averaging. • Contributions typically from pretax income. • Early withdrawal not available.

payment of predetermined benefits, employers will have to ante up the difference through higher contributions to the plan.

On the other hand, participants bear a different kind of risk in defined benefit plans, namely inflation risk. While the *nominal* amount of their potential retirement benefits may have been preestablished, the *purchasing power* of those potential benefits is not, with the result that if the inflation rate is high, they might end up with the dollars they were promised and yet discover that those dollars wouldn't buy nearly as much as they thought they would. Conversely, in defined contribution plans, although the absolute (or nominal) level of benefits would always have been inde-terminate, it is more likely that purchasing power (or real benefits) would have been maintained since investment returns likely would have tracked or exceeded the inflation rate.

Qualified means that the plan receives special tax treatment because it has met certain requirements of the Internal Revenue Code: in essence, contributions to a qualified plan are tax-deductible by employers when made, but employees may defer paying taxes on those contributions until they actually are received by them in the form of benefits. Earnings on such qualified funds also accumulate on a tax-deferred basis.

Finally, a *cash-or-deferred arrangement* or CODA means that an eligible employee has the right to decide whether he wants his employer to con-tribute a specific amount to the plan on his behalf or to pay him an equiv-alent amount in cash.

In a nutshell, what this all means is that in a 401(k) plan, you may direct your employer to deduct a specific amount from your salary, to contribute that amount to your 401(k) plan instead, and to invest it in your behalf. That amount is the *defined contribution* and also is known as your *elective* contribution. Your employer will get a tax deduction for that contribution, just as if he or she had paid it directly to you as salary, but you won't have to pay taxes on it until you actually receive it (or whatever amount it has grown into), presumably years later at retirement. Meanwhile, those con-tributions will be invested on your behalf, and you won't have to pay any taxes on the earnings on those investments either until you actually receive them. It is these tax-deductible features (for your employer) and tax deferral features (for you) that are a consequence of the plan's being *qualified.*

In 1993, approximately 210,000 different corporations maintained 401(k) plans for their employees, and about 17.5 million Americans par-ticipated in those plans. Total assets of these plans, as of year-end 1993, approximated $475 billion, and the average participant's account balance exceeded $20,000. The average annual contribution by an employee was approximately $2800.

Stand-Alone and Matching Plans

A 401(k) plan may *stand alone*, which means that it permits elective contributions only, or it may permit additional employer contributions, and/or it may allow additional after-tax employee voluntary contributions. Additional employer contributions often take the form of *matches* of some or all of an employee's elective contributions.

For example, an employer might agree to match the first half of whatever an employee contributed. Thus, an employee earning, say, $30,000 who contributed 10 percent of his salary to a 401(k) plan, would see a total of $4500 contributed on his behalf ($3000 deferred from his salary and an additional $1500 match from his employer). But in the years the contributions were made, he only would pay taxes on $27,000 (his $30,000 salary less the $3000 he contributed; taxes on the $4500, as well as on all the subsequent earnings on the $4500 would be deferred until distributions to him actually were made, generally after he retired).

In certain situations, employees also might make additional voluntary contributions that would not be tax-deferrable in the years in which they were made. But any earnings on those contributions could be deferred until such time as distributions actually took place.

The amounts that may be contributed into a 401(k) plan are subject to four restrictions. First, The Internal Revenue Service (IRS) has established a dollar limit on contributions per employee. That limit is adjusted upward annually in line with increases in the cost of living. In 1991, the limit was $8475; in 1992, it was $8728; in 1993, it was $8994; and for 1994, it was increased to $9240.

Second, in addition to the dollar limit that the IRS establishes annually, the Code provides that *total* additions to an employee's defined contribution plans (which includes 401(k) plans) may not exceed the *lesser* of $30,000 or 25 percent of an employee's compensation. Total additions, for this purpose, include employer contributions, employee contributions, forfeitures, and some amounts relating to medical benefits. Since 401(k) contributions are deducted from compensation for tax purposes, this effectively means that 401(k) contributions are limited to 20 percent of compensation *before* such elective contributions.

For example, an individual earning $40,000 (before elective contributions to a 401(k) plan) would be limited under this provision to making contributions of no more than $8000 (since 20 percent of $40,000 equals $8000). Note that this figure may also be derived by calculating 25 percent of compensation *less* elective contributions, that is, $40,000 minus $8000 equals $32,000, and 25 percent of $32,000 equals $8000.

Third, the law limits the extent to which the percentage of elective contributions made on behalf of highly compensated employees may exceed the percentage of elective contributions made on behalf of nonhighly compensated employees. For this purpose, the term *highly compensated* was defined in 1994 as including those earning $66,000 annually or more. (The amount will be higher in future years since it is indexed to the inflation rate). The actual annual percentage deferred by the former group may not be more than 1.25 times the percentage deferred by the latter group or, alternatively, may not be more than double the percentage deferral of the latter group, if the difference is no more than two percentage points.

This brings us to the fourth and last point: largely because of the last restriction that bars companies from giving a substantially greater percentage of benefits to higher paid than to lower paid workers, a company itself may establish a limitation within its plan providing, for instance, that elective contributions may not exceed some fixed percentage of an employee's gross compensation. That could have reduced the amount a particular employee would have been permitted to contribute in 1994 to less than $9240, but it could not have increased it to any more than that.

If, for example, an employee earned $45,000 in 1994, and his company's 401(k) plan limited elective contributions to 8 percent, he could have contributed a maximum of $3600 (8 percent of $45,000 equals $3600), rather than $9240. But if he earned $130,000, he could not have contributed $10,400 even though 8 percent of $130,000 equals $10,400; in that case, he still would have been limited to $9240.

How 401(k) Plans Can Invest

401(k) plans may be established to invest in just one or a number of different asset classes. At one extreme are plans that may be set up to allow plan participants to invest only in stock of the employer's company, or only in money market instruments, or only in some other single asset class. Much more typical, however, are those plans that provide participants with a menu of choices from at least three or four different asset classes, usually including money market instruments, common stocks, bonds, and a guaranteed investment contract (GIC). Sometimes the choices may be even greater including, for example, international stocks, small capitalization stocks, junk bonds, or balanced funds.

When a 401(k) plan is established to invest in just one asset class, such as company stock, the actual investment process may be handled internally, i.e., by an officer or employee of the sponsoring corporation functioning, in this instance, in the sole interest of plan participants. Since no great investment expertise would be required to make monthly purchases, say, of company stock for a 401(k) plan, that kind of internal management could be acceptable for small single option plans.

When a plan is established to invest in several different asset classes, however, the services of a professional investment management organization, such as a bank, insurance company, or mutual fund management company generally are retained. In fact, the investment services of such a professional investment management organization usually are integrated with the accounting, record keeping, and reporting functions that often are assumed by the same organization.

Such inherently more complex plans generally allow participants to select from among a family of mutual funds or commingled accounts, all of which are managed by the bank, insurance company, or mutual fund manager that was retained for that purpose. In some instances, more than one organization might be retained. Thus a mutual fund management company might be hired to manage stocks, bonds, and cash equivalents, and an insurance company retained to provide a GIC option. Or if company stock is to be a choice, an outside manager may be retained to manage all investments *except* company stock, while purchases of company stock may be handled internally. In the very largest plans, participants might be given even more choices, including the opportunity to select from families of funds managed by two or even more different investment management companies.

When several choices are provided, plan participants generally have the right to invest different percentages of their assets in different funds. A conservative investor, for instance, might choose to invest 50 percent in a bond fund, 25 percent in a GIC contract, and 25 percent in a money market fund; a middle of the road investor might invest 50 percent in a common stock fund and 50 percent in a bond fund; and an aggressive investor might invest 50 percent in a common stock fund and 50 percent in a small capitalization stock fund.

Increasingly, plans have been offering more and more options to employees. This positive trend has been encouraged by the U.S. Dept. of Labor, which decreed that as of January 1, 1994, 401(k) plan participants will be considered to be in control of their accounts and plan sponsors (i.e., employers) will be relieved of much of their fiduciary responsibilities if the following three criteria are met:

1. Plan participants must be given a choice of investing in at least three different asset classes, such as a money market fund, a common stock fund, and a bond fund. Simply providing a choice of three common stock funds would not satisfy this test, however, since the three options would not be sufficiently different.

2. Employees must be provided with information on all of these options in order that they might make intelligent informed choices in their own self-interest.

3. Plan participants must be provided with the opportunity to transfer funds among these choices at least four times a year.

By permitting employees to select from several different asset classes those specific investments that they deem most suitable for them—considering the point where they are in their own financial life cycle, the level of risk they are willing to assume, and their own investment predilections—these plans allow for a degree of investment personalization or individualization that clearly can be in the participants' best interest. But that would only be the case if the plan participants also were provided with adequate information about their options and had the knowledge to evaluate that information intelligently.

By allowing participants to switch from one asset class to another at least quarterly, these plans also enable participants to change their asset allocations as their circumstances change, or as they believe appropriate in light of their own perception of evolving economic or market conditions. Again, this can be a big plus.

But these options (to select from a large menu of choices and to transfer frequently from one asset class to another) can be a two-edged sword. If plan participants are uninformed or unduly emotional or financially naive, they may end up making all the wrong choices at all the wrong times. Later in this book, we will attempt to help you to avoid those pitfalls, i.e., we will show you how to interpret and evaluate the kind of information that you're likely to receive, so that you may make your own rational investment decisions and choices and avoid the potential problems that can result from information and options overload.

Investors in 401(k) plans are generally provided with valuations of their holdings at least quarterly. Depending on the technological reporting expertise of the management organization retained, valuations may even be available as frequently as daily through the use of Touch-Tone telephone services.

Your tax-deferred elective contributions into a 401(k) plan and any after-tax voluntary contributions that you might be permitted to make, as well as all of the earnings generated by those contributions, are nonforfeitable. That means that they belong to you in their entirety and cannot be taken back by your employer under any circumstances.

Under certain circumstances, an employer's matching or nonelective contributions to a plan also may be nonforfeitable. However, those contributions usually are made subject to a vesting schedule, in which case you might forfeit some or all of those matching grants if you were to leave your job within less than 5 to 10 years.

Thus, an employer who chose to "match" half your contributions, could establish, for instance, a five-year vesting schedule for those contributions. In the example given earlier, in which an employee earning $30,000 annually elected to contribute $3000 annually and his employer matched an additional $1500, if the employer also made his match subject to five years vesting (20 percent annually), only $300 of the $1500 annual match would vest in each of the next five years. Thus, if the employee left his job after three years, his $3000 elective contribution would not be forfeitable, but he would retain only $900 (60 percent) of his employer's original $1500 match; the remaining $600 of his employer's match would have to be forfeited.

How and When Can You Get Money Out of a 401(k) Plan?

Distributions from a 401(k) plan may only be made under the following circumstances:

1. Death, disability, retirement, or other termination of service
2. Attainment of the age of 59½
3. Participant hardship (subject to strict guidelines)
4. Certain unusual situations involving termination of a plan without the establishment of a successor defined contribution plan or the merger or sale of the company.

When distributions from 401(k) plans are made, they may be eligible for 5- or 10-year income averaging or capital gains treatment, or they may be taxed, in part or whole, as ordinary income. This is a very complicated area of the Tax Code, with your options dependent on a number of factors, including the number of years you participated in the plan before the distribution is to be made, the manner in which those distributions are to be made, and your age as of January 1, 1986. We will discuss these tax questions in greater detail in Chapter 12, but, even so, if you are approaching the point where you anticipate receiving distributions from your 401(k) plan soon, you should be sure to consult with your accountant or tax attorney before arranging to accept those distributions.

In the event that you leave your job before retirement, you may or may not be permitted to leave your 401(k) plan with your former employer. If you can, no additional contributions could be made into that plan, but it would continue to generate a tax-deferred return on the assets already in place. Of course, if your new employer offered a 401(k) plan, you could participate in that plan, too, notwithstanding the continued existence of the plan that you previously established with your former employer.

If you are not permitted to leave your 401(k) plan with your former employer or if you simply prefer not to, you might instead receive a lump sum distribution from that plan, which you might be able to roll over into your new employer's qualified retirement plan or into your own IRA. In either event, the transfer from one plan to the other would incur no additional tax liability if it were handled correctly.

Under certain circumstances, a 401(k) plan participant may borrow as much as 50 percent of the vested interest in his plan up to a maximum of $50,000. These loans are subject to a large number of restrictions, however, beginning with the fact that such loans only may be made from plans that have made provisions for them. Approximately two-thirds of all plans have such loan provisions, according to a 1991 survey by Hewitt Associates.

Interest rates charged on such loans generally are competitive or lower than bank rates, but the interest paid is not tax-deductible. The accounts themselves serve as collateral for the loans, but spousal consent may be required and repayment schedules are strict.

What Are 403(b) Plans?

403(b) plans are very similar to 401(k) plans in that they, too, are qualified defined contribution retirement plans established by employers to provide employees with retirement income and to allow employees to defer receipt of income until the end of their employment or even later. However, these plans differ from 401(k) plans in the following respects:

1. Most important, they are available only to employees of schools, churches, and certain other tax-exempt organizations. Employees of these organizations simply are not allowed to participate in 401(k) plans, and 403(b) plans are the alternative that the government has provided.

   In most cases, therefore, choosing between a 401(k) plan and a 403(b) plan will be a nondecision since the choice will have been made for you. If you are employed as a schoolteacher or a secretary at a church, you may be offered the opportunity to participate in a 403(b) plan, but you won't be offered a chance to participate in a 401(k). If you're a furniture salesman or work for an aerospace or automotive company, you may be given an opportunity to participate in a 401(k) plan, but no 403(b) plan will be offered to you. In these cases, the only choice you'll have to make is whether or not to participate in the one (401(k) or 403(b)) plan offered to you.

There is one exception: if you hold two jobs, one, for instance, during the day as a computer programmer and a second at night as a schoolteacher, you may be offered the opportunity to participate in a 401(k) plan through your computer company employer and in a separate 403(b) plan through the school where you teach. In that event, you might choose to participate in neither, either, or both. Participation in both could prove particularly beneficial.

2. Another small difference between 401(k) plans and 403(b) plans is that, as of this writing, investors in 403(b)s are permitted to make slightly larger contributions than are permitted in 401(k)s: in 1994, the 403(b) limitation was $9500 compared to $9240 in 401(k)s. Currently, however, the maximum amount that may be contributed to 403(b)s is not indexed to inflation, and it will not be until the amount that may be contributed to 401(k) plans "catches up" (probably in 1995 or 1996). Once that happens, i.e., when the amount that may be contributed to 401(k)s reaches $9500 also, both the amounts that may be contributed to 403(b)s and the amounts that may be contributed to 401(k)s will be indexed in the same manner, and this distinction will disappear.

3. Additionally, money that was in 403(b) plans *prior* to January 1, 1987, would not have to be withdrawn until the 403(b) planholder turned 75 (not 70½ as in the case of 401(k) planholders).

4. Insofar as money contributed to a 403(b) plan *after* January 1, 1987, is concerned, planholders who work in a church or government job must begin withdrawals by age 70½ *or at retirement, whichever comes later.* Other employees with 403(b) plans, however, would have to begin making withdrawals by age 70½ (just as is true of 401(k) planholders).

5. Finally, as noted, the Internal Revenue Code provides that, under certain circumstances, distributions from 401(k) plans may be eligible for 5- or 10-year income averaging or capital gains treatment. There is no such provision regarding distributions from 403(b)s.

What Are Individual Retirement Accounts (IRAs)?

An IRA is a personal, tax-deferred retirement plan that may be established by anyone under the age of 70½ who receives compensation. This includes employees and self-employed individuals, whether or not they partici-

pate in any other qualified retirement plans, such as 401(k)s, 403(b)s,
Keoghs, or SEPs. Under certain circumstances, however, some IRA contributions by participants in other qualified retirement plans may not be
fully tax-deductible. IRAs also may be established by anyone, of whatever
age, seeking to defer taxes by rolling over eligible distributions from qualified retirement plans.

IRAs differ from 401(k) plans in several important respects:

1. IRAs are trust or custodial accounts that individuals generally must
   establish on their own. Sometimes, employers establish "employer-
   sponsored IRAs" as an accommodation to some or all of their employees, but this is the exception, not the rule. The trustee or custodian of an
   IRA must be a bank, savings and loan company, brokerage house,
   insurance company, or another person who is acceptable to the IRS and
   is qualified to administer the IRA in a manner consistent with legal
   requirements.

2. Investments in a 401(k) plan are limited to the options provided by that
   particular plan; you could not choose any manager or asset class you
   wanted but would have to select only from among the choices provided you by your employer. The chances are that those choices would
   satisfy your needs but, even so, they probably would be limited to just
   three or four or, even in the broadest plans, at the most, a couple of
   dozen.

   In your own IRA, on the other hand, subject to certain restrictions,
   you could select the specific investment manager, asset class, or mutual
   fund you wanted from among thousands and thousands of available
   investment alternatives. Among those restrictions, however, is a prohi-
   bition against investing IRAs in life insurance or collectibles (including,
   with some exceptions, works of art, rugs, antiques, metals, gems,
   stamps, coins, alcoholic beverages, or any other tangible personal
   property specified by the IRS).

3. An individual may contribute up to 100 percent of his compensation to
   an IRA annually but only to a maximum of $2000 (compared to $9240
   to a 401(k) plan in 1994). In addition, if one spouse is working and the
   other is not, the working spouse may contribute an additional $250 on
   his nonworking spouse's behalf, or a total of $2250 to his own and his
   "spousal" IRA. Contributions need not be split equally between the
   two IRAs, but the maximum annual contribution in either one would
   be limited to $2000.

4. If an individual is an active participant in a qualified retirement plan,
   IRA contributions may not be fully deductible for tax purposes if the
   individual's adjusted gross income exceeds $40,000 (if filing a joint

return), $25,000 (if unmarried), or zero (if married and filing a separate return). For married couples filing jointly, if either spouse is an active participant in a qualified retirement plan, both are considered active participants in determining how much each may contribute to an IRA.

5. If, in any given year, individuals are ineligible to make a fully tax-deductible IRA contribution, they still could make a nondeductible contribution of the difference between (1) the lesser of $2000 (or $2250 in the case of a spousal IRA) or 100 percent of their total compensation and (2) their IRA deduction limit. Should they choose to do this, their excess contributions themselves would not be tax-deductible in the years in which they were made, but any earnings on those contributions would be tax-deferred until distributed.

6. Borrowing from an IRA is not permitted, whereas loans from qualified retirement plans, such as 401(k) plans, are allowed, subject to severe restrictions.

7. In general, IRA distributions *may* begin at age 59½ and *must* begin by age 70½. Distributions made prior to age 59½ are subject to a 10 percent penalty tax, unless such distributions are made because of the IRA owner's death or disability or if the payments are part of a series of substantially equal periodic payments made over the life expectancy of the IRA owner (or the life expectancies of the IRA owner and his designated beneficiary).

8. IRA distributions are taxed as ordinary income when made, as is the case with distributions from 403(b) plans. Distributions from 401(k) plans, on the other hand, under certain circumstances may be eligible for 5- or 10-year income averaging or capital gains treatment.

What Are Keogh Plans and Simplified Employee Pension Plans (SEPs)?

Keogh plans are qualified retirement plans maintained for the benefit of employees of unincorporated businesses or for self-employed individuals (whether sole proprietors or partners). Participants may contribute up to the lesser of $22,500 or 25 percent of earned income annually. These contributions, like contributions to a 401(k), 403(b), or IRA, may be deducted from gross income for tax purposes. Taxes on those contributions and on plan earnings may be deferred until distributed. Distributions may not be made prior to age 59½ and must begin by age 70½.

SEPs, on the other hand, are not qualified retirement plans but are individual retirement accounts established for an employee to which an employer makes direct tax-deductible contributions. SEPs may only be established by companies with fewer than 26 employees and then only when at least 50 percent of eligible employees elect to defer part of their compensation to the SEP.

SEPs provide the owners of small businesses with a means of providing pension benefits to their employees and realizing the tax benefits inherent in qualified retirement plans while avoiding the complicated and sometimes burdensome rules involved in the establishment of qualified retirement plans. But there are tradeoffs that the employer must make, too, since a SEP may be more expensive for him to maintain. For one thing, many of the employees whom he or she would not have had to cover under a qualified plan (such as part-time and seasonal workers) might have to be covered under a SEP. Additionally, all employees in a SEP must be immediately fully vested so that the employer could not structure his or her plan as an inducement to reducing employee turnover by favoring long-term employees.

Contributions to SEPs are limited to the lesser of 15 percent of an employee's compensation (not including the SEP contribution) or $30,000. Elective deferrals also are subject to the same absolute limits as are contributions to 401(k) plans, that is, $9240 in 1994, with those amounts scheduled to rise in future years in line with increases in the cost of living.

Distributions from a SEP generally are subject to the same rules as those applicable to an IRA, which means, among other things, that they are taxable as ordinary income in the year received and that they are not subject to favorable tax elections such as income averaging or capital gains treatment. Distributions from a SEP may not begin before age 59½ and must begin by age 70½.

3

The Two Most Important Rules in Retirement Planning: Start Your 401(k) Plan Early and Invest As Much As Possible

If your goal is to create as large a 401(k) fund as possible (as we believe it should be), then (1) you ought to begin investing in that plan *as soon* as possible and (2) you should invest *as much* as you can possibly afford all along the way.

Rule 1 for Successful Retirement Planning: Start Saving (and Investing) As Early As Possible

This may be the single most important rule you can learn in retirement planning. It works for two reasons:

1. It does not take a financial expert to realize that *the earlier you begin saving, the more you will have contributed to your retirement fund.* If you save

$2000 annually from age 40 until age 60, for example, you will have contributed just $40,000 to your retirement fund, whereas if you save $2000 annually from age 20 to age 60, your total contribution will amount to $80,000. That's just simple arithmetic.

2. That, of course, was not a very profound thought, but this next concept, while easy to understand, really is: *the earlier you begin saving, the longer your funds will benefit from the magic of compounding.* And that will make a much bigger difference over time than the total amount you contributed in the first place.

In Chapter 1, we showed how relatively small annual price increases of 4 to 5 percent or investment returns of 8 percent resulted in dramatic changes in the overall price level (the inflation index) or the market value of an investment portfolio after a period of years. In part, that simply reflected the cumulation of annual changes but, in larger part, it resulted from compounding.

A change of 4 percent per year for 10 years, for instance, when it is compounded, doesn't produce a total change of 40 percent (10 × 4 percent), but, rather, 48 percent. A compound change of 5 percent annually doesn't produce a cumulative change of 100 percent after 20 years (20 × 5 percent) but, rather, 165 percent. And a compound change of 10 percent annually won't produce a change of 400 percent after 40 years (40 × 10 percent) but, rather, 4426 percent!

In Table 3-1, you will be able to see how these two factors combine to justify your beginning to fund your 401(k) plan as early as possible.

If you invest $2000 a year for the first eight years of a 40-year period (a total of just $16,000), with annual compounding at 10 percent, your plan will be worth $531,188 at the end of the 40th year, and you will have earned more than someone who invested $2000 a year from years 9 through 40 (a total of $64,000), whose plan would only be worth $442,496 at the end of that time. The latter's total contribution would have been four times as great as yours, yet it would have earned 27 percent less.

Of course, the ideal situation would be one in which you began your contributions early and maintained them consistently, year in and year out, throughout your entire preretirement period. If you were to do that, your plan would be worth nearly a million dollars after 40 years, although your total contributions would only have amounted to $80,000. Investment earnings alone would have provided the remaining $893,684!

The desirability of starting a retirement plan early is especially evident if you compare the results of plans started at 5-year intervals between the ages of 25 and 60, that is, anywhere from 40 to only 5 years before retirement. In Table 3-2, we have calculated the values of plans started at just such five-year intervals, on the assumptions that $2000 contributions were

Table 3-1. The Power of Compounding ($)

	Early funding		Late funding		Consistent funding	
Year	Contribution	Year-end value	Contribution	Year-end value	Contribution	Year-end value
1	$2,000	$ 2,200	$ 0	$ 0	$2,000	$ 2,200
2	2,000	4,620	0	0	2,000	4,620
3	2,000	7,282	0	0	2,000	7,282
4	2,000	10,210	0	0	2,000	10,210
5	2,000	13,431	0	0	2,000	13,431
6	2,000	16,974	0	0	2,000	16,974
7	2,000	20,871	0	0	2,000	20,871
8	2,000	25,158	0	0	2,000	25,158
9	0	27,674	2,000	2,200	2,000	29,874
10	0	30,441	2,000	4,620	2,000	35,061
11	0	33,485	2,000	7,282	2,000	40,767
12	0	36,834	2,000	10,210	2,000	47,044
13	0	40,517	2,000	13,431	2,000	53,948
14	0	44,569	2,000	16,974	2,000	61,543
15	0	49,026	2,000	20,871	2,000	69,897
16	0	53,929	2,000	25,158	2,000	79,087
17	0	59,322	2,000	29,874	2,000	89,196
18	0	65,254	2,000	35,061	2,000	100,315
19	0	71,779	2,000	40,767	2,000	112,546
20	0	78,957	2,000	47,044	2,000	126,001
21	0	86,853	2,000	53,948	2,000	140,801
22	0	95,583	2,000	61,643	2,000	157,226
23	0	105,092	2,000	69,897	2,000	174,989
24	0	115,601	2,000	79,087	2,000	194,688
25	0	127,161	2,000	89,196	2,000	216,357
26	0	139,877	2,000	100,316	2,000	240,193
27	0	153,865	2,000	112,548	2,000	266,413
28	0	169,252	2,000	126,003	2,000	295,255
29	0	186,177	2,000	140,803	2,000	326,980
30	0	204,795	2,000	157,083	2,000	361,878
31	0	225,275	2,000	174,991	2,000	400,266
32	0	247,803	2,000	194,690	2,000	442,493
33	0	272,583	2,000	216,359	2,000	488,942
34	0	299,841	2,000	240,195	2,000	540,036
35	0	329,825	2,000	266,415	2,000	596,240
36	0	362,808	2,000	295,257	2,000	658,065
37	0	399,089	2,000	326,983	2,000	726,072
38	0	438,998	2,000	361,881	2,000	800,879
39	0	482,898	2,000	400,269	2,000	883,167
40	**0**	**531,188**	**2,000**	**442,496**	**2,000**	**973,684**
Total Contributions		16,000		64,000		80,000
Total Earnings		515,188		378,496		893,684

Table 3-2. Retirement Plan Values (Assuming Annual $2000 Contributions and 10% Compounding)

Age	Years to retirement	Total contributions ($)	Total earnings ($)	Plan value at retirement ($)
60	5	10,000	3,431	13,431
55	10	20,000	15,061	35,061
50	15	30,000	39,897	69,897
45	20	40,000	86,003	126,003
40	25	50,000	166,359	216,359
35	30	60,000	301,881	361,881
30	35	70,000	526,240	596,240
25	40	80,000	894,384	974,384

made annually to each plan and that the value of each plan compounded at 10 percent annually.

The differences are truly striking (Figures 3-1 and 3-2). If you had begun such a plan very late in life at age 60, you would have contributed a total of $10,000 and ended up with just $13,431, realizing a total return of 34.3 percent on your overall investment. If you had begun your plan just five years earlier, however, at age 55, you would have contributed $20,000, or twice as much, but you would have ended up with $35,061 or nearly three

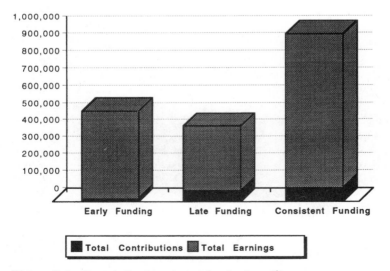

Figure 3-1. Cumulative investment fund values ($).

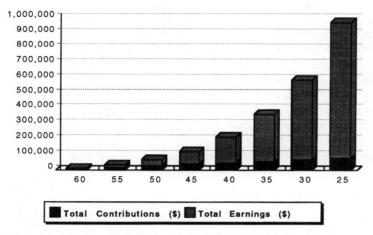

Figure 3-2. Ultimate pretax value of 401(k) plans begun at different ages ($).

times as much. And your total return would have been more than twice as high, amounting to 75.3 percent.

If you had started your plan much earlier, at age 35 for example, you would have contributed a total of $60,000, and your portfolio would have been worth $361,881. Your total return would have been a whopping 503 percent. And if you had had the foresight to have started your plan when you were only 25 years old, you would have contributed $80,000 and ended up with $974,384. Your return would have been a stupendous 1118 percent.

It is easy to apply this first rule to 401(k) plan investing. The ideal time to begin your retirement planning is right after graduation from high school or college when you enter your first job. If your first employer offers a 401(k) plan to his employees (and 19 out of 20 large employers do), you would have to be permitted to invest in it within one year of your employment. The rules regarding 401(k) plans simply don't allow your employer to limit participation only to higher paid employees or only to those who may have worked for him for several years. So you'd be able to start investing for your future retirement through your company's 401(k) plan after just 12 months of work, if not sooner.

And it would be convenient for you to do so. Chances are that shortly after beginning work you would receive a package of materials about your company's 401(k) plan that would spell out for you how much you'd be permitted to invest and what you might invest in (e.g., equities, bonds, GICs, company stock). Then, once you signed up and made your choices, the amount you selected automatically would be deducted from your paycheck to be invested in your behalf in the 401(k) options you designated. Nothing could be simpler or more painless.

Of course, other qualified pension benefit plans might also be made available to you by your employer but, unlike 401(k)s, if they provide for immediate 100 percent vesting, they could require that you wait as long as two years before participating. And in plans that don't provide for immediate 100 percent vesting, vesting schedules might result in your having to forfeit some or all of your accumulated benefits in the event that you were to leave your company after only a short stay. In the case of 401(k) plans, however, any money you contributed would remain yours, no matter when you left.

You also might open an IRA on your own at the same time that you began participating in your company's 401(k) plan and, if you could afford it, that would be an excellent idea. But that would not be nearly as convenient: it would be up to you to seek out the specific financial institution (probably a bank or mutual fund management company) through which to invest, and it would be up to you to write out large checks for your contributions rather than simply relying on relatively smaller (and less painful) automatic payroll deductions. Also, these IRA contributions would not be matched by your employer, as discussed later.

Rule 2: Save (and Invest) As Much As Possible

If the first and most important rule of retirement planning is to start as *early* as possible, the second and next most important rule is to save (and invest) as *much* as possible. Again, this would not appear to be a very profound thought, but its consequences are considerable.

In Table 3-3, we have calculated the differences in the ultimate values of your 401(k) retirement plan nest eggs if you were to save 2, 6, or 10 percent

Table 3-3. Retirement Nest Eggs Assuming Different Contribution Levels (Pretax $ Except as Otherwise Indicated)

		Percentage of salary contributed		
Age	Plan year	2%	6%	10%
25	1	520	1,560	2,600
30	5	4,277	12,832	21,387
35	10	10,769	32,307	53,845
40	15	21,546	64,639	107,732
45	20	38,963	116,889	194,815
50	25	66,571	199,715	332,859
55	30	109,713	329,140	548,568
60	35	176,390	529,170	881,950
65	40	254,531	763,595	1,272,660

of your salary annually, starting at age 25, and we have depicted this graphically in Figure 3-3. For the purposes of this exercise, we have assumed an annual starting salary of $26,000, annual compensation increases of 5 percent, and investment compounding at only 8 percent annually.

On this basis, the difference between saving 2 percent of your salary (starting at age 25) and saving 10 percent turns out to be the difference between retiring with a nest egg of $254,531 and retiring with a portfolio valued at more than $1.25 million. Quite a difference!

So the ideal situation is to start your retirement plan early and to contribute as much as possible to that plan every year. But few of us do what we ideally should and, more than likely, you're older than 25 and didn't get around to starting your retirement plan at that age. Now you're 35 or 45 or even 55. Is there anything you can do? Fortunately, the answer is: Yes.

You may recall that in the introduction to this book, we quoted an old maxim, "It's never too early to plan for your retirement." But you also may recall that we amended it to read, "It's never too early to plan for your retirement, *but if you haven't started yet and you're still gainfully employed, it's probably not too late, either.*" And that is where investing as much as possible comes in.

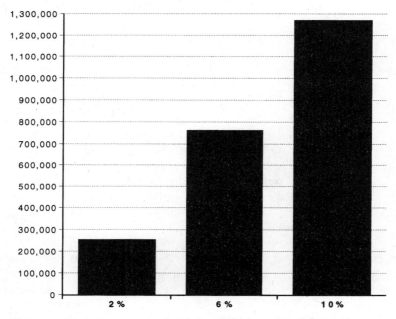

Figure 3-3. Ultimate pretax fund values ($) assuming different percent contributions starting at age 25.

If you didn't start your plan early, you still can start now and, by investing substantially larger amounts than you otherwise would have, you may be able to make up some or even all of the difference. It won't be easy, but that is the price that must be paid for starting a retirement program late in life.

Let us assume that you were earning $23,600 at age 25 and that you received 5 percent annual salary increases until you retired at age 65. Assume further that you had the foresight to enroll in your company's 401(k) retirement plan at that early age, that you contributed just 5 percent of your earnings to that plan annually, and that the plan generated an average annual compound return of 10 percent. Under those circumstances, you would be able to retire at age 65 with a nest egg of $1 million.

In Tables 3-4 and 3-5, we have calculated how much more you would have to invest if you started at ages beyond 25, in order to achieve a comparable retirement nest egg of approximately $1 million.

Yes, it is doable, but it won't be easy. By increasing the size of your contributions, you can compensate for a late start, but the later you begin, the more difficult it will be. If you delay starting until you're 35, for instance, you'll have to contribute 9 percent of your annual salary (or a little more than one monthly paycheck per year) in order to build that $1 million retirement nest egg by the time you're 65. And if you were 45, you would have to contribute 18 percent (or slightly more than two months' salary) annually to achieve that goal.

In the latter case, the chances are that you wouldn't be able to invest the entire 18 percent in your company's 401(k) plan because of the legal restrictions on the size of 401(k) contributions as a percentage of compensation. But you still could invest as much as possible in your company's 401(k) plan and supplement that by establishing a separate retirement plan on your own with the difference.

If you wait until you're 55, however, the sad news is that you probably won't make it. It still would be theoretically possible, of course, but it would require you to save 43 percent of your income annually and it's doubtful if most people could handle that. If you waited that long, you certainly should get started right away and contribute as much as you can but, realistically, you should recognize that your retirement nest egg almost surely will amount to less than $1 million.

In this case, you might consider the first two alternatives we mentioned at the beginning of Chapter 2. Perhaps you should delay your retirement for an extra year or so, if possible, which will reduce your potential requirements and, at the same time, buy you a little more time to build your retirement fund. Or perhaps you should consider lowering your sights regarding the standard of living that you hope to maintain in your retirement years.

Table 3-4. Retirement Plans Started at Ages 25 and 35
($ Except as Otherwise Indicated)

		Plan started at age 25			Plan started at age 35		
Age	Salary	Contri-bution (5% of salary)	Earnings (10% of plan value)	Plan value	Contri-bution (9% of salary)	Earnings (10% of plan value)	Plan value
25	$ 23,600	$1,180	$ 0	$ 1,180	$ 0	$ 0	$ 0
26	24,780	1,239	118	2,537	0	0	0
27	26,019	1,301	254	4,092	0	0	0
28	27,320	1,366	409	5,867	0	0	0
29	28,686	1,434	587	7,888	0	0	0
30	30,120	1,506	789	10,183	0	0	0
31	31,626	1,581	1,018	12,782	0	0	0
32	33,208	1,660	1,278	15,721	0	0	0
33	34,868	1,743	1,572	19,036	0	0	0
34	36,611	1,831	1,904	22,770	0	0	0
35	38,442	1,922	2,277	26,970	3,460	0	3,460
36	40,364	2,018	2,697	31,685	3,633	346	7,439
37	42,382	2,119	3,168	36,972	3,814	744	11,997
38	44,501	2,225	3,697	42,895	4,005	1,200	17,202
39	46,726	2,336	4,289	49,520	4,205	1,720	23,127
40	49,063	2,453	4,952	56,926	4,416	2,313	29,855
41	51,516	2,576	5,693	65,194	4,636	2,986	37,477
42	54,092	2,705	6,519	74,418	4,868	3,748	46,093
43	56,796	2,840	7,442	84,699	5,112	4,609	55,814
44	59,636	2,982	8,470	96,151	5,367	5,581	66,763
45	62,618	3,131	9,615	108,897	5,636	6,676	79,075
46	65,749	3,287	10,890	123,074	5,917	7,907	92,900
47	69,036	3,452	12,307	138,834	6,213	9,290	108,403
48	72,488	3,624	13,883	156,341	6,524	10,840	125,767
49	76,112	3,806	15,634	175,781	6,850	12,577	145,194
50	79,918	3,996	17,578	197,355	7,193	14,519	166,906
51	83,914	4,196	19,736	221,286	7,552	16,691	191,149
52	88,110	4,405	22,129	247,820	7,930	19,115	218,194
53	92,515	4,626	24,782	277,228	8,326	21,819	248,340
54	97,141	4,857	27,723	309,808	8,743	24,834	281,916
55	101,998	5,100	30,981	345,889	9,180	28,192	319,288
56	107,098	5,355	34,589	385,833	9,639	31,929	360,855
57	112,453	5,623	38,583	430,038	10,121	36,086	407,061
58	118,075	5,904	43,004	478,946	10,627	40,706	458,394
59	123,979	6,199	47,895	533,040	11,158	45,839	515,392
60	130,178	6,509	53,304	592,852	11,716	51,539	578,647
61	136,687	6,834	59,285	658,972	12,302	57,865	648,814
62	143,521	7,176	65,897	732,045	12,917	64,881	726,612
63	150,697	7,535	73,205	812,785	13,563	72,661	812,836
64	158,232	7,912	81,278	901,975	14,241	81,284	908,360
65	166,144	8,307	90,197	1,000,479	14,953	90,836	1,014,149

Table 3-5. Retirement Plans Started at Ages 45 and 55
($ Except as Otherwise Indicated)

		Plan started at age 45			Plan started at age 55		
Age	Salary	Contri-bution (18% of salary)	Earnings (10% of plan value)	Plan value	Contri-bution (43% of salary)	Earnings (10% of plan value)	Plan value
45	$ 62,618	$10,645	$ 0	$ 10,645	$ 0	$ 0	$ 0
46	65,749	11,177	1,065	22,887	0	0	0
47	69,036	11,736	2,289	36,912	0	0	0
48	72,488	12,323	3,691	52,926	0	0	0
49	76,112	12,939	5,293	71,158	0	0	0
50	79,918	13,586	7,116	91,859	0	0	0
51	83,914	14,265	9,186	115,311	0	0	0
52	88,110	14,979	11,531	141,820	0	0	0
53	92,515	15,728	14,182	171,730	0	0	0
54	97,141	16,514	17,173	205,417	0	0	0
55	101,998	17,340	20,542	243,298	43,859	0	43,859
56	107,098	18,207	24,330	285,835	46,052	4,386	94,297
57	112,453	19,117	28,583	333,535	48,355	9,430	152,082
58	118,075	20,073	33,354	386,961	50,772	15,208	218,062
59	123,979	21,076	38,696	446,734	53,311	21,806	293,179
60	130,178	22,130	44,673	513,538	55,977	29,318	378,474
61	136,687	23,237	51,354	588,128	58,775	37,847	475,097
62	143,521	24,399	58,813	671,340	61,714	47,510	584,321
63	150,697	25,619	67,134	764,092	64,800	58,432	707,553
64	158,232	26,900	76,409	867,401	68,040	70,755	846,348
65	166,144	28,244	86,740	982,386	71,442	84,635	1,002,425

Maximizing Retirement Plan Contributions Through Your 401(k) Plan

As discussed in Chapter 2, the amount that you will be able to invest in your 401(k) plan will vary depending on (1) your income; (2) the relationship between the amount of contributions made by highly compensated versus nonhighly compensated employees; (3) your allowable maximum individual contribution under the law; and (4) the terms of the particular plan your company has established. Under present law, this means that *total* additions to an employee's defined contribution plans (which includes 401(k) plans) may not exceed the *lesser* of $30,000 or 25 percent of an employee's compensation in any given year. And since 401(k) contributions are deducted from compensation for tax purposes, this means that 401(k) contributions are limited to 20 percent of compensation *before* such elective contributions. In addition, the law specifically provides that the maximum you could have contributed to a 401(k) plan in 1994 was $9240, an amount that will be adjusted upward annually in line with the rate of inflation in future years.

This $9240 annual amount is a meaningful sum and is a strong argument for investing in a 401(k) plan. To put it in context, consider that the maximum amount you currently may invest in a 401(k) plan (if permitted by your particular plan) could be more than four times as great as what you might invest in your own IRA. And while the amount you can contribute to your IRA has been fixed by law at $2000 (or $2250 including a spousal IRA), the amount you will be allowed to contribute to your 401(k) plan is expected to continue to increase year after year after year.

Of course, the amounts that may be contributed to Keogh plans and SEPs may be even larger than the sums that may be contributed to 401(k)s, and if you are a participant in a Keogh plan or SEP, you're very fortunate. But realistically speaking, Keoghs and SEPs generally are available only to the self-employed and the employees of relatively small companies; for the employees of larger corporations, 401(k) plans and IRAs often are their only real options.

A Big Bonus: Employer Matching Contributions

Moreover, if your goal is to invest as much as possible for your future retirement, many 401(k) plans provide you with another terrific opportunity that does not exist in other kinds of plans: the opportunity to receive matching contributions from your employer. In essence, this is a chance to get more money from your employer—the equivalent of a raise or bonus, if you will—simply by participating in a 401(k) plan, which you probably would have wanted to participate in anyway.

Employer matches work like this: employers agree to contribute to your 401(k) plan on your behalf an amount of money equivalent or proportionate to the amount of your own contribution. This may be accomplished in several ways.

In the very best plans, your employer's contribution may be a 100 percent match: if you contribute, say, 4 percent, your employer will contribute an additional 4 percent; if you contribute 7 percent, your employer will contribute another 7 percent; if you contribute 10 percent, your employer will contribute another 10 percent, and so on.

In other cases, however, your employer may agree only to match a portion (e.g., one-half) of your contribution. In such instances, if you were to contribute 4 percent, your employer would contribute 2 percent; if you contributed 7 percent, your employer would contribute 3.5 percent; if you contributed 10 percent, your employer would contribute 5 percent, and so on.

In yet other situations, your employer might agree to match your contributions in their entirety, but only up to a certain amount, say, 5 percent of your salary. In such instances, if you contributed 3 percent, your employer would contribute another 3 percent; if you contributed 4 percent, your employer would contribute another 4 percent; and if you contributed 5 percent, your employer would contribute 5 percent. But if you contributed any more than that, say 6, 8, or 10 percent, your employer's contribution would be limited to 5 percent.

Or your employer might agree to match a portion of your contributions (e.g., one-half), but only up to a certain ceiling, for instance, 5 percent. In such instances, if you contributed 3 percent, your employer would contribute 1.5 percent; if you contributed 4 percent, your employer would contribute 2 percent; and if you contributed 5 percent, your employer would contribute 2.5 percent. But if you contributed any more than that, say 6, 8, or 10 percent, your employer's contribution still would be limited to 2.5 percent.

Finally, your employer could make a company match (of whatever amount) contingent on your investing in a particular one of the options available to you through the 401(k) plan—typically, company stock. In such situations, you would get the match on whatever 401(k) funds you invested in your company's stock but not on whatever other amounts you might invest in stocks, bonds, GICs, money market instruments or any of the other 401(k) choices available to you. Whether to take advantage of such an opportunity or not would depend on your particular circumstances; we shall have more to say about this later.

If they wish, employers may provide that their matches to 401(k) plans are immediately 100 percent vested and therefore nonforfeitable by employees, but more often they make those contributions subject to a vesting schedule instead. That means that if you leave their employ before becoming fully vested in the plan, you would forfeit some or all of the benefits attributable to your employer's matching contributions (although benefits resulting from your own contributions would, of course, remain nonforfeitable). In providing that their matching contributions be subject to a vesting schedule, employers hope to reduce employee turnover by creating an additional incentive for employees to remain on the job.

Employers may not establish any vesting schedule they wish, however. They could not, for instance, provide that you would only become vested in annual 5 percent increments over a period of 20 years nor that you would become fully vested after 10 years but would not be vested at all before that. Rather, vesting schedules must fulfill one of the following two legal minimum requirements:

1. *Five-year "cliff" vesting.* Your 401(k) plan may provide that you will not be vested at all in the benefits attributable to your employer's

matching contributions for five years but that you will be fully vested after five years of service. That means that if you left your job after only three or four years, you would forfeit any benefits attributable to your employer's matching contributions, but if you left after five years, all those benefits would be yours to keep.

2. *Seven-year graded vesting.*   Alternatively, your plan may provide that you would not be *totally* vested for seven years, but in that case, you would have to become at least *partially* vested long before then. This schedule provides that if you were to leave your job before completing three years of service, all of your employers's matching contributions could be forfeitable. If you were to leave after at least three but within less than four years, however, you would have to be at least 20 percent vested, which means that you would have to be permitted to keep at least one-fifth of your employer's matching contributions and one-fifth of the earnings on those contributions; if you were to leave after four years but in less than five, you would have to be at least 40 percent vested; if you were to leave after five years but in less than six, you'd have to be at least 60 percent vested; and if you were to leave after six years but in less than seven, you'd have to be at least 80 percent vested.

Note that both of these schedules refer to years of service, i.e., years of employment, not years of plan participation. Thus, if your plan provided for a one-year waiting period before you were permitted to participate, you would be fully vested under five-year cliff vesting after participating in the plan for just four more years, not five (assuming you joined at your earliest possible opportunity). And if your plan provided for seven-year graded vesting, you would become vested in at least 20 percent of the benefits attributable to your employer's matching contributions after only two years in the plan, not three. Under seven-year graded vesting, you'd also become fully vested after six years in the plan, rather than seven (also assuming you signed on at your earliest opportunity).

Indeed, if you only began to participate in your company's 401(k) plan after you'd worked at your company for five years, you'd immediately be fully vested not only in the benefits attributable to your own contributions but also to those resulting from your employer's matching contributions if the plan utilized a five-year cliff vesting schedule. And if it used a seven-year graded vesting schedule, you'd immediately be 100 percent vested in your own contributions and 60 percent vested in your employer's matching contributions and would become 100 percent vested in your employer's matching contributions in just two more years.

Employers may, of course, make their vesting schedules more generous than this and, in fact, many do, but, except for multiemployer plans established pursuant to collective bargaining agreements, they may not make them more onerous. (In that exceptional case of multiemployer plans, 10-year cliff vesting is permitted.)

One popular approach employed by many plan sponsors has been to provide for vesting over five years in 20 percent annual increments; from the point of view of the employee, that combines the benefit of five-year cliff vesting (total vesting after five years) with the benefit of graded vesting (partial but increasing vesting during each of the first four years), while from the point of view of the employer, it still creates an incentive for employees not to leave.

Let's take a look at the effect that matching contributions could have on a typical retirement plan. In Table 3-6, we have assumed that Robert, a 22-year-old new employee, has been hired at a starting salary of $25,000 annually; that he will receive 5% annual salary increases over the next 43 years, at which time he will retire at age 65; and that his company has a 401(k) plan in which he will participate, joining after one year.

We have further assumed that the plan permits Robert to contribute a maximum of 10 percent of his annual income; that contributions at that level never would violate legal limits, which will continue to be increased annually in line with the rate of inflation; and that he will, in fact, contribute at that maximum level. We have also assumed that the assets in Robert's 401(k) plan will generate a 10 percent annual return.

Finally, we have assumed that the company is offering a 50 percent match of his contributions and that its vesting schedule provides that he will become vested in the benefits attributable to those matched contributions over five years at the rate of 20 percent per year.

There are several points worth noting from Table 3-6.

1. In his first year in the plan, Robert will contribute $2625 (10 percent of his salary of $26,625) to his 401(k) plan and his employer will contribute an additional $1312 (5 percent of his salary) on his behalf. Robert will be fully vested in his own contribution immediately, which means that even if he quits his job right after making that contribution, the $2625 would remain his. However, after one year in the plan, he will only be 40 percent vested in his employer's contribution, which means that if he leaves then, he would forfeit $800 (60 percent of his employer's contribution), and only $512 of that employer match would remain his.

2. The reason that Robert would immediately become vested in 40 percent of his employer's contribution rather than 20 percent is that he already worked for his employer for a year before he joined the plan, and vesting is calculated on the basis of total years of employment, not total years in the plan.

3. Because Robert will not have been fully vested in his employer's contributions until he has been employed for five years, the *accrued* value of his plan would have exceeded its *vested* value during his first four years in the plan. After that, the accrued and vested values would have been identical, which means that he would be immediately vested in every additional dollar contributed to the plan, whether by himself or his employer, and in all earnings on those contributions.

4. Robert's annual contribution to the plan will not exceed the current (1994) $9240 limit for 27 years when he reaches the age of 49. That should present no problem, however; there can be little doubt that, in line with inflation and assuming no change in the basic provisions of the law, the maximum annual limit will have been increased to well above that level by that time.

5. Additionally, Robert's contribution, together with his employer's matching contribution, will not exceed the $30,000 limit applicable to all defined contribution plans until the year of his retirement—43 years after the start of his employment. In theory, if there is no change in the law, this conceivably could present a tiny problem, but it seems overwhelmingly likely that this limit, too, will be raised with the passage of time. And the 25 percent of compensation limitation never would come into play since Robert always would be contributing 10 percent of his earnings and his employer another 5 percent for a total of just 15 percent.

6. During his working career, Robert will have contributed a total of $375,358 to his plan. Earnings on his contributions will have been more than six times as great, however, amounting to $2,359,389. As a result, through the magic of compounding, the value of that portion of the plan attributable to his own contributions and the earnings on those contributions will amount to $2,734,746 when he retires.

7. In addition, Robert's employer will have contributed a total of $187,679 on Robert's behalf, through matching contributions, and earnings on those contributions will have amounted to an additional $1,179,694. Thus, the value of that portion of the plan attributable to his employer's matching contributions and the earnings on those contributions will amount to another $1,367,373 by the time he retires.

8. The bottom line is that Robert will be able to retire with a total retirement fund from his 401(k) plan of more than $4 million pretax—nearly 11 times as much as he personally would have contributed to the plan over his entire working career. The increase will have reflected a combination of earnings on his contributions, his employer's matching contributions, and earnings on his employer's matches. See Figure 3-4.

Table 3-6. Accrued and Vested 401(k) Plan Values (Including Employer Matches) ($ Except as Otherwise Indicated)

Age	Salary	Employee contribution @10%	Return on employee account @10%	Accrued and vested value of employee account	Employer match @ 50%	Return on employer account	Acrued value of employer account	Vested value of employer account	Accrued value of total account	Vested value of total account
22	$ 25,000	$ 0	$ 0	$ 0	$ 0	$ 0	$ 0	$ 0	$ 0	$ 0
23	26,250	2,625	0	2,625	1,312	0	1,312	525	3,938	3,150
24	27,562	2,756	262	5,644	1,378	131	2,822	1,693	8,466	7,337
25	28,941	2,894	564	9,102	1,447	282	4,551	3,641	13,653	12,743
26	30,388	3,039	910	13,051	1,519	455	6,526	6,526	19,577	19,577
27	31,907	3,191	1,305	17,547	1,595	653	8,773	8,773	26,320	26,320
28	33,502	3,350	1,755	22,652	1,675	877	11,326	11,326	33,978	33,978
29	35,178	3,518	2,265	28,435	1,759	1,133	14,217	14,217	42,652	42,652
30	36,936	3,694	2,843	34,972	1,847	1,422	17,486	17,486	52,458	52,458
31	38,783	3,878	3,497	42,348	1,939	1,749	21,174	21,174	63,521	63,521
32	40,722	4,072	4,235	50,655	2,036	2,117	25,327	25,327	75,982	75,982
33	42,758	4,276	5,065	59,996	2,138	2,533	29,998	29,998	89,994	89,994
34	44,896	4,490	6,000	70,485	2,245	3,000	35,243	35,243	105,728	105,728
35	47,141	4,714	7,049	82,248	2,357	3,524	41,124	41,124	123,371	123,371
36	49,498	4,950	8,225	95,422	2,475	4,112	47,711	47,711	143,133	143,133
37	51,973	5,197	9,542	110,162	2,599	4,771	55,081	55,081	165,243	165,243
38	54,572	5,457	11,016	126,635	2,729	5,508	63,318	63,318	189,953	189,953
39	57,300	5,730	12,664	145,029	2,865	6,332	72,514	72,514	217,543	217,543

40	60,165	6,017	14,503	165,548	3,008	7,251	82,774	82,774	248,322	248,322
41	63,174	6,317	16,555	188,420	3,159	8,277	94,210	94,210	282,631	282,631
42	66,332	6,633	18,842	213,896	3,317	9,421	106,948	106,948	320,843	320,843
43	69,649	6,965	21,390	242,250	3,482	10,695	121,125	121,125	363,375	363,375
44	73,132	7,313	24,225	273,788	3,657	12,113	136,894	136,894	410,682	410,682
45	76,788	7,679	27,379	308,846	3,839	13,689	154,423	154,423	463,269	463,269
46	80,627	8,063	30,885	347,793	4,031	15,442	173,897	173,897	521,690	521,690
47	84,659	8,466	34,779	391,038	4,233	17,390	195,519	195,519	586,558	586,558
48	88,892	8,889	39,104	439,031	4,445	19,552	219,516	219,516	658,547	658,547
49	93,336	9,334	43,903	492,268	4,667	21,952	246,134	246,134	738,402	738,402
50	98,003	9,800	49,227	551,295	4,900	24,613	275,648	275,648	826,943	826,943
51	102,903	10,290	55,130	616,715	5,145	27,565	308,358	308,358	925,073	925,073
52	108,049	10,805	61,672	689,192	5,402	30,836	344,596	344,596	1,033,787	1,033,787
53	113,451	11,345	68,919	769,456	5,673	34,460	384,728	384,728	1,154,184	1,154,184
54	119,124	11,912	76,946	858,314	5,956	38,473	429,157	429,157	1,287,471	1,287,471
55	125,080	12,508	85,831	956,653	6,254	42,916	478,327	478,327	1,434,980	1,434,980
56	131,334	13,133	95,665	1,065,452	6,567	47,833	532,726	532,726	1,598,178	1,598,178
57	137,900	13,790	106,545	1,185,787	6,895	53,273	592,894	592,894	1,778,681	1,778,681
58	144,795	14,480	118,579	1,318,845	7,240	59,289	659,423	659,423	1,978,268	1,978,268
59	152,035	15,204	131,885	1,465,933	7,602	65,942	732,967	732,967	2,198,900	2,198,900
60	159,637	15,964	146,593	1,628,490	7,982	73,297	814,245	814,245	2,442,736	2,442,736
61	167,619	16,762	162,849	1,808,101	8,381	81,425	904,051	904,051	2,712,152	2,712,152
62	176,000	17,600	180,810	2,006,512	8,800	90,405	1,003,256	1,003,256	3,009,767	3,009,767
63	184,800	18,480	200,651	2,225,643	9,240	100,326	1,112,821	1,112,821	3,338,464	3,338,464
64	194,040	19,404	222,564	2,467,611	9,702	111,282	1,233,805	1,233,805	3,701,416	3,701,416
65	203,742	20,374	246,761	2,734,746	10,187	123,381	1,367,373	1,367,373	4,102,119	4,102,119

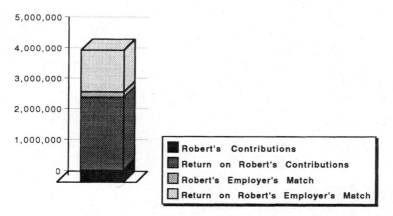

Figure 3-4. The value of Robert's 401(k) plan at retirement ($).

But suppose Robert didn't contribute quite that much or suppose his employer provided for a match of all of his contributions or none or provided for a match under some other terms. How would Robert have fared? In Table 3-7, we have calculated what would have happened had Robert contributed anywhere from 1 to 10 percent of his compensation annually and had his employer (1) matched his contributions in their entirety, (2) matched half of his contributions, (3) matched the first 5 percent of his contributions in their entirety, (4) matched half of the first 5 percent of his contributions, or (5) provided no matching program at all.

Table 3-7. Value of Robert's Retirement Nest Egg Under Varying Assumptions ($ Except as Otherwise Indicated)

% Elective contribution	Terms of employer's matching contributions				
	100% match	50% Match	100% match on first 5%	50% Match on first 5%	Zero match
10	$5,469,492	$4,102,119	$4,102,119	$3,418,432	$2,734,746
9	4,922,543	3,691,907	3,828,644	3,144,958	2,461,271
8	4,375,594	3,281,695	3,555,170	2,871,483	2,187,797
7	3,828,644	2,871,483	3,281,695	2,598,009	1,914,322
6	3,281,695	2,461,271	3,008,221	2,324,534	1,640,848
5	2,734,746	2,051,060	2,734,746	2,051,060	1,367,373
4	2,187,797	1,640,848	2,187,797	1,640,848	1,093,898
3	1,640,848	1,230,636	1,640,848	1,230,636	820,424
2	1,093,898	820,424	1,093,898	820,424	546,949
1	546,949	410,212	546,949	410,212	273,475

The differences are striking. If Robert had contributed just 1 percent of his salary annually and if his employer had made no matching contributions, he would retire with a nest egg valued at a little more than $250,000. But if he had contributed 10 percent annually and if his employer had matched his contributions in their entirety, his retirement nest egg would amount to nearly $5.5 million—20 times as much! Investing as much as you possibly can afford and getting an employer match really do make a difference.

4

Eight More Rules for Successful 401(k) Plan Investing

In addition to the two most important rules for successful 401(k) retirement plan investing

1. *Start saving (and investing) as early as possible*
2. *Save (and invest) as much as possible*

there are eight other retirement planning rules that it would also pay you to understand. These are:

1. *Personalize your retirement investment plan.*
2. *Avail yourself of tax-deferral opportunities.*
3. *Invest for maximum potential total return.*
4. *Invest in equities if possible.*
5. *Diversify your investment holdings.*
6. *Review and modify your portfolio to adjust to changing circumstances.*
7. *Utilize professional management.*
8. *Attempt to provide for emergency access to your retirement funds.*

Let's see how these additional eight rules apply to 401(k) plan investing.

Rule 1. Personalize Your
Retirement Investment Plan

A retirement investment plan might be well designed and make perfect sense for your brother-in-law or your neighbor or your co-worker and yet be totally inappropriate for you for a number of reasons. You may, for example, be initiating your plan at a much earlier or later age than your brother-in-law is beginning his and that alone would directly affect how much you should contribute to your plan and what asset classes you ought invest in. Or you might have much more grandiose (or much more modest) aspirations regarding how you hope to live in your retirement years and that, too, would have a tremendous effect on how much you should be investing and in what asset classes.

Or you might have a lot more or a lot less money to work with than your neighbor does, either because your income is much higher or much lower than his or hers or because your current financial requirements are much greater or less than his or hers are. Perhaps he or she is supporting aged parents or paying alimony and child support from a prior marriage while supporting a family of six, whereas both your parents and those of your spouse are deceased or independently wealthy; you never were married before; and you are the parent of an only child and have no intention of raising any more; or vice versa.

Or maybe your risk tolerance is simply much higher than your co-worker's so that you might be willing to invest in speculative asset classes in the hopes of generating higher returns whereas he or she wouldn't. Or, again, it could be the other way around: you might be unwilling to make such investments even if it could be proven to your satisfaction objectively that it would be economically sensible for you to do so; in your judgment, the emotional cost you might incur as the value of your portfolio fluctuated sharply during interim periods might far overweigh your potential increase in returns. But only you can make that decision.

Or it might simply be that your cousin, your neighbor, or your friend works for a company that provides very generous pension benefits, whereas your company is much more frugal. Or that the asset classes in which they can invest through their companies' 401(k) plans are much more diversified or at least very different from those available to you.

For any or all of these reasons, as well as many, many more, you might find that a program designed for another just wouldn't work for you, just as someone else's custom-tailored suit might be elegant and finely made but wrong for you because it just didn't fit. Thus, just as you might be better off with a much less expensive suit that at least fits or, better yet, an equally well-made suit that was designed just for you, you would be better off with a retirement investment plan designed with *you* in mind.

Of course, it is easy to say that you should individualize or personalize your retirement investment program, but you may find that that's more easily said than done. Indeed, in at least some respects, you *won't* be able to individualize your plan. A part of your retirement income, for instance, may be expected to come from social security benefits, and there's not much you'll be able to do that will affect the level of those benefits.

The amount you will receive from that source will depend on the law, the inflation rate, and your career earnings, and you couldn't very well ask the government to invest the funds that will generate your particular benefits differently from everyone else's in order that you might realize higher returns, even if you were willing to incur the incremental risk that that might entail. (Actually, social security funds only may be "invested" in government securities, which really means that the government simply lends money to itself and the whole social security program is nothing more than a "pay-as-you-go" plan, with benefits a function of taxes and political considerations, rather than investment returns.)

Similarly, if you're a participant in a traditional defined benefit or profit-sharing plan provided by your company, you probably won't have much, if any, say as to how assets in that plan are allocated nor the specific investments that are made, which means that you won't be able to do much to affect your level of benefits from that source either.

But, as we have seen, your company pension and social security benefits probably won't be enough to assure you of a comfortable retirement, and you will have to supplement those benefits with income generated from a plan or plans you set up yourself during your working years. And it is those plans, whether 401(k), 403(b), IRA, or whatever, that generally will provide you with the opportunity to individualize in your own best interest.

In those plans, within limits, you generally will be able to determine the level of your contributions and your allocation of funds to different asset classes. A *default position* may be suggested to you—to commit all your assets to just one balanced mutual fund, for instance—and while that sometimes may make sense, more often you will be better off personalizing or individualizing your portfolio to a greater degree in order to reflect your personal needs, objectives, and risk constraints.

What might you do? While you probably won't be able to determine which specific securities should be bought or sold for your account, you generally will be able to decide which asset classes to invest in and in what proportions, which managers to retain (when offered a choice of more than one), and when to shift your funds from one asset class or from one manager to another. And these decisions can have a substantial impact on the returns you will realize, the benefits you ultimately will receive, and your peace of mind, both before and after retirement.

Your investments in a SEP, Keogh, or a company's defined benefit or defined contribution plan generally are lumped together with those of all other participants whose interests may or may not coincide with your own. In those situations, not only won't you usually have any control over what's bought or sold, but you won't even have a say in the allocation of your funds or what asset classes your funds are invested in.

One of the biggest advantages of 401(k) plan investing, however, is the control it gives *you* over your *own* investments. To be sure, in 401(k) plans you usually can't pick individual stocks or bonds either, but you generally will be allowed to decide which asset classes you want to invest in. And you usually will be able to establish whatever asset allocation you deem most appropriate for yourself.

Indeed, although some 401(k) plans still provide plan participants with only limited options for investing their funds, the vast majority now allow and encourage employees to choose from among an array of cash equivalent, fixed income, equity, and specialized products. These might include money market funds, guaranteed investment contracts (GICs), company stock, common stock index funds, and balanced funds, as well as actively managed commingled or mutual funds concentrating in blue chip equities, emerging growth or small capitalization stocks, government securities, corporate bonds of varying maturities, high yield ("junk") bonds, and foreign or international securities. (A preliminary study done by Hewitt Associates in 1993 indicated that more that 70 percent of all 401(k) plans already offered more than three options to plan participants, even before new government regulations intended to encourage the expansion of such offerings took effect.) Additionally, participants usually are not limited to investing in only one or two of these asset classes but are often given a choice of four or more, being permitted to allocate their assets among them as they deem appropriate.

This is a tremendous advantage provided by 401(k) plan investing since it allows you to individualize your portfolio in a way that sharply distinguishes it from those of your co-workers whose interests might not coincide with your own. If your plan provides you with even just four options, say, a money market fund, a fixed income fund, an equities fund, and a small capitalization stock fund and if it simply allows you to invest in any or all of those funds in increments of 25 percent, you'll be able to structure your own portfolio in 35 different ways.

Later in this book, we'll describe in greater detail several of the asset classes that frequently are used as investment vehicles in 401(k) plans and we'll explain their different risk-reward characteristics. Then we'll show you how you might go about deciding how much risk you should assume in your own 401(k) investment program and what other factors you should consider when determining which asset classes in what combinations might be most suitable for you. Finally, we'll provide you with several specific examples of different asset allocations that might be appropriate for a variety of 401(k) plan investors.

Rule 2. Avail Yourself of Tax-Deferral Opportunities

In general, investment portfolios are established with after-tax dollars, and the returns on those plans are, themselves, taxable. If you set up a home purchase fund or a college education fund, for instance, in all likelihood, the monies that you contribute to those plans will have come from your salary or wages, *after* you paid taxes on them. Then, whatever income may be earned in those plans, whether from interest, dividends, or capital gains, would itself be taxable.

There are exceptions, two minor and one major, to this general taxability principle. The first minor exception is that you could invest in tax-free instruments, such as municipal bonds in any of these funds. If you did, the interest that you would receive on those securities would not be taxable, although any capital gains still would be. But the reason that this exception is only of minor interest is that the securities and credit markets are relatively efficient, which means that the *gross* interest returns realizable on nontaxable securities generally are comparable to the *net* after-tax returns available from taxable issues of comparable risk. So this is not a big loophole.

The second minor exception relates to the possibility of establishing trust funds or otherwise transferring college education funds from a parent in a high-tax bracket to a minor child in a lower bracket, in order to reduce, if not entirely eliminate, taxes payable on the investment income of such funds. This did work for a while, but the loopholes in the tax laws that permitted it have since been closed, which is why today it is only of minor interest.

This brings us to the major exception, which really is of considerable importance in the area of retirement planning. As a matter of public policy (and recognizing that social security certainly won't be enough), the U.S. government has sought to encourage individuals to provide for their future retirements by establishing their own retirement plans in their preretirement years. To that end, various provisions have been written into the tax laws providing for the establishment of all sorts of retirement accounts with important tax-deferral features. Included in this category are IRAs, Keogh plans, SEPs, 403(b) plans, and, of course, 401(k) plans.

These plans differ among themselves in several respects (as we discussed in Chapter 2), but they have three important features in common.
First, subject to certain limitations, monies contributed to such plans may
be deducted from income for tax purposes in the years in which contributions are made. Second, taxes are not payable on the earnings of any of
these plans until those earnings actually are withdrawn. And third, all of
these plans are *retirement* plans, which means that they may not be established for any other purposes, such as providing for college educations,
home purchases, or whatever.

Now the question is: should you establish your own retirement fund
within the framework of one or more of these not only legally approved
but actually federally encouraged tax-deferred funding vehicles, or
should you not bother and just establish your plan on your own, ignoring
any tax-deferral opportunities? The answer is clear: under almost all circumstances, it will pay you to take advantage of these tax-deferral opportunities. In the long run, it will make an enormous difference, allowing
you to accumulate a much larger retirement nest egg than otherwise
would have been the case. This is so for three reasons:

1. Since initial contributions may be deducted from income for tax purposes, your initial tax bite will be reduced, allowing you to contribute
   more money to your plan to begin with. Eventually, you will have to
   pay taxes on these funds but "eventually" may be 20, 30, or 40 years
   away. Meanwhile, you effectively would have received an interest-free
   loan from the U.S. government with the right to invest the proceeds of
   that loan in your own self-interest.

2. No taxes will be payable on the earnings of the plan until they, too, are
   withdrawn. Eventually, of course, these taxes will have to be paid but,
   as we said, "eventually" is a long time away. And this only means that
   your interest-free loan will grow larger and larger over time.

3. Finally, when it does come time for you to pay the taxes you deferred,
   current laws allow you to do so over a period of years during your
   retirement when your tax bracket presumably will be lower than it was
   at the time your original tax-deferred contributions were made and
   lower than it was during all the years in which those contributions
   were compounding in value. And under certain circumstances, you
   might be able to take advantage of special income averaging or capital
   gains provisions in the tax laws that also could reduce your tax liability. (Of course, there is always the risk that more punitive tax laws will
   be passed in the future.)

Let's see how this might work for you if you were earning $23,600 at age
25 (when you began a tax deferral retirement plan), if you received 5 per-

cent annual salary increases until you retired at age 65 and if you contributed 5 percent of your earnings to your retirement plan annually. (These were the assumptions we made in Table 3-4 in Chapter 3.) If your plan generated a return of 10 percent annually (as we assumed), you would be able to retire at age 65 with a nest egg of $1,000,479.

Results would be far different, however, if the plan were not tax-deferred. You still would have retired at age 65 with a $1 million nest egg *if*, over the years, you had treated the taxes payable on the earnings of your plan as just another living expense and had paid those taxes out of ordinary income. But that may have been easier said than done.

In the first decade, when such taxes would have amounted to no more than a few hundred dollars a year, you might have been able to absorb that expense with little difficulty. But in the final two decades preceding your retirement, when taxes on those earnings would have risen to thousands of dollars annually, that might not have been so easy. So in those years, you may have had to dip into the plan itself to pay those taxes.

Indeed, if we assume that taxes (including state taxes) on plan earnings approximated 30 percent and if those taxes were paid out of the plan itself, that would have had the effect of reducing the plan's after-tax annual return from 10 to 7 percent. And if that happened, you would have ended up not with $1 million, but with only half that amount (see Table 4-1).

Now, let's look at what would have happened if you had established a 401(k) plan or some other tax-deferred retirement plan instead. For starters, you would have been able to contribute more to your retirement plan every year without adversely affecting your standard of living. Assume, for example, that you were in the 30 percent tax bracket (federal and state) and had been contributing 5 percent to a taxable retirement plan annually. Then, by subtraction, we could conclude that you were spending 65 percent of your income annually (65 percent in expenses + 30 percent in taxes + 5 percent in plan contributions = 100 percent). In dollars in the first year it would be: $15,340 in expenses + $7080 in taxes + $1180 in plan contributions = $23,600.

If, instead of contributing to a taxable plan, however, you had contributed to a tax-deferred 401(k) account, you could have deducted the amount of your retirement plan contribution from your taxable income and not have had to pay any taxes on it. In the 30 percent tax bracket, you could contribute $1686 to your retirement plan in that first year, rather than $1180. By deducting that $1686 from your taxable income, your taxes would have been reduced from $7080 to $6574, a savings of $506. And it was that $506 tax savings that, when added to the $1180, would have permitted you to contribute the larger total of $1686 to your retirement plan.

Note that this would have had no effect on your spending. Whether you invested $1180 in a taxable plan or $1686 in a tax-deferred 401(k) account,

Table 4-1. Taxable Versus Tax-deferred Retirement Plans ($ Except as Otherwise Indicated)

Age	Salary	Expenses at 65%	Taxes at 30%	Taxable contributions				Taxes	Tax-deferred contributions		
				Contributions to plan	Plan earnings	Taxes on earnings	Plan value		Contributions to plan	Plan earnings	Plan value
25	$23,600	$15,340	$7,080	$1,180	$0	$0	$1,180	$6,574	$1,686	$0	$1,686
26	24,780	16,107	7,434	1,239	118	35	2,502	6,903	1,770	169	3,624
27	26,019	16,912	7,806	1,301	250	75	3,978	7,248	1,858	362	5,845
28	27,320	17,758	8,196	1,366	398	119	5,622	7,611	1,951	585	8,381
29	28,686	18,646	8,606	1,434	562	169	7,450	7,991	2,049	838	11,268
30	30,120	19,578	9,036	1,506	745	223	9,477	8,391	2,151	1,127	14,546
31	31,626	20,557	9,488	1,581	948	284	11,722	8,810	2,259	1,455	18,259
32	33,208	21,585	9,962	1,660	1,172	352	14,203	9,251	2,372	1,826	22,456
33	34,868	22,664	10,460	1,743	1,420	426	16,941	9,713	2,490	2,246	27,192
34	36,611	23,797	10,983	1,831	1,694	508	19,957	10,199	2,615	2,719	32,526
35	38,442	24,987	11,533	1,922	1,996	599	23,276	10,709	2,746	3,253	38,525
36	40,364	26,237	12,109	2,018	2,328	698	26,924	11,244	2,883	3,852	45,260
37	42,382	27,548	12,715	2,119	2,692	808	30,928	11,807	3,027	4,526	52,813
38	44,501	28,926	13,350	2,225	3,093	928	35,318	12,397	3,178	5,281	61,272
39	46,726	30,372	14,018	2,336	3,532	1,060	40,126	13,017	3,337	6,127	70,737
40	49,063	31,891	14,719	2,453	4,013	1,204	45,388	13,668	3,504	7,074	81,314
41	51,516	33,485	15,455	2,576	4,539	1,362	51,141	14,351	3,679	8,131	93,125
42	54,092	35,160	16,227	2,705	5,114	1,534	57,425	15,069	3,863	9,313	106,301

43	56,796	36,918	17,039	2,840	5,743	1,723	64,285	15,822	4,056	10,630	120,987
44	59,636	38,763	17,891	2,982	6,429	1,929	71,767	16,613	4,259	12,099	137,345
45	62,618	40,702	18,785	3,131	7,177	2,153	79,921	17,444	4,472	13,735	155,552
46	65,749	42,737	19,725	3,287	7,992	2,398	88,803	18,316	4,696	15,555	175,803
47	69,036	44,873	20,711	3,452	8,880	2,664	98,471	19,232	4,931	17,580	198,314
48	72,488	47,117	21,746	3,624	9,847	2,954	108,989	20,193	5,177	19,831	223,322
49	76,112	49,473	22,834	3,806	10,899	3,270	120,424	21,203	5,436	22,332	251,091
50	79,918	51,947	23,975	3,996	12,042	3,613	132,849	22,263	5,708	25,109	281,907
51	83,914	54,544	25,174	4,196	13,285	3,985	146,344	23,376	5,993	28,191	316,091
52	88,110	57,271	26,433	4,405	14,634	4,390	160,994	24,545	6,293	31,609	353,993
53	92,515	60,135	27,755	4,626	16,099	4,830	176,889	25,772	6,607	35,399	396,000
54	97,141	63,142	29,142	4,857	17,689	5,307	194,128	27,061	6,938	39,600	442,538
55	101,998	66,299	30,599	5,100	19,413	5,824	212,817	28,414	7,285	44,254	494,076
56	107,098	69,614	32,129	5,355	21,282	6,385	233,069	29,835	7,649	49,408	551,133
57	112,453	73,094	33,736	5,623	23,307	6,992	255,007	31,326	8,031	55,113	614,277
58	118,075	76,749	35,423	5,904	25,501	7,650	278,761	32,893	8,433	61,428	684,138
59	123,979	80,586	37,194	6,199	27,876	8,363	304,473	34,537	8,855	68,414	761,406
60	130,178	84,616	39,053	6,509	30,447	9,134	332,295	36,264	9,297	76,141	846,844
61	136,687	88,846	41,006	6,834	33,230	9,969	362,390	38,077	9,762	84,684	941,291
62	143,521	93,289	43,056	7,176	36,239	10,872	394,934	39,981	10,250	94,129	1,045,670
63	150,697	97,953	45,209	7,535	39,493	11,848	430,114	41,980	10,763	104,567	1,161,000
64	158,232	102,851	47,470	7,912	43,011	12,903	468,134	44,079	11,301	116,100	1,288,401
65	166,144	107,993	49,843	8,307	46,813	14,044	**509,210**	46,283	11,866	128,840	**1,429,107**

you still would have the same $15,340 left to provide for current consumption.

Moreover, you would be able to do this every year. In fact, you actually would be able to contribute approximately 7.14, rather than 5 percent, of your income each year to a tax-deferred retirement plan while still having the same amount of disposable income left to spend.

But the situation gets even better. You would not have to pay any taxes on any of the earnings in the tax-deferred account until you actually began making withdrawals from the plan in retirement, so that you would not have to withdraw any monies from the plan in your preretirement years in order to pay taxes. And that would allow all of your retirement funds to continue to compound in value over time.

As a result of 40 years of compounding, a tax-deferred 401(k) retirement plan would be worth nearly three times as much as a taxable plan in your 65th year, or $1,429,107 as opposed to $509,210. (Actually, it's not quite that good since you would have to pay taxes on that tax-deferred $1,429,107 eventually, whereas taxes already would have been paid on the $509,210. But even if you ultimately had to pay taxes at the same 30 percent rate in effect when you were younger, that would only reduce the value of his plan by $428,732, and your portfolio still would be worth over $1 million).

Moreover, the chances are that taxes would be payable at a much lower rate than 30 percent and then not all at once, and the value of that tax-

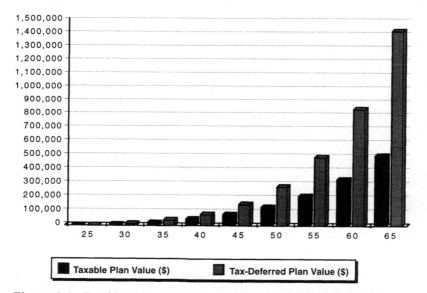

Figure 4-1. Taxable versus tax-deferred 401(k) plan values at different ages.

deferred portion of the plan would continue to compound to your benefit. And if, when taxes eventually were payable, your effective tax rate were, say, 20, instead of 30 percent, that would increase the value of your account by yet another $142,911, even without allowing for the benefit of continued compounding.

401(k) plans, just as Keoghs, SEPs, 403(b)s, and other qualified defined benefit and defined contribution plans are, of course, *tax-advantaged:* you pay no taxes on contributions to those plans nor on earnings on those contributions until benefits actually are received. And this is true no matter what tax bracket you might be in.

IRAs are similarly tax-advantaged but *not* if you're an active participant in a qualified retirement plan and your income exceeds certain predetermined levels. So, in addition to the advantages of being able to accept larger contributions more conveniently, 401(k) plans would appear to have an edge over IRAs in terms of the tax advantages they provide too.

Rule 3. Invest for Maximum Potential Total Return

Intuitively, this rule seems obvious. Shouldn't one *always* invest for maximum total return? After all, why should one ever seek to realize a *lesser* return than he otherwise might achieve?

Yet, there actually *are* many instances in which one should *not* invest for maximum total return. The primary reason is that a direct correlation exists between risk and reward, so that the greater the reward one seeks, the greater the risk that generally must be assumed. Hence, if risk is a limiting factor, one might decide to follow an investment course leading to a *less* than maximum total return in order to avoid incurring an unacceptable level of risk.

Additionally, there are other securities and portfolio attributes, such as liquidity, that relate inversely to potential return. Usually, some price must be paid for liquidity, for instance, so that if liquidity is an important portfolio consideration, some return may be sacrificed to that end as well.

It is for these reasons that rolling over short-term money market instruments for a number of years generally will produce a lower average annual total rate of return than would investing in a static portfolio of longer term fixed income securities, even those of the same issuer. Since the credit risk inherent in short-term instruments generally is less than that of longer term securities (all other things being equal) and since their liquidity usually is higher, short-term interest rates typically are lower than long-term rates, producing a lower average annual total return over time.

If you are investing to accumulate assets to provide for a vacation or a down payment on a house in just a few years, you might willingly accept a less than maximum rate of return in order to assure the liquidity of your funds and limit the risk that market reverses might wreak havoc with your plans at just the wrong moment. Or if you are well into retirement, you might do the same thing, recognizing that you might not have many years left in which to make up any losses you might incur by adopting a more aggressive market approach.

Recognizing these realities, many investors focus not on *absolute* total return, but on *relative risk-adjusted* total return, when structuring their investment programs. In other words, they try to maximize total return, but only within the context of some specific risk level, knowing that they probably could achieve a higher return if they were willing to accept greater risk, but unwilling to assume such incremental risk. And, in the examples given above (investing in a vacation fund or a home purchase fund or in the later years of retirement), such a conscious sacrifice of potential absolute return in order to minimize risk and maximize liquidity certainly is sensible.

Such considerations are *not* nearly as important in the early years of structuring retirement plans, however. If you expect to require all the money in your portfolio shortly (as, for example, from a home purchase fund) or if you expect to be making regular withdrawals relatively soon (such as from a retirement fund when you are very close to or already in retirement), these concerns over risk and liquidity are wise. But that is generally not the case in the early or even middle years of your retirement planning, although this distinction is often overlooked.

If you are in your twenties or thirties or forties (or even early fifties), you will have anywhere from 10 to more than 40 years before you will have to start making withdrawals from your retirement fund. In such situations, the assumption of some risk is not nearly as dangerous, since time is on your side, and the higher potential return trade-off makes it worthwhile. Even if you should lose money in some years by adopting a more aggressive investment strategy, there likely would be enough other years in which your returns would be sufficiently above average to more than offset those losses. (See Figure 4-2.)

Additionally, liquidity need not be of major concern. If you were to purchase bonds maturing at staggered intervals beginning in the first year of your retirement, for example, what would it matter to you if the prices of those bonds were above or below what you paid for them in the 10th year before they were due to mature?

All of this being the case, your goal in a retirement fund should be to invest in a manner to maximize return, without undue concern over risk (as measured by interim price fluctuations) or liquidity. Indeed, even a

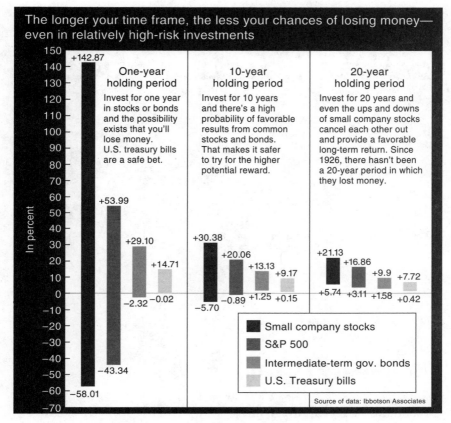

Figure 4-2. Best/worst total returns—1926 to 1993.

small increase in the annual return you realize in your retirement plan could have an enormous impact on the total value of that plan after a period of years. As indicated in Figure 4-3, starting with an initial investment of only $10,000, a retirement plan growing at 6 percent annually would be worth a little over $100,000 in 40 years. But one growing at 8 percent annually—just two percentage points higher annually—would grow to over $200,000 or more than twice as much. And one growing at 10 percent a year, would be worth more than twice as much as that—or more than $450,000.

But how should you attempt to maximize your return? Certainly, we cannot mean to suggest that anything goes, nor that the most speculative

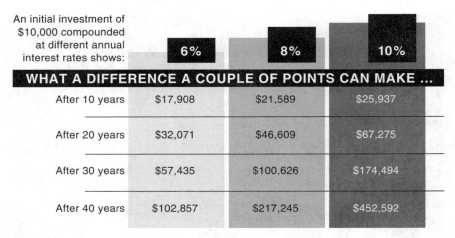

An initial investment of $10,000 compounded at different annual interest rates shows:	6%	8%	10%
WHAT A DIFFERENCE A COUPLE OF POINTS CAN MAKE ...			
After 10 years	$17,908	$21,589	$25,937
After 20 years	$32,071	$46,609	$67,275
After 30 years	$57,435	$100,626	$174,494
After 40 years	$102,857	$217,245	$452,592

Figure 4-3. Impact of retirement plan annual return on long-term plan total value.

venture capital opportunities would necessarily represent appropriate investments for your retirement plan. So what would?

Rule 4. Invest in Equities If Possible

While it is true that highly speculative venture capital investments (or commodities or risk arbitrage deals, for that matter) wouldn't represent appropriate investments for your retirement plan, common stocks generally would. Admittedly, equities are riskier holdings than money market instruments, GICs, or other fixed income securities, but the higher rates of return generated by common stocks *over time* justifies the assumption of such incremental risk.

For the past several decades, common stocks have generated higher rates of return on average than have fixed income securities or cash equivalents. Of course equities were riskier holdings, too, in that they fluctuated more widely in price than did those fixed income alternatives. But that higher risk affects only those investors with relatively short-time horizons; those with longer horizons discovered that, over time, the incremental risks of equity ownership were more than offset by the higher returns.

In Figure 4-4, we have indicated total returns for four different asset classes, ranging from treasury bills (most conservative) to small capitalization common stocks (most aggressive) during the 68-year period from 1925 through 1993. What is immediately evident is how much better off an investor with a very long-time horizon would have been had he or she invested aggressively in equities, rather than conservatively in fixed income securities.

A $1000 investment in treasury bills over the entire period would have grown in value to $11,730 while a $1000 investment in long-term U.S. government bonds would have increased in value to $28,030. By contrast, a $1000 investment in large company stocks would have appreciated in value to $800,080 while a comparable $1000 investment in small company stocks would have increased in value to $2,757,150!

Most 401(k) plans provide you with an opportunity to seek maximum total return by concentrating your investable funds in equities, rather than

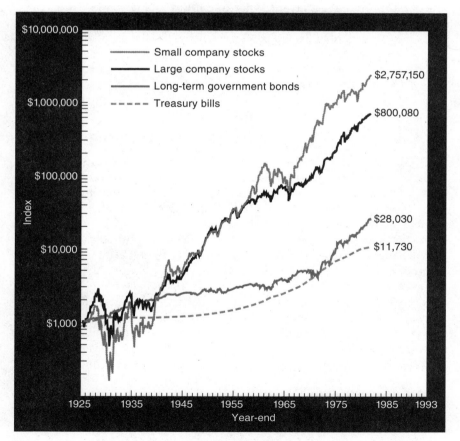

Figure 4-4. Wealth indices of investments in the U.S. capital markets. (*Ibbotson Associates*)

money-market instruments, fixed income securities, balanced funds, or GICs. This is an opportunity most long-term investors should seize.

Ironically, however, despite such overwhelming evidence of the long-term outperformance of equities relative to fixed income securities and cash equivalents, many investors, unduly concerned over risk and liquidity, have persisted in investing the bulk of their retirement funds in bank certificates of deposit, GICs, corporate and government bonds, or bond funds. And, in general, that has been a big mistake.

Indeed, in a nationwide survey of 1,000 401(k) plan participants, The Frank Russell Company found that 38 percent of their average assets had been allocated to GICs, 16 percent to money market funds, 7 percent to fixed income funds, and 16 percent to balanced funds, with only 23 percent committed to equities. That mix produced a real (i.e., after inflation) rate of return of only 3 percent, whereas a more balanced mix with greater equity exposure consisting of 45 percent in large capitalization stocks, 10 percent in international equities, 5 percent in small capitalization stocks and 40 percent in fixed income would have generated a significantly higher 5 percent rate of return. This extra 2 percent per year compounded makes a big difference over the long run.

Rule 5. Diversify Your Investment Holdings

Risks come in many varieties. There is *market risk,* for example, or the possibility that the securities market may decline and take your stocks and bonds down with it. There is *credit risk,* or the chance that the company whose bonds you purchased might default on its obligations to pay interest and repay principal when due. There is *reinvestment risk,* which is the chance that interest rates may decline, with the result that funds that become available upon the maturation of high-yield (based on cost) fixed income securities could not be rolled into new bonds at equivalently attractive rates.

There is *business risk,* or the chance that the company in which you invested (whether by purchasing its stocks or its bonds) will fare poorly, lose competitive position, or even go bankrupt, causing you to lose some or even all of your original investment. And there is *inflation risk,* or the possibility that the overall price level will rise so steeply over time that even if your investments appreciate in nominal terms, they may not appreciate in *real* terms.

We already have argued that the relative risk of investing in common stocks rather than fixed income securities in retirement plans is worth incurring. In effect, our reason was that the market fluctuations, which inevitably occur during normal business and credit cycles, need not be a major concern if one's time horizon is long enough. And historically, the returns generated by common stocks have greatly exceeded those from money-market instruments and fixed income securities over long enough periods of time.

To be sure, there will be interim bear markets during which times your investment holdings may be worth less than they were a year or two earlier, or even decline below what you originally paid for them. But since time immemorial, bear markets have been followed by bull markets and, after 20 or 30 or more years, common stock prices invariably have stood above their levels decades earlier.

Moreover, this has been true not only in nominal terms, but also in *real* (inflation-adjusted) terms. That is, over extended periods, common stocks have provided investors with total returns that not only have been positive but also have generally exceeded the rate of inflation.

What is true of an overall asset class, in this case common stocks, however, is not necessarily true of each component of that class. In other words, while stocks in general may be expected not only to appreciate over time, both in nominal and in real terms, not every single stock in which you might invest will do likewise. Some stocks, unfortunately, may advance, but not as fast as the inflation rate, so that while they may appreciate in nominal terms, they still may decline in real terms. Worse yet, some may actually decline in value, even in nominal terms. And, in the worst of all possible worlds, some may become totally worthless.

The solution to this problem is to *diversify* your holdings. By purchasing a large number of different common stocks, you will reduce greatly the risk that your total equity portfolio might become worthless, decline in nominal value, or simply fail to keep pace with inflation. Even if one or two of your holdings do decline, those losses likely will be more than offset by gains in the others. Indeed, for portfolios with relatively long-time horizons that are very broadly diversified, these risks may be reduced to close to zero.

Diversification in 401(k) Plans

Diversification of the investments in your 401(k) plan can be accomplished on three levels. First, you probably will be able to *diversify your overall portfolio by asset class*, manager, or both, by allocating your assets among several different options. As we have noted, although some 401(k) plans provide plan participants with only limited choices in which to invest, nearly three-quarters allow employees to diversify their holdings among at least three different options, such as money-market funds, GICs, company stock, and both actively and passively managed foreign and domestic stock and bond funds.

Second, you generally will be able to *diversify your funds within each asset class* since the options provided by most plans usually consist of commingled or mutual funds, rather than discrete securities (other than company stock). Usually these commingled or mutual funds are themselves broadly diversified. Passively managed funds are necessarily broadly diversified in order to replicate the indices they are designed to track, but even *actively managed funds* (those in which the goals are to outperform their respective market indices) generally are diversified within their own universes.

Finally, you will be able to *diversify your portfolio over time*, through an automatic program of *dollar cost averaging*. This would result from the fact that the contributions to your plan (both your own and your employer's matches, if any) would be made automatically at regular intervals.

The advantage of dollar cost averaging is that you would purchase more shares of your employer's stock, or more shares of the mutual fund, or more units of the commingled fund in which you elected to invest, when the prices of those shares or units were low than you would when they were high. As a consequence, your *average share cost* would be lower than it would have been had you purchased the same *number* (rather than the same dollar value) of shares each time. (See Table 4-2.)

Here's how it would work out if you were to invest, say, $300 monthly through your 401(k) plan for one year in a mutual fund whose shares (1) rose in price, (2) declined in price, or (3) fluctuated in price, simply ending the year where they began.

Average share *cost* was calculated by dividing the $3600 invested over the course of a year by the number of shares purchased during the year. In the rising market example, it amounted to $29.40 ($3600 divided by 122.46 shares); in the declining market instance, it amounted to $13.64 ($3600 divided by 263.96); and in the fluctuating market case, it was $19.64 ($3600 divided by 183.30).

Average share *price*, on the other hand, was calculated by adding up the prices of the shares in each of the 12 months and dividing by 12. In the rising market example, average price was $31 ($20 + $22 + $24 + $26 + $28 + $30 + $32 + $34 + $36 + $38 + $40 + $42 = $372 divided by 12 = $31). In the declining market instance, it was $14.50 ($20 + $19 + $18 + $17 + $16 + $15 + $14 + $13 + $12 + $11 + $10 + $9 = $174 divided by 12 = $14.50). And in the fluctuating market case, it was $20.25 ($20 + $22 + $24 + $26 + $24 + $22 + $20 + $18 + $16 + $14 + $17 + $20 = $243 divided by 12 = $20.25).

Note that in each of these three instances, the average *cost* of a share of stock would have been *less* than the average *price* of a share of stock over the same period. That is usually the way dollar cost averaging works.

Ending market value in each case was calculated by multiplying the total number of shares purchased over the course of the year by the price of the stock in the final month (December). Thus, in the rising market case, ending market value amounted to $5,143.26 (122.46 × $42); in the declining market case, it amounted to $2,375.68 (263.96 × $9); and in the fluctuating market instance, it came to $3,666.07 (183.30 × $20).

Of course, even dollar cost averaging could not guarantee you against loss. If the price of the security you purchased kept declining, you still would end up losing money (as is evident in the declining market case in Table 4-2, wherein a loss of $1,224.32 is incurred). But in most cases of rising or fluctuating prices, a program of dollar cost averaging would generate a profit over time.

Rule 6. Review and Modify Your Portfolio to Adjust to Changing Circumstances

We have suggested that your 401(k) portfolio be heavily exposed to equities in order to maximize potential total return and that it be well diversi-

Table 4-2. The Advantages of Dollar Cost Averaging ($ Except as Otherwise Indicated)

Month	Amount invested	Rising Prices		Declining Prices		Fluctuating Prices	
		Price per share	No. of shares bought	Price per share	No. of shares bought	Price per share	No. of shares bought
January	$ 300.00	$ 20	15.00	$ 20	15.00	$ 20	15.00
February	300.00	22	13.64	19	15.79	22	13.64
March	300.00	24	12.50	18	16.67	24	12.50
April	300.00	26	11.54	17	17.65	26	11.54
May	300.00	28	10.71	16	18.75	24	12.50
June	300.00	30	10.00	15	20.00	22	13.64
July	300.00	32	9.38	14	21.43	20	15.00
August	300.00	34	8.82	13	23.08	18	16.67
September	300.00	36	8.33	12	25.00	16	18.75
October	300.00	38	7.89	11	27.27	14	21.43
November	300.00	40	7.50	10	30.00	17	17.65
December	300.00	42	7.14	9	33.33	20	15.00
Total	$3600.00		122.46		263.96		183.30
Average share cost		29.40		13.64		19.64	
Average share price		31.00		14.50		20.25	
Ending market value		5,143.26		2,375.68		3,666.07	
Profit (or loss)		1,543.26		(1,224.32)		66.07	

fied in order to limit risk. But that does not mean that you should be 100 percent invested in common stocks at all times, nor that your stocks, once purchased, never should be sold.

To be sure, substantial equity exposure makes the most sense throughout most of your preretirement years—certainly through your twenties, thirties, and forties and probably into your early fifties as well. But as you come closer to use of the retirement funds, your portfolio mix should be modified to reduce your risk exposure so that a shift of some assets from equities into fixed income securities begins to make more sense. And once you have retired, your asset mix probably should be adjusted still further in the direction of greater fixed income exposure, depending on the size of your estate, tax considerations, and other important factors.

There are other reasons which could justify your making changes in your portfolio besides the simple passage of time. Perhaps those responsible for managing your account have done a poor job and you think a new investment management team might do a better one. Or perhaps a major change in market conditions or a sharp rise or decline in the level of interest rates significantly altered the relative attractiveness of different asset classes. Under such circumstances, changes in your financial plan may or may not be called for, but a review of your holdings certainly would be in order.

How well do 401(k) plans score on this important issue of accommodating your need to make portfolio changes from time to time? Fortunately, very well indeed.

401(k) plans have been offering more and more options to employees, and they have improved their flexibility in permitting the making of portfolio changes. Both of these positive trends were encouraged by the Labor Department, which decreed that as of January 1, 1994, employees would be considered to be in control of their accounts if (1) they were given a choice of investing in at least three different asset classes, (2) they were provided with information on all of these options in order to make intelligent decisions, and (3) they were permitted to transfer funds among these choices at least four times a year. As a result, the overwhelming majority of 401(k) plans now do allow portfolio changes at least quarterly.

Rule 7. Utilize Professional Management

Investing can be fun. Reading financial publications, company reports, investment advisory services, and brokerage house recommendations with an eye toward selecting stocks in which to invest can be challenging, enjoyable, and even a profitable hobby. And you may do it very well if you have adequate background and training and sufficient time to devote to it.

Similarly, it can be fun to paint or panel your basement, to build a new porch or a new deck for your pool, or to repair a leaking roof. And you might take justifiable pride in doing those jobs well.

But just because you enjoy making some home improvements and can do it well, doesn't mean that you would be likely to undertake a major project such as replacing all the wiring in your home or all of the pipes. For big jobs like that, you surely would turn to professional electricians or plumbers.

Similarly, when it comes to structuring your overall retirement investment plan, it makes the most sense for you to utilize the services of professional money managers. Intrinsically, they may not be any smarter than you (just as the electricians and plumbers you called may not have been any smarter than you), but that is their job. And just as you shouldn't act as your own lawyer or doctor, you also really shouldn't consider being your own portfolio manager where large sums of money and your entire future are at stake.

Of course, there's no reason why you couldn't still invest small amounts for yourself, if that's something you enjoy doing (just as you could continue to undertake small home improvement projects if that gave you pleasure). But you should distinguish such fun investing from your serious retirement investment program.

In addition to professional expertise, there are three other important benefits you would realize by utilizing professional portfolio management for your retirement plan. First, your plan almost assuredly would be adequately diversified (see rule 5) as an automatic by-product of professional management. Thus, if you decide to invest in common stocks in your retirement plan and alternatives are available to you, you'd generally be better off if you didn't try to select individual stocks on your own, but rather invested in a professionally managed mutual fund or other commingled account instead. Inevitably, that fund or account would be diversified so that you would realize the advantages of both professional management and diversification all in one.

Second, if you invested in a *balanced* mutual fund or commingled account, whose policy it was to adjust its asset allocation of stocks, bonds, and cash in light of changing market conditions, then the professional managers of that fund also would be relieving you of at least some of the responsibility of deciding when to change your portfolio mix (see rule 6). Of course, any changes they made would only reflect their judgment as to the relative attractiveness of different asset classes at different times in the abstract and wouldn't take into consideration changes in your own personal circumstances. You'd still be responsible for that.

Finally, you'd probably benefit from economies of scale. The professional manager of a mutual or commingled fund can buy and sell blocks of securities for your retirement plan in conjunction with his transactions for other investors in his fund. Consequently, the commission charges applicable to the small proportion of those trades attributable to your own account usually would work out to be lower than the commissions you would have incurred had you attempted to replicate your share of those transactions in a personal account of your own.

In most 401(k) plans, the investment decision-making process has been delegated to professional investment managers, including mutual fund management companies and the investment management affiliates or subsidiaries of banks or insurance companies. This is as it should be. Professional investment management companies have the experience, expertise, and resources that an individual, acting on his own, necessarily would lack, and your interests are well served as a result of such delegation.

Rule 8. Attempt to Provide for Emergency Access to Your Retirement Funds

Under all but the most extreme circumstances, the funds you set aside for your ultimate retirement should be allowed to remain where they are until you actually do retire—or even longer. If, instead, you look upon your retirement plan as nothing more than another savings account, to be drawn upon as desired (to purchase new furniture, pay for a vacation, finance your daughter's wedding or whatever), you will discover that when the time does come to retire, you'll have a lot less money to live on than you expected. Even if the funds you withdrew from time to time during your working years eventually were repaid, you would have lost the very important benefit of compounding that, as we have seen, can have a huge impact on the final value of your retirement fund. Additionally, penalty taxes paid on premature withdrawals from retirement plans could further deplete your assets.

Under most circumstances, then, you definitely should *not* look upon your retirement plan as a source of funds to be tapped at whim, to whatever degree you legally might be able to do so. But having said that, what should you do in the event of a *real* emergency? Suppose that you or a loved one were to suffer a catastrophic accident or illness against which you were not fully insured. Or suppose you lost your job and found that it took you much longer than you ever had expected to find a new one. What should you do then?

In such situations, of course, you first would turn to whatever emergency funds you had set aside for such purposes and then would dip into, possibly even deplete, your general savings. Next, you might borrow some money from close friends or relatives or even take out an equity loan or a second mortgage on your home. But suppose doing all that still was not enough. In that event, you might find that the *only* asset left for you to tap was your retirement fund and, under such circumstances, it could make sense for you to do so.

But would you be able to? Some sources of potential retirement income, such as your social security account, simply wouldn't be available to you even in the event of most emergencies. Your company's qualified retirement plan, on the other hand, may not allow you to make an outright withdrawal but may allow you to take out a loan equivalent to a portion of the value of your interest in the plan, subject to a strict repayment schedule and reasonable interest charges.

What you really should be concerned about, however, is your potential access to the assets in those retirement accounts you may have set up to supplement your potential social security benefits and your employer's pension plan. That would include your IRA, your 401(k) plan, or any other retirement account you might have established.

If all of your supplemental retirement money were in a taxable account that you had set up on your own, you would have no difficulty taking out any money you may need or want early. After all, such a fund would only be a "retirement fund" in your own eyes: it would have been accorded no preferential legal or tax treatment to distinguish it from any other bank account or mutual fund account or investment portfolio you may have, so that you could liquidate all or any part of it whenever you wished. But if you were to set up your retirement fund in that way just to have easy potential access to your money in the event of emergency, you'd be paying an enormous price in terms of the loss of tax benefits that you would incur. And psychologically it could be a bad thing, too, making it all too easy for you to deplete your fund long before you retired. We would not recommend it.

If your supplementary retirement funds were all in IRAs, instead, you'd realize the benefits of tax deferrability (within limits), but you still would be permitted to make withdrawals at any time, even before retirement. Unfortunately, however, IRA regulations provide that you'd have to pay 20 percent federal withholding taxes and 10 percent penalty taxes on premature withdrawals, diminishing the relative attractiveness of this option too.

Most 401(k) plans also permit outright preretirement "hardship" withdrawals, under special circumstances, although here, too, 20 percent withholding taxes and 10 percent penalty taxes (on withdrawals made if you are under 59½ years of age) would have to be paid. And many 401(k) plans also permit you to borrow against them.

In fact, in the event of emergency, there are three ways in which you might be able to get at your 401(k) funds before retirement: (1) you could leave your job and take the money in your plan with you rather than allowing it to remain where it was or rolling it into your new employer's 401(k) plan or into an IRA you set up yourself; (2) you could apply for a "hardship" withdrawal; or (3) you could borrow against the value of your assets in the plan.

Under most circumstances, the first of these approaches would be unrealistic. It is unlikely that you would choose to leave your job voluntarily at a time of personal emergency simply to gain access to the funds in your 401(k) plan. To do so might actually worsen your economic plight, rather than improve it.

There are some instances in which you might be *forced* to leave your job, however, and should that occur, it's nice to know that the very fact of your separation would enable you to gain early access to the assets in your 401(k) plan. Suppose, for instance, that you were forced to leave your job because of illness (your own, perhaps, or that of a loved one for whom you had to assume the role of primary care giver). Or suppose that you were laid off or fired from your job and were unable to find another one for an extended period. In either of those cases, you might discover that all you had to fall back on were the funds in your 401(k) plan, and it would be comforting to know that under those circumstances, they could be made available to you.

Whenever employees leave their jobs before retirement, they have to decide what to do with the funds in their former employers' 401(k) plans. When they are not simultaneously confronted by some emergency, that may be a difficult decision, but it is not necessarily an unpleasant one. Sometimes they are permitted to leave their funds in their former employers' 401(k) plans and, if their separation was amicable, that may be an easy and acceptable solution. Often, however, they prefer to sever their connections with their former employers entirely, choosing not to leave their 401(k) plan assets there, even when they have the right to do so.

Under those circumstances, or when they are not offered the opportunity of leaving their funds in their former employers' 401(k) plans, there are three options available to them: (1) they may roll those funds into their new employers' plans (assuming they have new employers with 401(k) plans that would accept such rollovers); (2) they may roll the funds into new or existing IRAs; or (3) they may withdraw the funds in their 401(k) plans for current consumption or for some other investment purpose.

Most of the time, their decision will be to roll the funds into their new employers' plans or into their own IRAs, which really is what generally makes the most sense. If done correctly, transfers of that sort are deemed to be nontaxable transactions, enabling participants to keep their assets intact and retain the tax-deferred status of those funds. That way, their funds would continue to compound in value tax-free until they actually withdrew them at retirement.

If, on the other hand, they were to withdraw their funds when they left their jobs and before the age of 59½, they would have to pay a 20 percent withholding tax on those funds as soon as they were withdrawn. Subsequently, participants would have to pay ordinary income taxes on those funds as if they all were earned in the year of their withdrawal. Then, they would have to pay a 10 percent penalty tax on top of all that. Finally, by the time they retired, those funds would no longer be available to them. All in all, it would add up to a very steep price for them to pay for immediate access to their funds.

If participants were confronted by a genuine emergency, however, that still might be the best (or only) thing for them to do. Thus, in the examples we proposed earlier—if they were forced to leave their jobs because of illness or to care for a loved one or if they were fired or laid off and unable to find new employment—withdrawing their 401(k) funds and paying a very steep price may be their only choice.

The second approach—to apply for a "hardship" withdrawal—usually isn't an attractive alternative either, but sometimes it can become necessary too. The tax implications of making a hardship withdrawal from a 401(k) plan before age 59½ are virtually identical to those of making a premature withdrawal upon leaving your job: just because you remain employed or designate the withdrawal as being made for hardship purposes won't change the facts that you still will have to pay ordinary income taxes on the value of the assets you withdraw in the year in which you withdraw them, plus a 10 percent penalty tax. And you still will lose the future potential benefits of compounding and tax deferrability, just as if you had left your job, withdrawn your 401(k) funds at that time, and failed to roll them over into another tax-deferred plan.

The only real advantage of making a hardship withdrawal rather than leaving your job in order to get at your 401(k) funds is that you won't have to give up your job to do it—but that can be a very big advantage. So if your plan does provide for hardship withdrawals, you may be able to take your money out, pay your taxes and penalties, and still remain in your present employment. That, of course, could be very important to you since, at a time of emergency, having to leave your job to get at your funds could make matters worse for you, rather than better.

But there are disadvantages in your banking on being able to make a hardship withdrawal rather than having to leave your job in order to get at your money. For one thing, your plan simply might not have any hardship withdrawal (or borrowing) provisions at all, which would mean that the only way you could withdraw your money before retirement would be to leave your job. Or, even if your plan did provide for hardship withdrawals, you might discover that your personal emergency, while real enough to you, still didn't qualify as a hardship for the purpose of making a premature withdrawal under the law or under the terms of your particular plan.

Assuming that your plan does provide for hardship withdrawals, it would still be necessary under the law that your withdrawal, in order to qualify, meet two criteria:

1. The withdrawal would have to be made because of your "immediate and heavy financial need."

2. It would have to be "necessary" in order for you to satisfy that need.

In order to determine whether these two standards are met, plans may apply either of two methods known as the "facts and circumstances" test and the "safe harbor" test. If they wish, they may use either of these tests for one determination and the other for the second, or they may use the same method for both.

The *facts and circumstances test* is as it sounds: the decision as to whether or not your requested withdrawal would qualify as a hardship withdrawal would be based on a review of all the relevant facts and circumstances in your particular case.

Plans utilizing the facts and circumstances test to determine whether an "immediate and heavy financial need" exists generally establish rules regarding the purposes for which hardship withdrawals will be permitted. While they can allow hardship withdrawals for any reason, if the surrounding circumstances are deemed to create an immediate and heavy financial need, it generally is the case that the need to pay such things as funeral expenses would qualify, whereas the need to purchase a boat or television set would not.

Under the facts and circumstances test, a hardship withdrawal would be deemed "necessary" if the amount of the withdrawal did not exceed the amount required to relieve the financial need and if that need could not have been satisfied through recourse to any other sources that were reasonably available. These resources would include all of your assets as well as those of your spouse and minor children. In general, a hardship withdrawal would be deemed necessary if the need could not have been relieved through the liquidation of assets, reimbursement by insurance, cessation of elective and voluntary contributions under the plan, other withdrawals or nontaxable loans from all plans in which you participate, or borrowing from commercial sources on reasonable terms.

Under the "safe harbor" test, on the other hand, a hardship withdrawal will be considered an "immediate and heavy financial need" if the withdrawal was made for any of the following specific purposes:

1. Payment of medical expenses for you, your spouse, or your dependents
2. Purchase of your principal residence (excluding mortgage payments)
3. Payment of educational expenses for the following year for yourself, your spouse, or your dependents
4. Payment of amounts necessary to prevent your eviction from your principal residence or foreclosure on the mortgage of your principal residence
5. Any other specific events that might be prescribed by the IRS.

Under the "safe harbor" test, your withdrawal will be considered "necessary" if the amount of the withdrawal does not exceed the amount required to relieve the financial need and you made all other withdrawals (other than hardship) and took all nontaxable loans available to you under all of your employer's plans. In addition, your maximum elective contribution in the following taxable year will be reduced by the amount of the elective contribution you made in the year in which you made your hardship withdrawal, and you won't be allowed to make any contributions to your employer's plans for 12 months after receipt of the hardship withdrawal.

The third way in which you may have access to the assets in your 401(k) plan even before retirement would be by borrowing against the value of those assets. If your plan provides for such loans (as approximately two out of three do), this may be a *much better approach* for you to take than to apply for a hardship withdrawal or actually separate from service in order to gain access to your funds for three reasons:

1. Your plan's loan provisions may not be as rigid as its hardship withdrawal provisions: you may not have to prove that you had an "immediate and heavy need" nor that the loan would be "necessary" to satisfy that need in order to make the loan.
2. No taxes would be withheld when you borrowed, and you would not have to pay ordinary income taxes or penalty taxes when making the loan.
3. You would be more likely to repay the loan than to replenish a fund depleted by a hardship withdrawal; hence, it would be more likely that your retirement funds would be there when you eventually needed them at retirement.

On the other hand, borrowing from a 401(k) plan is no "free lunch" either. For one thing, you would not necessarily be able to borrow *all* the money in your 401(k) plan but only the lesser of (a) $50,000 or (b) the greater of 50 percent of the present value of your vested interest or

Table 4-3. Potential Borrowing Power in Your 401(k) Account ($)

Vested interest in account	Amount you could borrow
1,000	1,000
3,000	3,000
5,000	5,000
10,000	10,000
15,000	10,000
20,000	10,000
25,000	12,500
50,000	25,000
75,000	37,500
100,000 or more	50,000

$10,000. That means that if your vested interest amounted to only $10,000 or less, you'd be able to borrow all of it, but if it amounted to $100,000 or more, you'd be limited to only $50,000. Table 4-3 shows what you'd be able to borrow assuming different vested interest levels.

The interest rate you would be charged on a loan from your 401(k) plan would be competitive with bank rates, but the interest you paid would not be tax-deductible (unlike the interest on a home equity loan). However, the interest you paid on your 401(k) plan loan actually would be paid to yourself: it would accrue in your account as earnings, and when you eventually withdrew funds at retirement, you'd have to pay taxes on those interest earnings.

If you borrow no more than 50 percent of your vested interest in your plan, you would not require any additional collateral for the loan since the assets in the account themselves would serve as adequate collateral. However, if you borrowed more than 50 percent, additional collateral could be required.

Loans from 401(k) plans for any purpose other than the purchase of a primary residence would have to be repaid within five years; if they were not repaid, they would be treated as taxable distributions. (If a loan were made to purchase a primary residence, however, the five-year repayment schedule would not apply.) Additionally, the loan repayment schedule would have to provide for level amortization, which means that repayments of principal and interest would have to be made in approximately equal installments at least quarterly during the term of the loan. Finally, spousal consent to the loan might be required under certain circumstances.

5

Investment Considerations in 401(k) Plans: Common Stocks, Bonds, and Mutual Funds

Congratulations! You've decided to enroll in your company's 401(k) plan as soon as possible and to invest the maximum allowable to get the biggest bang for the buck from your employer's match and to maximize the total amount you'll receive at retirement. Now it just remains for you to decide exactly how to allocate your contributions.

But that's no easy job. After all, you may not be a financial expert, and a lot of the terms in your 401(k) plan's descriptive material may be Greek to you. What, for instance, is the difference between a "global" stock fund, a "foreign" stock fund, and an "international" stock fund? They certainly sound the same. "Active" investing sounds as if it should be better than "passive" investing—but is it really? Indeed, what do "active" investing and "passive" investing really mean anyway?

Should you put all your money into your own company's stock? That could indicate your corporate loyalty and, if you're working for the company, shouldn't you want to invest in it too? Or would that provide you with inadequate diversification? Maybe you should put all your money into a common stock fund instead. But if you do put all your money into a common stock fund, which one should it be? The blue chip fund? The small capitalization fund? Or one of those foreign sounding funds?

Or maybe you should only put some of your money in stocks and the rest in bonds—but which bond fund should you invest in? The government bond fund? The corporate bond fund? Or the high-yield bond fund? High yield sounds good, but didn't someone once tell you that "high-yield bonds" was just a euphemism for "junk bonds"? And why would you want to invest in "junk"?

If you do decide to put some money in stocks and some in bonds, how much should you allocate to each? Maybe you should just put all your money into the balanced fund, instead, and let a professional investment manager allocate your assets for you. But would he really know what was best for you?

Or maybe you should just invest in the GIC, the guaranteed investment contract. After all, it's guaranteed, isn't it? But *what* really is guaranteed? And by whom?

Before you can decide which of the asset classes available to you through your 401(k) plan are most appropriate for you and in what proportions, it first is necessary that you understand just what those different asset classes represent. So let's begin with a minicourse in financial terminology and the principles of investment.

Owning and Loaning

In general, when you invest, it will either be as the *owner* (or one of the owners) of a business or as a *creditor* to it. In the first instance, if the company in which you are investing is a *corporation* (as opposed to a partnership or single proprietorship), you would become a *stockholder* by buying shares of the company's stock. The shares that you would own would be evidence of your ownership interest in the corporation's fortunes, i.e., in its assets and earning power.

If, however, you were to invest by *lending* money to the corporation, you would do so by buying the company's notes, bonds, money market instruments, or other evidences of its debt to you. If you bought bonds, for instance, you would become a *bondholder* and the bonds that you own would be evidence of the corporation's financial obligation to you, indicating, among other things, how much the corporation owed you, when it agreed to repay you, and how much interest it would pay you along the way.

There are some big advantages (and some big disadvantages) in being a bondholder rather than a stockholder. One of the biggest advantages is that interest on the money owed you would have to be paid to you before any dividends could be paid to the owners of the corporation (its stockholders). Moreover, you would be promised that on a date certain the money you loaned to the company would be repaid to you in its entirety. At that time, you would have to be repaid before any distributions could be made to stockholders.

If the company should fare badly, lose money, or even go into receivership, you would have a legal claim on its assets. If it were to go bankrupt, you could even sue to get your money back before anything could be paid to stockholders.

Those would all be advantages as compared to the rights of stockholders who would not be assured of anything since corporations are not under the same legal obligation to pay dividends on their stock as they are to pay interest on their bonds. And there is no date certain on which the money that a stockholder invested would be returned to him by the company. The only way he could get his money back would be by selling his stock to someone else (or, possibly, through a settlement in the event of the company's liquidation).

On the other hand, if a company fared well, it would be its stockholders, not its bondholders, who would benefit disproportionately. Bondholders would get the interest they were promised and their principal back at maturity, but that's all: everything over and above that would go to the stockholders.

The Basic Principles of Investing in Bonds

When bonds are originally sold by corporations, they generally are issued in $1000 *face amount* denominations. The rate of interest that the company is committed to pay is called the *coupon rate*. Thus, if the company offers to pay, say, $60 in interest annually on each $1000 bond, that would be expressed as a 6 percent coupon; if it agreed to pay $85, the coupon would be 8.50 percent.

The date on which the company promised to return the money that you loaned it, often 10, 20, or more years in the future, is known as the *maturity date*. Thus, the one-line description of an issue as "IBM 8⅜ of 2019" translates into "bonds issued by the International Business Machines Corporation with an 8.375 percent coupon that will mature in the year 2019." If you owned one of those bonds, it would mean that you loaned $1000 to IBM; you will receive $83.75 in interest from IBM annually until the year 2019; and in the year 2019, the bond will "mature" and you will get your $1000 back.

Similarly, "General Motors 8⅞ of 1999" would translate into "bonds sold by General Motors Corporation with an 8.875 percent coupon that will mature in the year 1999." If you owned one of those bonds, it would mean that you loaned $1000 to General Motors; you will receive $88.75 in interest from General Motors annually until the year 1999; and in that year the bond will "mature" and you will get your $1000 back.

When bonds are originally issued, their terms vary substantially from company to company and from time to time based on a number of variables. Obviously, every company would like to pay as little in interest as possible while every potential creditor would like to receive as much as possible. The rate that a company actually pays will reflect the following:

- The perceived financial strength of the corporation (investors will demand higher interest rates from companies they view as being riskier borrowers than they will from companies they consider financially secure)

- The maturity date (investors generally will demand higher annual rates for lending money for longer than for shorter periods)

- The overall level of competitive market interest rates (when rates in general are high, any company, risky or not, will have to pay higher rates of interest in order to compete for investors' available funds than that same company would have to pay when rates are low and vice versa)

- The special features of convertibility and callability, which we shall explain later

By convention, a bond selling for $1000 is described in newspapers' financial tables as selling for 100, and other prices are expressed proportionately. Thus, if you read in the paper that a bond is selling at 100, you know that it's selling for $1000; if it's quoted at 97½, you know that it is selling for $975 in the open market (or at a *discount* of $25 or 2½ points from the face value per bond); and if it's quoted at 101⅜, it's selling for $1013.75 in the open market (or at a *premium* of $13.75 or 1⅜ points per bond).

If you hold a bond until maturity, it might not matter to you whether it sold at a premium or at a discount along the way. After all, the amount you would receive at maturity would be the face amount of the obligation, or the original $1000 denomination, and the company's obligation to you would not be affected by fluctuations in the price of the bond in the open market prior to maturity.

Why, then, would a bond ever sell at a premium or discount? In other words, why would you ever be willing to pay more than $1000 for a bond if you knew that $1000 was all you would get back at maturity (seemingly assuring you of a loss)? Conversely, why would you ever be willing to sell a bond originally issued for $1000 for, say, only $975, if you knew that if you just held on you'd get the full $1000 at maturity? And yet this happens all the time.

To understand why this occurs, one first must understand the difference between current yield and yield to maturity. *Current yield* is simply the annual interest paid divided by the price of the bond. Thus if a bond pays $82.50 annually in interest and the bond sells at $965 (a discount of $35 or 3½ points), the current yield would be 8.55 percent ($82.50 divided by $965). (Note that this could also be determined by dividing the coupon rate, 8.25 percent, by the quoted price of the bond, 96½.) Or, if the bond sells at $1032.50 (a premium of $32.50 or 3¼ points), the current yield would be 7.99 percent ($82.50 divided by $1032.50 or 8.25 percent divided by 103¼).

Yield to maturity, on the other hand, is a calculation of the average annual *total* return, consisting not only of interest but also of the gain or loss of principal, that a bondholder would realize by buying the bonds at a discount or premium and holding them until maturity. In the previous example, if maturity were just 10 years away and the bond were purchased today at $965, the investor would not only receive interest of $82.50 annually but also would receive another $35 at maturity (the difference between $1000 and $965). Spread out over 10 years, that $35 would be equivalent to additional earnings of $3.50 annually and when that is factored in, the yield to maturity turns out to be 8.75 percent or 0.20 percent *higher* than the current yield.

Conversely, if the bond were purchased today at $1032.50, the investor would still receive $82.50 annually in interest, but he also would *lose* $32.50 at maturity (the difference between $1000 and $1032.50). Amortized over 10 years, that $32.50 would be equivalent to a loss of $3.25 annually; when that is factored in, the yield to maturity becomes 7.80 percent or 0.19 percent *lower* than the current yield.

(Note that whenever a bond sells at a premium, its yield to maturity will be less than its current yield. When it sells at a discount, its yield to maturity will be greater than its current yield. And when it sells exactly at face value, also known as *par,* its yield to maturity and its current yield will be identical.)

Now let's return to our original question: why might a bond sell at a discount or premium to face value, i.e., for more or less than the $1000 that the investor would expect to receive at maturity? It is because it is only at that discounted or premium price that the issue's yield to maturity would become competitive with the returns available from comparable issues at that time.

Remember that when a bond is originally issued, the coupon rate at which it is sold will be dependent on a number of factors, including the perceived investment quality of the issuing company, the number of years until maturity, and the general level of market interest rates. At one point in time, for instance, the hypothetical ABC Company, perceived as being very financially sound, might be able to sell its bonds to yield 6 percent, whereas its less highly regarded competitor, the XYZ Company, might have to pay 7 percent.

At some future date, however, should overall interest rates decline, ABC Company might be able to issue new bonds with only a 5 percent coupon, and XYZ Company might be able to sell bonds with a 6 percent coupon. But a year later, should rates again rise, ABC Company might have to pay interest on its new bonds of 8 percent, and XYZ Company might have to pay interest of 9 percent.

Moreover, that all assumes that the relative quality of the ABC Company and the XYZ Company didn't change over time. But suppose one deteriorated and/or the other improved. Even if overall market interest rate levels didn't change from one year to another, the ABC Company might have to pay more, for example, 7 percent, to borrow money if its earning power or its competitive position deteriorated substantially. Conversely, if the XYZ Company's financial position improved, it might find that it could borrow money by issuing new bonds at only 6 percent rather than 7 percent.

As things change, i.e., as the overall level of interest rates rises or falls or the quality of the issuing company improves or declines, the bonds that a company previously issued also would have to rise or fall in price in order to remain competitive with any new bonds being issued by the same or other companies. If they did not, during a period of rising interest rates, no one would buy a previously issued bond with a lower coupon, and in a period of declining rates, no one would sell a bond with a higher coupon that he bought at an earlier time. But since previously issued bonds do rise and fall in price, their yields to maturity will remain competitive with the yields on new issues.

Here's how it might work out in practice. In Table 5-1, we assume that the ABC Company and the XYZ Company each issued 20-year bonds at 5-year intervals: in 1990, 1995, and 2000. The first bonds that ABC Company issued in 1990 bore a 6 percent coupon while those that XYZ Company sold were priced to yield 7 percent. Over the next five years, however, two things happened: ABC Company's financial position deteriorated (although not down to the level of the XYZ Company's), and the overall level of interest rates rose by about one percentage point (or 100 basis points). As a result, the bonds that XYZ Company sold in 1995 could only be sold with an 8 percent coupon while those that ABC Company issued bore a coupon of 7.5 percent.

Over the next five years, conditions changed again: XYZ Company's financial position improved dramatically so that it actually came to be considered a better credit risk than ABC Company, and the overall level of interest rates declined by one-half of one percentage point (50 basis points). As a result, XYZ Company was able to sell new 20-year bonds in the year 2000 on a 6.5 percent yield basis while ABC Company sold its new bonds at 7 percent.

Over the next 15 years, both ABC Company and XYZ Company maintained their relative financial positions and investment grades. Interest rates fluctuated widely, but, surprisingly, they ended the years 2005, 2010, and 2015 exactly where they had been in the year 2000.

Under these circumstances, here's what would have happened to the prices of all of the bonds that the ABC Company and the XYZ Company issued in the years 1990, 1995, and 2000:

There are a few other things you ought to know about bonds. First, some are *convertible*, which means that under certain circumstances, at the option of the bondholder, they may be converted into or exchanged for

Table 5-1. ABC Company and XYZ Company Bond Yields at Different Times

	ABC Company				XYZ Company			
Year	Coupon and maturity	Price	Current yield	Yield to maturity	Coupon and maturity	Price	Current yield	Yield to maturity
1990	6s of 2010	100	6.00	6.00	7s of 2010	100	7.00	7.00
1995	7.5s of 2015	100	7.50	7.50	8s of 2015	100	8.00	8.00
	6s of 2010	86	6.98	7.46	7s of 2010	91	7.69	7.96
2000	7s of 2020	100	7.00	7.00	6.5s of 2020	100	6.50	6.50
	7.5s of 2015	105	7.37	7.00	8s of 2015	115	6.96	6.51
	6s of 2010	93	6.45	6.94	7s of 2010	104	6.73	6.47
2005	7s of 2020	100	7.00	7.00	6.5s of 2020	100	6.50	6.50
	7.5s of 2015	104	7.21	6.96	8s of 2015	111	7.21	6.54
	6s of 2010	96	6.25	6.94	7s of 2010	102	6.86	6.53
2010	7s of 2020	100	7.00	7.00	6.5s of 2020	100	6.50	6.50
	7.5s of 2015	102	7.35	7.03	8s of 2015	106	7.55	6.60
	6s of 2010	99	6.06	7.04	7s of 2010	101	6.93	5.97
2015	7s of 2020	100	7.00	7.00	6.5s of 2020	100	6.50	6.50
	7.5s of 2015	101	7.46	6.43	8s of 2015	101	7.92	6.97
	6s of 2010	———Matured———			7s of 2010	———Matured———		
2020	7s of 2020	100	7.00	7.00	6.5s of 2020	100	6.50	6.50
	7.5s of 2015	———Matured———			8s of 2015	———Matured———		
	6s of 2010	———Matured———			7s of 2010	———Matured———		

common shares of the issuing corporation on the basis of a previously established exchange ratio.

This can be a big plus for investors. If a company does very well and its common stock rises sharply in price, the price of its convertible bonds will rise too, irrespective of interest rate levels, since the bonds could be converted into shares of the company's stock at the investor's option. On the other hand, if the stock declined in price, the bonds usually wouldn't decline proportionately as much (and, indeed, might not even decline at all) because they would retain their underlying investment value, being priced on the bases of their yields to maturity.

Of course, there is no such thing as a free lunch, and convertible bonds are no exception. Because convertible bonds offer attractive conversion features, they usually are originally priced to yield less than comparable straight bonds that are not convertible. And they usually will continue to yield less than comparable nonconvertible bonds in the open market.

If *convertibility* is a plus for investors, however, *callability* is a negative. What it means for a bond to be callable is that the issuing company, at its option rather than the bondholder's, may "call" them (or buy them back) from bondholders before maturity. Of course, with rare exceptions, companies only would want to do that when interest rates have fallen. Then they could buy back their old bonds at par (or at a small premium above par) and sell new bonds, carrying a lower interest rate, thereby saving money.

While this would be good for the companies involved, it would be a negative for bondholders. That is because the holders of callable bonds run the risk of being forced to reinvest the money they had invested in those bonds long before they matured and at much lower rates than they had been counting on.

Finally, it is important to note that it is not only corporations that sell bonds. Bonds and other fixed income securities of varying maturities also may be sold by the federal government and its agencies as well as by states, cities, and various municipal authorities, such as housing, bridges, tunnels, and sewers.

In general, United States government obligations are considered to be the safest or least risky of all fixed income obligations. As a result, they usually are priced to yield less than even the highest quality corporate issues. The gross yield on state and municipal obligations also is usually below that of corporate issues because the interest on such issues often is tax-exempt. This latter feature, the tax-exempt status of many municipal obligations, is generally *not* of interest to investors in 401(k) plans, however, since those plans already have a tax-deferred status of their own. As a consequence, municipal bond funds seldom are an option in 401(k) plans.

We now can see what the key advantages and disadvantages to investing in bonds and other fixed income securities might be:

1. The biggest advantage is that the return on your investment (the bond's yield to maturity) is fixed and known in advance. You know exactly what payments you'll receive (interest payments and the face value of the bond) and when you'll receive them (the interest payment dates and the maturity date), subject only to any possible call features.

   But the flip side of this is that you couldn't receive any more than that. Hence, if inflation continues to erode the purchasing power of the dollar, the interest and principal payments you receive might be worth a lot less than you expected in *real* terms. That is what is known as the *inflation risk* in bonds.

2. You may be reasonably confident that you'll get your original investment back on a specific future date (the maturity date), assuming the issuer remains in business (although, as noted above, the purchasing power of the funds you get back may be lower than that of the funds you originally invested). If the company whose bonds you purchased went bankrupt, however, you might not get back your entire investment, although you likely would get something (assets in liquidation might be worth less than even the face amount of bonds outstanding); this is known as the *business risk* or *credit risk* in bonds.

3. If the company whose bonds you own fares badly, you will be entitled to receive the interest due you on your bonds before stockholders get anything. And if the company is forced to liquidate, your claim on the company's assets will take precedence over the claims of stockholders. But no matter how well the company does, you won't get any more (unless the bonds are convertible).

4. If the bonds in which you invested are convertible, you will have an opportunity to share in the benefit of rising stock prices, while being protected against suffering from any stock price declines by those bonds' underlying investment values. But you probably will have to pay a premium over conversion and investment values when you purchase those bonds, and yields on convertible bond issues are likely to be lower than on nonconvertible bonds of the same or equivalent issuers.

5. Finally, bond prices are likely to fluctuate over a more narrow range than are stock prices. They will fluctuate in line with overall interest rate levels, however, so that if interest rates rise, any nonconvertible bonds you owned would be likely to decline in price, even if the company that issued the bonds were doing very well and even if its stock price were rising. This is known as the *market risk* or *interest rate risk* in bonds.

The Basic Principles of Equity or Common Stock Investment

Just as there are advantages and disadvantages to investing in bonds and other fixed income securities, so, too, are there advantages and disadvantages in being a stockholder, rather than a bondholder. No matter how well a company does, for example, the holders of its nonconvertible fixed income securities never would receive more than the interest to which they were legally entitled plus the return of their original principal investments provided they hold to maturity. But there would be no limit to what stockholders might receive since any money the company earned, after paying the interest it owed to its bondholders, would belong to them. So if a company did well, very generous dividends might be paid, and the stock price could appreciate substantially.

As we have seen, the value of a bond may be precisely determined if we know the quality of the issuing company, the face amount of the bond (usually $1000), the coupon rate, the maturity date, the overall level of competitive interest rates, and any other special features such as convertibility or callability. With such information, investors can make very exact calculations of the relative value of different fixed income issues, down to fractions of a point.

But how would one determine the value of a stock? There is, after all, no fixed maturity date on which the investor would be assured of getting his money back. Moreover, the company may or may not be paying a dividend and, if it is, there is no guarantee that the dividend will be maintained. It could be eliminated in its entirety, reduced, or increased (unlike the coupon rate on a bond that remains constant).

The answer is that the value of a common stock is a function of the company's current and prospective earnings (which translate into its dividend-paying ability) and its underlying asset value. And since these variables cannot be determined with anywhere near the certainty of a bond's coupon rate or maturity date, the evaluation of common stocks is as much an art as a science. Nonetheless, intelligent security analysis can provide equity investors with reasonable estimates on which to base their investment decisions.

If you could know exactly how long a company would remain in existence, how much it would pay in dividends over its entire life span, and what, if anything, its stockholders would receive when the company eventually went out of business and liquidated any remaining assets, then you could calculate the discounted future value of that dividend stream and liquidating value and thereby establish a precise present value for the stock. It would be similar to calculating a yield to maturity for a bond except that the period in question would likely be very much longer and the annual dividend payments would be variable rather than constant.

In order to estimate the future dividends that a company might pay, however, it would be necessary to forecast a company's future earnings since it would only be from those earnings that dividends ultimately could be paid. Thus if a company were earning a lot or if its earnings were expected to grow rapidly, it would appear to be more likely that the company would pay out a lot of dividends over time than if its earnings were low or declining.

That does not mean, however, that if a company were earning a lot today or if its earnings were expected to increase dramatically over the next few years, it necessarily would be paying high dividends today or that it will be increasing its dividend rate anytime soon. Indeed, the very fact that it's earning a lot or that its earnings are increasing suggests that there may be a growing demand for its products or services; that being the case, stockholders might be better off in the long run if the company retained most or all of its earnings for plant expansion, increased marketing efforts or new product development, rather than paying out high dividends right away. In that way, the company may be able to pay even higher dividends in the future than otherwise would have been possible.

Consequently, a company's earning power and future earnings growth rate should be of greater importance to common stock investors than a company's present dividend rate since it is future earnings, not current dividend policy, that will determine what dividends will be paid over the company's entire life span. It is for this reason that, for instance, the ABC Company, paying a dividend of $2 a share, currently may sell at a lower price than the XYZ Company, even though the latter is paying a dividend of only 50 cents a share or perhaps no dividend at all.

It could be that the ABC Company is only earning $3 a share but is paying out most of that in dividends because it has no good opportunities for growth or expansion; if so, it is doubtful if its dividend will ever be increased and it may even be cut. But the XYZ Company may be earning $5 per share, even though its current dividend payments are nil or only nominal; it may be reinvesting most of its earnings for future expansion, in which case the expectation would be that it eventually would pay dividends that, in total, will vastly exceed those paid by ABC Company.

Or, even if the XYZ Company is now earning no more than or even less than the ABC Company, its growth prospects may be very much brighter. Perhaps the XYZ Company is only earning $2 a share today, but its earnings are expected to increase at a 20 percent rate annually over the next five years, whereas the ABC Company's earnings are only expected to increase at a 5 percent average annual rate. In that event, the XYZ Company would be earning nearly $5 a share in five years, whereas the ABC Company would only be earning about $3.80.

If the most important thing for bond investors to calculate is yield to maturity, the most important thing for common stock investors to calculate is *price-earnings ratio*, i.e., the price of a stock divided by its earnings per share. For by comparing the price-earnings ratios of two different stocks, even two selling at widely different prices, the investor would be able to make at least a preliminary judgment as to their relative attractiveness.

If the ABC Company, for instance, were selling at $45 a share, earning $3 a share, and paying a dividend of $2, its price-earnings ratio would be 15 times ($45 divided by $3) and its dividend yield would be 4.4 percent ($2 divided by $45). If XYZ Company were selling at $60 a share, earning $5 a share, and paying a dividend of 50 cents, its price-earnings ratio would be 12 times ($60 divided by $5) and its dividend yield would be only 0.8 percent (50 cents divided by $60). Under these circumstances, XYZ would be selling at a price $15 or one-third higher than ABC and it would be yielding much less (0.8 percent as compared to 4.4 percent) but, on the basis of its underlying earning power, as evidenced by its price-earnings ratio, it might well be the more attractive stock.

Of course, the calculation of price-earnings ratios alone would not be sufficient, in and of itself, to determine a stock's attractiveness. It would have to be considered within the context of such issues as the quality of a company's management, its financial position, the underlying cyclicality of its business, its competitive position within its industry, its research and development activities, and its overall growth prospects. Thus, just as a bond with a high yield to maturity would not necessarily be more attractive than one with a lower yield to maturity, if the latter were of higher investment grade, or were convertible, or were noncallable, so, too, a stock with a low price-earnings multiple would not always represent a more attractive investment opportunity than one carrying a higher multiple.

Diversification, Mutual Funds, and Commingled Funds

Whenever you invest in anything, whether stocks, bonds, real estate, art, postage stamps, baseball cards, or whatever, you'll generally find that you're better off spreading your funds among a number of investments rather than concentrating all of your money in just one or two items. It is the old principle of not putting all your eggs in one basket.

If you had put $1 million, representing all of your investable funds, into just one parcel of Texas real estate, for instance, you might have done very well for a time, but when the oil boom turned into an oil bust, you could have suffered a very substantial or, perhaps, even total loss. On the other hand, if you had divided your $1 million into, say, twenty $50,000 pieces and had invested in 20 different real estate parcels instead, some developed and some undeveloped, some commercial, some industrial, and some residential, some in California, some in Texas, some in New York, and some in Kansas, the chances of your having suffered a major overall disaster would have been greatly reduced.

Under those circumstances, even if the Texas oil boom went bust, so that the property you owned there lost value, the other properties you owned in Kansas or California still might have appreciated. And if the real estate boom in California collapsed, real estate values in New England or the South still might have held their own or even risen.

The same thing would be true of a portfolio of oil paintings, rare books, or common stocks. Impressionist painters and twentieth-century American novelists might move in and out of favor, and if all of your money were in Monet paintings or Henry Branch Cabell novels, you might do very well sometimes but very badly at other times. On the other hand, if your art or rare books collections were broadly diversified by artist or author and by period and style, you'd be much more likely to come out ahead over time.

The same thing is true of stocks and bonds. If all your investment money were in the common stock of General Motors, AT&T Corp., or IBM, there was a time when you would have done very well and a time when you would have done disastrously. But if your money were diversified among hundreds of different issues, large companies and small, cyclicals and noncyclicals, basic industrials, consumer goods companies, public utilities, high technology enterprises, and so forth, you'd be much more likely to come out ahead of the game.

Looked at another way, if one company in an expanding industry were to gain market share at the expense of another, you might do very well if you invested in the right one and very poorly if you picked the wrong one. But if you invested in both, you'd be ahead as long as the industry as a whole continued to grow. What you'd lose on one, you'd more than make up on the other. In effect, you would have converted individual bets on specific companies into a bet on an overall industry where your chances of success were greater.

Moreover, if you invested in the stocks of companies in several different industries or, better yet, several different economic sectors, your risk would be reduced still further. And if those industries or economic sectors were selected so that the factors that affected one bore *inversely* on the other, your chances of success would be even more greatly enhanced.

For example, if you were to put all your money into just one oil stock, your one-stock portfolio clearly would not be diversified. If you were to put your money into several oil stocks, you would be diversified, but only within one industry. And if you put your money into the stocks of companies in several industries, say oils, natural gas, and mining, your diversification would be even greater. But all of those stocks still might tend to move in the same direction—up or down—if the identical factors, such as worldwide trends in commodity prices, affected them.

If, on the other hand, you were to put your money into a combination of, say, oil stocks and airline stocks, you would have diversified your portfolio much more effectively. That is because airline stocks and oil stocks are *negatively correlated*, which simply means that they tend to move in opposite directions under similar conditions.

Think about it. Since fuel costs constitute a large part of airline companies' expenses, an increase in oil prices will tend to reduce airlines' profits even as it increases the earnings of the oil companies themselves, and vice versa. So if oil prices go up, it's bad for the airlines and good for the oils, and if oil prices go down, it's bad for the oils and good for the airlines.

This principle, to seek negative correlations or negative covariance among the components of their portfolios, is followed by most professional managers of commingled and mutual funds, and it is a practice that you might attempt to emulate in your own 401(k) plan. That is, if you are offered several mutual funds, you might attempt to purchase the shares of funds that are negatively, rather than positively, correlated with one another. For example, a foreign stock fund and a domestic stock fund would be more likely to be negatively correlated than would two domestic stock funds, and a small-capitalization U.S. fund and a large capitalization domestic fund would be more likely to be negatively correlated than would two large capitalization funds. So you might seek to diversify your investments in that manner.

Similarly, if all your money were invested in a single series of bonds of one issuer, you might do well—or poorly. But if you were to diversify your fixed income investments among a number of different issuers of varying investment grades and with staggered maturities, you'd be much more likely to do well overall.

This is the diversification principle underlying the creation of mutual funds and commingled funds. Such funds seek to invest in a broad array of financial instruments with the goal of diversifying away much of the risk inherent in individual companies. And it is these mutual funds and commingled funds that will provide you with most of the options in your 401(k) plan.

From the point of view of 401(k) investors, the distinction between mutual funds and commingled funds is a legalistic but not a substantive one. In general, commingled funds are managed by the trust departments of banking institutions, whereas mutual funds are operated by independent investment companies (which may, themselves, be subsidiaries or affiliates of banks or insurance companies). In both cases, however, the net effect would be to permit individual investors to pool their assets in a single fund in which the investors would retain proportionate interests. The fund, in turn, would invest in a diversified portfolio of securities.

The Most Popular 401(k) Plan Options

With the exception of stock in your employer's company and GICs, the alternatives generally available to investors in 401(k) plans seldom include individual stocks, bonds, or investment contracts. Rather, they generally include mutual funds or commingled funds that invest in the securities of a large number of different companies, which is good because it provides individual participants with a degree of investment diversification that they might have been hard-pressed to achieve on their own, given their more limited individual resources.

If you looked hard enough, you probably could find a commingled or mutual fund that invested in any particular kind of security you might think of, from options to blue-chip stocks, from Japanese securities to U.S. government obligations, from junk bonds to convertibles. But it is doubtful that you could find any one fund that invested in *all* such classes of securities. Rather, funds tend to fall into one of three categories:

- Those that invest entirely in fixed income securities (including money-market funds)
- Those that invest entirely (or primarily) in equities
- Balanced funds (which invest both in equities and fixed income securities)

Even within these more limited categories, moreover, most funds tend to specialize, to a greater or lesser degree, in just one particular area, with one investing, for example, only in small capitalization stocks, another in corporate bonds with maturities of more than 10 years, a third in Asian securities, and a fourth only in the stocks of companies in energy-related industries. Not every such fund would be appropriate for 401(k) investing, and not all find their way into 401(k) programs, but many do. So let's take a look, in the next two chapters, at the kinds of funds you're most likely to find in your own 401(k) plan.

6

Fixed Income Alternatives in 401(k) Plans

The fixed income investment alternatives available to participants in 401(k) plans run the gamut from the most conservative of investments (U.S. government money-market funds in which the risks are virtually nil but where potential returns are likely to be commensurately relatively low) to much more speculative mutual funds and commingled funds specializing in junk bonds, foreign securities, or convertible debentures (in which both risks and potential returns can be considerable). An array of funds that invest in all kinds of fixed income securities of differing quality and maturities and in a variety of styles, as well as *guaranteed investment contracts* (GICs) offered by insurance companies, are found in between.

Since GICs are the most popular choice of 401(k) plan participants, currently accounting for about two-thirds of all employee retirement plan assets, let's first examine what they're all about before turning our attention to the fixed income funds.

What Are GICs?

A guaranteed investment contract (GIC), also known as a guaranteed *income* contract, is a contract between an insurance company and a corporate profit-sharing or pension plan (such as a 401(k) plan), whereby the plan invests a sum of money with the insurance company for a specified period of time, and the insurance company, in turn, pays interest on the loan at a fixed rate over the life of the contract. The insurance company then invests the borrowed funds in a portfolio of securities, including bonds and mortgages, usually structured to mature around the time that the GIC is scheduled to expire.

In this way, the insurance company (which hopes to profit by generating returns on its portfolio in excess of the interest rate it has guaranteed) assumes all market, credit, and reinvestment risks on the portfolio. The assumption of those risks by the insurance company, rather than the plan participant, and the assured rate of interest (which historically has been relatively high) explain the tremendous popularity of GICs among 401(k) plan participants.

What many plan participants do not realize, however, is that the word *guaranteed* only refers to the rate of interest to be paid on the contract. There is no U.S. government agency guarantee of interest or principal comparable to the Federal Deposit Insurance Corporation (FDIC) guarantee on bank deposits. Thus, while it is true that the insurance company does assume all market, credit, and reinvestment risks on the portfolio, it is still the plan participant who must assume the credit risk that the insurance company could run into such serious difficulties that it might be forced to default on interest and principal payments when the GIC matures.

Admittedly, this is not a very great risk and may even be a reasonable risk to assume (depending on the level of interest rates that are offered and what alternative investment opportunities are available). Moreover, the risks inherent in GICs can be further reduced if a plan diversifies by purchasing GICs from several, rather than just one, issuer. But some risk still does persist (as attested to by the well-publicized problems of a few insurers in the early 1990s), and you should be aware of it.

In light of all this, have 401(k) plan participants done well by investing a high percentage of their assets to GICs? Probably not. Long-term compounded rates of return on GICs, as on other fixed income securities, have fallen short of long-term returns on equities and are likely to continue to do so. With the exception of those 401(k) plan participants, therefore, who already are retired or who are very close to retirement, it generally makes more sense to minimize fixed income exposure (including GICs) and maximize equity exposure instead.

Fixed Income Funds: A Plethora of Choices

In addition to GICs, however, there are innumerable other mutual and commingled funds that concentrate wholly or primarily on fixed income securities. These fixed income funds may be classified in at least six different ways:

1. As foreign, domestic, or both
2. As government, corporate, or both
3. By the investment quality grades of their investments
4. In terms of the maturity of the issues in which they invest
5. As actively or passively managed
6. In terms of their investment styles

Domestic, International, and Global Bond Funds

Most fixed income funds that are offered as choices in 401(k) plans are *domestic funds,* which means that they invest only in the U.S. dollar-denominated liabilities of the U.S. government itself, U.S. government agencies, or U.S. companies. Some 401(k) plans, however, do offer fixed income funds that invest only in *foreign securities* (issued by foreign companies, foreign governments, or both), or in both foreign and domestic securities. A fund that invests only in foreign securities generally will be described as *foreign* or *international.* One that invests both in U.S. *and* foreign securities usually will be described as *global.*

The risk inherent in international or global bond funds may be greater than that of domestic funds for three reasons. First, the credit ratings of U.S. government issues are generally higher than those issued by most foreign governments; indeed, the possibility of default on U.S. government obligations is virtually nil, whereas the risk of default on foreign governments' issues, while low, still exists.

Second, foreign governments' regulation of securities issued by companies under their jurisdictions often are not as strict as those in the United States, and the information available on foreign corporate issues often is not as comprehensive as that available on U.S. issues. Hence, investment decisions based on such information may be less reliable. And this might be true whether the issuer were a foreign company itself or a U.S.-based international company making a particular offering in Italy or Germany, denominated, for example, in liras or deutsche marks.

Finally, and most important, one incurs a *currency risk* by investing in foreign bonds. Even if the foreign issuer pays interest and principal in timely fashion, foreign bonds, denominated in yen, francs, lira, marks, or whatever, could decline sharply in value in U.S. dollars if the U.S. dollar itself should rise sharply in value against those other currencies.

Of course, just as international and global bond funds are riskier investments than domestic bond funds, they also do provide investors with the possibility of greater reward—for the same reasons. For one thing, inherently riskier securities generally are forced to pay higher interest rates than are less risky securities. For another, limited information allows knowledgeable professional investors to capitalize on opportunities in less efficient market sectors. Finally, currency risks can cut both ways: if the U.S. dollar were to *decline* in value against, say, the Japanese yen or German deutsche mark, bonds denominated in yen or deutsche marks would produce currency *gains* (in U.S. dollars) for American investors.

Moreover, there is at least one way in which international and global bond funds actually may be *less* risky than domestic bond funds. Over the long term, interest rates in different markets tend *not* to move in tandem, so that a decline in the value of fixed income securities in one market (because of a rise in interest rates there) might well be offset by a rise in the value of fixed income securities in another country (where interest rates were falling). That geographic diversification could result in reduced volatility and a stabilization of returns from global and international bond funds as compared to domestic funds.

U.S. Treasury, U.S. Agency, and Corporate Bond Funds

The safest, most risk-free, and most creditworthy of all fixed income securities are U.S. government debt instruments, including treasury bonds, bills, notes, and savings bonds that the government has pledged to repay. That is because these securities, known as *government obligations* or *treasuries* are backed by the full faith and credit of the U.S. government, which, if necessary, could always simply print money to pay principal and interest.

On the other hand, the debt issues of federal agencies, including the *Federal National Mortgage Association* (FNMA, or Fannie Mae), *Student Loan Marketing Association* (SLMA, or Sallie Mae), *Resolution Funding Corporation* (REFCORP) and the Federal Land Banks, among others, are known not as government obligations but as *government securities* or *agencies* or *agency securities* and are *not* backed by the full faith and credit of the U.S. government (although most people believe that the government still would always recognize a moral, if not legal, obligation not to allow them to default). Thus, these issues, while boasting very high-credit ratings, are not quite as creditworthy as treasuries and generally are priced to provide slightly higher yields.

Corporate obligations run the gamut from very high to very low quality, depending on the issuers and the terms of their debt covenants. Even the most creditworthy of corporate issues, however, could not be deemed to be of as high quality as treasuries because no company, no matter how solid, would ever be in a position to print money to fulfill its obligations as could the U.S. government.

Some funds available through 401(k) plans invest only in treasuries, others only (or primarily) in agencies, and still others mostly in corporates, while some invest in any or all of these securities depending on the assessments of their relative values at different times by the funds' managers. Investors in funds that limit their holdings only to treasuries would, of course, bear the least risk, but their returns over time likely would be lower than those realized by investors in funds that also traded in agencies and/or corporates.

Money Market, Intermediate-Term, and Long-Term Bond Funds

Some fixed income funds invest in securities of virtually any maturity. A fund restricted to investing only in U.S. government obligations, for instance, might invest in treasury bonds (long-term debt instruments with maturities of 10 years or longer), treasury notes (intermediate-term instruments with maturities of 1 to 10 years), or treasury bills (short-term securities with maturities of less than 1 year). Similarly, a domestic fund restricted to investing only in corporate fixed income securities might invest in a company's 60-day commercial paper or in bonds due to mature in 5, 10, or 20 years, or even longer. And a domestic fixed income fund that was not restricted to either governments or corporates might invest in any or all of the above.

While some fixed income funds have been designed with that much latitude, however, most are limited to investing in debt instruments whose maturities fall within a specific range, say, 3 to 5 years or 7 to 10 years. At one extreme are the *short-term, money-market,* or *cash equivalent* funds, which generally are limited to investing in securities with maturities of less than one year and whose *average* maturities usually are measurable in days. A government money-market fund thus would generally be limited to investing in treasury bills (although it might also invest in government notes or bonds as their maturity dates approached). And a corporate money-market fund, which was not restricted to investing only in treasuries, also might invest in commercial paper issued by industrial corporations and in bank certificates of deposit.

At the opposite maturity extreme are the *long-term* bond funds (whether government, corporate, or both), which invest in issues with maturities of longer than 10 years. And in between are the *intermediate-term* bond funds whose average maturities generally range from 5 to 10 years.

In general, the returns provided by bond funds will vary directly with
their maturities. In other words, the returns from long-term bond funds
will be greater over time than those from intermediate-term bond funds,
and the returns from intermediate-term bond funds will be greater than
those from short-term or money-market funds.

There is, of course, a reason for this. Returns generally are higher on
long-term securities than on those with short-term maturities because
yields to maturity on long-term securities are higher than those on short-
term issues. And the reason this is true is that the risks of investing in long-
term securities are greater than the risks of investing in short-term ones.

In Chapter 5, we described some of the basic risks inherent in investing
in fixed income securities including: (1) business (or credit) risk; (2) inflation (or purchasing power) risk; and (3) market (or interest rate) risk. In all
three of these cases, risk increases as maturities stretch out. Consider:

Business (or Credit) Risk. If you purchase the commercial paper or
very short-term notes of a financially solid corporation, there may appear
to be little likelihood that the company's fortunes would be reversed
overnight, seriously jeopardizing the value of your investment. But if you
buy from the same corporation long-term bonds that might not mature for
20 years or more, your risk necessarily would be greater. After all, how
confident can one really be in forecasting what will happen a generation
from now?

Inflation (or Purchasing Power) Risk. One of the biggest risks in
fixed income investing is that the money that will be returned to you
when your securities eventually are redeemed may be worth a lot less in
real terms (or in terms of purchasing power) than the funds you originally
invested. When investing in short-term securities, this risk is minimal:
investors at least may make reasoned guesses as to what the inflation rate
is likely to be over the next several months or the next year or two. But no
one can really forecast with any high degree of confidence what the inflation rate is likely to average over the next five years, let alone the next 10
or 20.

Market (or Interest Rate) Risk. Again, how much more likely is it
that interest rates will rise sharply over a period of several years than over
just the next several months? This represents a risk for the holders of
bonds that will not mature for several years but not for the purchasers of
money-market instruments or short-term notes. More importantly, however, even should interest rates rise very sharply in the near term, fixed
income securities with short maturities will retain most of their value
since they would be redeemed soon, whereas long-term bonds would not.

It is for these reasons that fixed income investors, recognizing the inherently greater risk of investing in long-term than in short-term securities, generally demand higher returns from the former than from the latter. And it is for these reasons that investors willing to accept the incremental risks of going out long generally will realize higher returns over time than will more conservative and short-term oriented fixed income investors.

Investment Grade Bond Funds and Junk Bond Funds

Just as some domestic funds are permitted to invest in fixed income securities of any maturity while others are restricted to narrower maturity ranges, and just as some funds may invest in any combination of treasuries, agencies, and corporates while others are limited to investing only in treasuries, so, too, may some funds invest in fixed income securities with all different credit ratings while others are restricted to investing only in securities that fall within a specific credit rating range.

But what actually is a credit rating? Several rating agencies, including Standard & Poor's, Moody's Investors Service, and Fitch Investors Service, evaluate the investment or credit risk of specific fixed income securities, assigning ratings to those issues reflecting their own opinions of the creditworthiness of corporate obligors with respect to their specific obligation. In the case of Standard & Poor's, these assessments are based on a number of considerations including:

1. The likelihood of default as evidenced by the capacity and willingness of the obligor to make timely payment of interest and principal in accordance with the terms of the obligation

2. The nature and provisions of the obligation

3. The protection afforded by and relative position of the obligation in the event of bankruptcy, reorganization, or other arrangement under the laws of bankruptcy and other laws affecting creditors' rights.

Based on these considerations, Standard & Poor's rates corporate debt issues as follows:

Investment Grades: AAA, AA+, AA, AA–, A+, A, A–, BBB+, BBB, and BBB–. The grades from AAA to BBB– are commonly known as "investment grade" ratings. The highest, AAA, is reserved for those obligations for which the capacity to pay interest and repay principal is extremely strong. Debt rated from AA+ to AA– has a strong capacity to pay interest and repay principal and differs from AAA-rated debt only in small degree. Debt rated below AA– has a strong capacity to pay interest

and repay principal but becomes less adequate to pay and more suscepti-
ble to the adverse effects of changes in corporate circumstances and economic conditions with lowered ratings.

**Speculative Grades: BB+, BB, BB–, B+, B, B–, CCC+, CCC, CCC–,
CC, and C.** Debt rated below BBB– is considered speculative with
respect to the issuer's capacity to pay interest and repay principal in
accordance with the terms of the obligation. Although such debt generally does have at least some protective characteristics, those are out-
weighed by large uncertainties or major risk exposure to adverse
conditions.

Bonds rated below BBB– are commonly referred to as *junk bonds,* which
means that they have been issued by companies without long records of
sales and earnings or by companies of questionable creditworthiness. In
the 1980s, junk bonds were a popular means of financing takeovers and
leveraged buyouts.

Bonds rated BB+ to B– have less near-term vulnerability to default than
other speculative issues but do face major ongoing uncertainties or exposure to adverse conditions that could lead to inadequate capacity to meet
timely interest and principal payments.

Debt rated CCC+ and lower on the other hand, has a currently identifi-
able vulnerability to default and is dependent upon favorable conditions
to enable it to continue to make timely payments of interest and principal;
in the event of adverse conditions, it is unlikely to do so.

As might be expected, all other things being equal, there is an inverse
correlation between the ratings assigned to different bond issues and the
yields those issues provide, with the lowest rated issues generally yielding the most (provided they are not in default) and the highest rated issues
yielding the least. This is just one more example of the inevitable trade-off
that exists between risk and reward in the world of investments.

As a practical matter, what this means is that bond funds that are
restricted to investing only in investment grade issues (those rated BBB–
or higher) generally will yield less and often provide lower total returns
over extended periods of time than will those that invest in more specula-
tively rated issues. But over shorter periods, such investment grade funds
also will tend to be less risky and less volatile.

Not surprisingly, speculative or junk bond funds seldom are marketed
as such; rather, they tend to be promoted as high-yield funds, which, to
give the devil his due, they certainly are. But investors should be aware
that that euphemistic "high-yield" appellation may mask speculative or
"junk" characteristics, and, therefore, they should be wary of investing in
this arena without further investigation.

This is not to say, of course, that one *never* should invest in speculative, junk, or high-yield funds. In fact, well-managed funds in this sector frequently have generated very handsome returns for their shareholders, commensurate with their risk, and 401(k) investors with long-time horizons certainly may consider them as equity alternatives in the more aggressive sector of their portfolios. In doing so, however, they ought to realize the risks inherent in such investments and remember that their risk exposure is not necessarily lowered by investing in a "bond fund" rather than a "stock fund."

Active Management, Passive Management, and Index Funds

An *actively* managed fund is one whose manager seeks to select specific securities from a given universe in order to outperform the average of that universe. A *passively* managed fund, on the other hand, is one whose manager simply seeks to structure a diversified portfolio whose return will replicate, or at least approximate, the average return generated by a particular securities universe.

Any fund, whether a bond fund or a stock fund, may be managed actively or passively, even if it is subject to very specific restrictions. For example, a corporate bond fund might be limited to investing only in investment grade issues (those rated BBB– or higher by Standard & Poor's) and only in issues with maturities of ten years or less. Such a fund still could be actively managed if the manager attempted to invest in A-rated bonds which, in his opinion, really deserved to be AA-rated, on the assumption that those bonds eventually would be upgraded by Standard & Poor's and that, when that occurred, they would rise in price. Or the fund could be actively managed if the manager intentionally adjusted the average maturity or investment grade of his portfolio from time to time, say, from 9.5 years to 6 years or from AAA-AA to A-BBB, depending upon his evaluation of the relative values of those subuniverses at different points in time.

That same corporate bond fund would be passively managed, however, if the manager simply purchased and held a portfolio of securities with an average investment grade of, say, AA-A and an average maturity of, say, eight years, in order to attempt to replicate the performance of the average of that universe. The averages of particular securities universes are calculated as *indexes,* and passively managed funds therefore have come to be known as *index funds.*

Now, it may seem that active investing makes all the sense in the world and that passive investing makes none at all, and for a long time that, indeed, was the conventional wisdom. After all, it was argued, why should anyone pay a manager to run a fund that seeks to achieve an average return comparable to that which would have been achieved by the indiscriminate purchase of all securities in a particular universe? Shouldn't one expect an experienced professional portfolio manager to be able to do better than that by focusing on undervalued securities and avoiding overvalued ones?

When individual investors dominated the securities markets, this reasoning did, indeed, make a lot of sense. Professional institutional investors were able to capitalize on market inefficiencies resulting from the mistakes or ignorance or lack of sophistication of the investing public. Under such circumstances, institutional investors understandably were expected to "beat the market." And many, if not most, did.

Over time, however, the demographics of market participation changed, and institutional investors themselves came to dominate the securities markets with individuals coming to play a smaller and smaller role. In fact, institutional portfolios came to *be* the market, so that it no longer made sense to expect all, or even most, institutional investors to "beat the averages." To continue to expect that would be tantamount to expecting all, or most, institutional investors to outperform themselves or, in other words, for a majority to be above average. But that would be a logical impossibility.

Concurrently, a school of thought began to develop, first in academia but then in the investment community itself, to the effect that, unless he is just randomly lucky, it really is impossible for an investor to outperform a truly efficient market over time. (A perfectly "efficient" market would be one in which all information, which, if known, could affect the price of a security was, in fact, known by all market participants simultaneously, and any new information that could affect the value of a security would be instantaneously disseminated to all.)

Under conditions of such perfect market efficiency, it was argued, no investor could benefit by taking advantage of another's ignorance since, by definition, everyone would know everything that was relevant at the same time. The investment playing field would be perfectly level, and it would be only as a consequence of random luck that one investor might outperform another over a month or quarter or even year. And over time, it was expected that random luck would balance out.

Of course no one argued that securities markets were "perfectly efficient," since it was obvious that corporate insiders always would possess at least *some* relevant information to which the rest of the investing public (both individual and institutional) would not be privy and that the dissemination of news could not, in fact, be instantaneous but always would take at least some finite period of time. But considering how strict insider trading rules had become, how many thousands of market researchers and traders were poring over and analyzing the same data, and how swift (if not quite instantaneous) the electronic dissemination of news was in today's society, the advocates of passive investing concluded that the securities markets (at least the major U.S. markets) were efficient enough that no significant gains could be realized by active investors trying to beat the market.

In fact, the passive investing advocates argued, the very act of trying to beat the market by selling stocks perceived as overvalued and buying those perceived as undervalued would cause actively managed portfolios to *underperform* the market because the increased trading activity that active investing would entail would increase commission charges, thereby reducing portfolio values. And, in fact, in support of the position taken by the advocates of passive investing and index funds, it *is* the case that over extended periods of time, actively managed funds, on average, have tended to *underperform* the popular market indices!

On the other hand, advocates of active investing continue to argue that, even discounting the matter of inside information, all relevant investment information never *is* known by all market participants. They argue that smarter or more conscientious or more experienced or more talented investors always will have an edge on their less intelligent, less hard-working, less experienced, or less talented competitors because they will ferret out and interpret significant public (not inside) investment information that others simply overlook or ignore or fail to appreciate. Active investors point out that, in fact, some investors *have* consistently outperformed the market over periods as long as decades (a fact that passive investors dismiss as just a random event to have been expected of a small number of managers in a universe with thousands of participants).

So what is the truth? Does active investing make sense or not? Is passive investing just a way of seeking mediocre returns or will it result in the maximization of risk-adjusted returns over time?

Unfortunately, at this time, the jury remains out. Active investing may, or may not, add value overall (although the author is of the opinion that, in fact, it can). All that really is known with certainty is that the variability of rates of return for index funds, relative to the universes they were designed to track, is much less than the average variability of returns for actively managed funds participating in the same arenas. So if your objective is only to do as well as a particular index, if you want to avoid doing worse and are willing to forego the possibility of doing better, then passively managed index funds would make sense for you. But if your goal is to outperform a particular index, and if you're willing to incur the risk that in trying to do better, you might, in fact, do worse, then actively managed funds would make more sense for you.

Of course it doesn't have to be all one way or the other. You might, for instance, consider committing most of your 401(k) contributions to passively managed index funds and only a small amount to actively managed funds. In that way, you could assure yourself of generating an overall total return on your assets that would not fall too far short of the indices, even if your actively managed assets fared poorly, while preserving an opportunity of doing at least a little better if your actively managed assets fared well.

Different Styles of Fixed Income Management

Different active managers of fixed income funds may approach the management of their portfolios in different ways. Subject to the constraints of individual funds, three of the most popular fixed income management styles (exclusive of convertible bond management) are:

1. Interest Rate Anticipation. Some managers attempt to forecast the level of interest rates and adjust the maturities or durations of their portfolios accordingly. If they expect interest rates to rise sharply, they sell those securities in their portfolios with the longest maturities and buy those with shorter maturities instead; in that way, they shorten the average maturity of their portfolio to minimize their principal exposure. On the other hand, if they expect rates to decline precipitously, they lengthen the average maturity of their portfolio, thereby locking in currently higher yields and positioning themselves to capitalize on potentially rising bond prices.

The degree to which a manager might do this would depend, of course, on the overall maturity constraints established for his fund. Thus, the manager of a fund with no maturity constraints, could adjust the average maturity of his portfolio from, say, 18 years to 2 years and back again. (At least he could do so in theory; in practice, it is doubtful if any professional fixed income manager ever would make such big bets.) The manager of a long-term bond fund, however, whose portfolio was required to have a minimum maturity of 10 years, might only be able to adjust his portfolio from, say, 18 to 12 years or vice versa. The manager of an intermediate-term bond fund might be able to adjust the maturity of his portfolio from, say, 8 to 5 years or from 5 to 8 years. And the manager of a short-term bond fund might be able to adjust the maturity of his portfolio only from 18 months to 3 years and back again.

When these managers guess right, i.e., when interest rates move in the directions they forecast, they may realize substantial gains, and their funds may substantially outperform both the applicable bond market indices and any passively managed funds pegged to those indices. But interest rates are notoriously difficult to forecast and when these managers are wrong, which also happens, they may realize sizable losses, underperforming both the bond market averages and comparable passively managed bond funds.

2. Playing the Yield Curve. As we have noted, all other things being equal, fixed income securities with long maturities generally yield more than those scheduled for earlier redemption. And low-quality issues generally yield more than those of higher investment grades.

The difference between the yield to maturity on an issuer's 20-year bonds and on the same issuer's 10-year bonds is not fixed, however. Although the yield on the former will usually be higher than that on the latter, the spread between the two might be 100 basis points or 50 or only 10 and, in some unusual circumstance, might even turn negative. Similarly, the difference between the yield to maturity on BBB-rated bonds and on A-rated bonds of the same maturity also is not constant; although the yield on the former usually will be higher than the yield on the latter, the difference could be 15 basis points or 63 or 112.

Some managers attempt to capitalize on what they expect to be only temporary market aberrations by purchasing lower quality issues or issues with longer maturities and by selling higher quality issues or issues with shorter maturities when the spread between the yields on low- and high-quality issues or longer and shorter term maturities seems inordinately high. Conversely, they seek to purchase higher quality issues or issues with shorter maturities and to sell lower quality issues or issues with longer maturities when the spread between the yields on low- and high-quality issues or longer and shorter term maturities seems inordinately low.

This approach can work out well over long periods of time because market anomalies are corrected eventually (otherwise they wouldn't be anomalies!). But the risk is that what appears to be an anomaly may only be an early sign of the establishment of a new norm, in which case such an active trading strategy may generate nothing more than high transaction costs.

3. Anticipating Investment Grade Changes. From time to time, a major rating service, such as Standard & Poor's, may upgrade its rating for a particular issue from, say, BB to BBB or from BBB to A or may downgrade a rating from AAA to AA or from BBB to BB, based on its latest evaluation of the creditworthiness of the issuer or the particular security. Some managers attempt to anticipate such changes by purchasing those securities that they believe may be upgraded and selling those that they believe may be downgraded, reasoning that, if they are correct, they could stand to profit in two ways.

First, since higher rated issues tend to yield less than lower rated ones, any upgrade could result in a rise in price for an upgraded issue (in order to produce a decline in yield), and any downgrade could result in a decline in price (in order to produce a rise in yield). Second, any upgrade of an issue from below investment grade (below BBB−) to investment grade (BBB− and above) could make the issue eligible for purchase by banks and fiduciaries, which otherwise might not have been permitted to purchase it under various state regulations; that could increase demand for the issue, raising its price. Conversely, any downgrade of an issue from investment grade to below investment grade might make the issue ineligible for retention by banks and fiduciaries under state laws, thereby increasing selling pressure on the issue and lowering its price.

It might appear that this approach would represent an absolute plus-play: if a manager buys a bond expecting it to be upgraded, and the issue is upgraded, the bond will move up in price, but if the issue is not upgraded, it will stay where it is. So it would seem that the manager could win or break even but could not really lose.

In reality, however, it seldom works quite like that. The fact is that the bond market, even if not perfectly efficient, is reasonably efficient, and it is rare for a manager to correctly anticipate an upgrade or downgrade that other professional market participants didn't also consider to be at least a possibility. At a time, therefore, when 20-year BBB-rated bonds are yielding, say, 7.20 percent and 20-year A-rated bonds are yielding, say, 7.00 percent, a bond that is rated BBB but which many professional bond market participants think is likely to be upgraded to A, might already be yielding 7.10 percent, rather than 7.20 percent. Then, if the bond is upgraded, its yield might drop to 7.00 percent, but if it is not, its yield might rise to 7.20 percent. So the manager placing this bet could stand to lose, after all, if he or she turned out to be wrong.

7
Equity and Balanced Alternatives in 401(k) Plans

The range of equity or common stock investments offered through 401(k) plans is at least as broad as the number of fixed income alternatives. As an example, your 401(k) plan may allow you to invest in a portfolio consisting only of your own company's common stock. At the opposite extreme, you may be able to invest in one or more mutual or commingled funds whose portfolios are broadly diversified in their ownership of the common stocks of a whole array of well-established, blue-chip, big capitalization corporations.

In addition, your plan may allow you to invest in more speculative funds that might only purchase the stocks of small capitalization or emerging growth companies, or in funds that invest in the equities of companies in only one industry, or in funds that buy the stocks of corporations located in only one geographical corner of the world. Some of those funds may be actively managed while others may be passively managed. And some may utilize a *value* approach, while others employ a *growth* style.

In addition to all-equity funds, moreover, you may be offered a chance to invest in *balanced funds,* i.e., those that invest in *both* stocks and bonds. Here, too, you will discover major differences among funds depending on their fixed income and equity styles, the constraints imposed upon them in each area, and the balance they choose or are mandated to maintain between the two. In fact, with *two* components, fixed income and equity,

119

rather than just one, the permutations of choices among balanced funds are even greater than those among either stock funds or bond funds alone.

Why Not Just Invest in a Company Stock Fund?

But if investing in your own company's common stock is a choice available to you, why not just do that and be done with it? After all, you probably know more about your own company's operations than you'll ever be able to find out about any of the other companies in which you'd indirectly be investing through a mutual or commingled fund. And isn't it better to know what you're investing in than to invest in ignorance? Moreover, wouldn't investing in your company's stock fund indicate your loyalty and confidence in your company? And might that not help your career?

All of this is true, but, unfortunately, that's not all there is to it. Investing all your 401(k) assets in your own company's stock fund would constitute a classic example of putting all your eggs in one basket and, even though you may have determined that that was a sturdy basket, such a lack of diversification still would represent a very high-risk investment strategy, generally inappropriate for your retirement plan.

To be sure, if your company continued to do very well, your investments in your company's stock might produce larger returns than would a more broadly diversified portfolio. But should your company stumble (and even the best do from time to time), you'd have no positive returns from other sources to fall back on to offset your losses on your company's stock.

Moreover, while it is true that anytime you invest in just one security, you run this kind of risk, when the one investment is your own company's stock, your risk is even greater. That is because your financial future already is closely aligned with that of your company. If your company does well, your compensation is likely to increase through raises and bonuses. If it fares poorly, however, your compensation could stagnate or even decline.

Additionally, many companies have traditional pension or profit-sharing plans as well as 401(k) plans. If your company does, then your interest in your company's pension or profit-sharing plan already constitutes a kind of investment by you in your company. If the company does well, you'll get the benefits due you from the pension or profit-sharing plan at retirement and what you get from your 401(k) plan will just add to it. But if your company does badly, your pension turns out to have been underfunded, and your pension benefits are jeopardized, you'd almost surely be better off if your 401(k) plan had not also been invested in your company's stock.

Finally, in the worst case, your company could do so poorly that it was forced to downsize and you could find yourself unemployed. Should that occur, you might want to tap your 401(k) plan for hardship funds; if your

401(k) assets were invested wholly or primarily in company stock, however, you might be in serious financial difficulty.

In other words, if all goes well at your company and you invested heavily in the company's stock, you could make out very well: rising compensation and capital appreciation on your company's stock would represent a double bonanza. But if things went wrong at the company, you might suffer doubly too. And it's simply not worth incurring that downside risk in the hopes of realizing higher returns.

For these reasons, it generally is *not* a good idea to invest substantial amounts of your 401(k) plan assets in your own company's stock (especially if you already own stock or options on stock in the company). Indeed, recognizing this, most 401(k) plans that offer company stock as an alternative don't even permit a participant to invest 100 percent of his assets in company stock; rather, they limit such investments to no more than, say, 25 percent or 50 percent of the total. But even in such cases, our advice to you is that if diversified investment alternatives other than company stock are available to you, you'll generally be better off if you select one or some combination of those alternatives.

There is, however, one further complication. Some plans provide for employer matches of those of your 401(k) contributions that are invested in company stock but no matches of any of your contributions invested in any other plan options; given those circumstances, you might want to consider investing at least some of your 401(k) assets in company stock after all. That is because the company match would provide you with a cushion in the event the market declined and would provide you with considerable upside leverage in the event the market rose.

For example, if a $200 401(k) plan contribution could buy you $300 worth of your own company's stock or $200 worth of ABC Mutual Fund shares and if ABC Fund were to appreciate, say, 25 percent and your company's stock did nothing, you still would have been better off investing in your company's stock (which would still be worth $300) rather than in ABC Fund shares (which would only have grown in value to $250). And even if your company's stock were to *decline* 25 percent (to $225), ABC Fund shares still would have had to appreciate 12.5 percent to be worth as much.

Of course, this presupposes that you would be immediately vested in the company stock you acquired through your employer's match of your own 401(k) contribution or that you would remain in your company's employ long enough to become vested. If you wouldn't, then the apparent company stock windfall resulting from the match could prove illusory.

Equity or Common Stock Funds

As equity alternatives to company stock funds, there are numerous other mutual and commingled funds that concentrate wholly or primarily on common stocks. These equity funds also may be classified in at least six different ways:

1. As foreign, domestic, or both
2. By the capitalizations of the individual companies in which they invest
3. As concentrated in individual industries or broadly diversified
4. As traditional or socially responsible funds
5. As actively or passively managed
6. In terms of their investment styles

1. Domestic, International, Global, and Single Country or Regional Stock Funds

As is true of fixed income funds, most common stock or equity funds that are offered as choices in 401(k) plans are *domestic funds,* which means that they invest only (or at least primarily) in the stocks of U.S. companies. Some 401(k) plans, however, offer equity funds that invest only in *foreign* companies or in both foreign and domestic companies. A fund that invests only in the stocks of foreign companies generally will be described as *foreign* or *international* while one that invests both in U.S. *and* foreign securities, usually will be described as *global.*

In addition, some funds invest only in the stocks of companies in just one foreign country, such as Japan or Germany, or in the stocks of companies in only one geographical region, such as Southeast Asia, or the Pacific Rim, or Latin America, or Europe. These are known as *regional funds.*

Just as the risk inherent in international, global, or regional fixed income funds may be greater than the risk inherent in investing in their domestic counterparts, so, too, the risk inherent in international, global, or regional equity funds may be greater than that of domestic funds. For one thing, in many countries that are politically less stable than the United States, there is a risk of nationalization or expropriation without adequate compensation. For another, as noted in Chapter 6, foreign governments' regulations of securities generally are not as strict as those in the United States and the financial information provided to investors by foreign companies is seldom as comprehensive or reliable as that provided by U.S. companies.

Additionally, you would incur a *currency risk* by investing in foreign stocks similar to the currency risk you would incur by investing in foreign bonds. A Japanese or German company may do very well, its earnings may rise, its dividends may increase, and its stock price may climb—in yen or deutsche marks. Those earnings, dividends, and stock prices still could decline sharply in value in U.S. dollars, however, if the U.S. dollar were to rise against the yen or deutsche mark.

On the other hand, just as international, global, and regional stock funds may be riskier investments than domestic stock funds, they also may provide investors with the possibility of higher returns. For one thing, inherently riskier securities generally are priced to reflect their higher risk: the stock of a company that appears to be at some risk of being nationalized, for instance, is likely to sell at a lower price, relative to its underlying assets, earning power, and dividend-paying ability, than one for which such risk does not exist; then, if nationalization does not occur, the return on the riskier security from that lower price could be very substantial.

Moreover, as also is true in the fixed income sector, the limited dissemination of information on some companies in some markets may allow professional equity fund managers to capitalize on equity market inefficiencies. Too, currency fluctuations can provide gains as well as losses: if the U.S. dollar *declined* against the yen or deutsche mark, dividends denominated in yen or deutsche marks would be *higher* in U.S. dollars and stock prices denominated in yen or deutsche marks would generate currency *gains* in U.S. dollars.

Most important, however, the stocks of companies in emerging markets such as Southeast Asia, the Pacific Rim, or Latin America may provide investors with extraordinary growth opportunities not likely to be available from companies doing business in more mature markets such as the United States or Western Europe. Younger 401(k) plan participants who can afford the risk, therefore, might seriously consider committing some portion of their assets to a regional, global, or international equity fund if such options are available.

Moreover, recall that there is at least one way in which international and global bond funds actually may be *less* risky than domestic bond funds. Since, over the long term, interest rates in different markets tend not to move in tandem, a decline in the value of fixed income securities in one market might well be offset by a rise in the value of fixed income securities in another country, thereby providing greater diversification, reduced volatility, and a stabilization of returns from such bond funds as compared to domestic funds.

Similarly, there is at least one way in which international and global equity funds may be *less* risky than domestic equity funds. Just as, over the long term, interest rates in different markets tend not to move in tandem, neither do worldwide economic activity or securities markets. When one country's or region's economy is in recession, another's may be booming, and when one's stock market is declining, another's may be soaring. Hence, a decline in the value of equities in one market might well be offset by a rise in the value of common stocks in another, providing investors in global or international equity funds with greater diversification, lower volatility, and more stable returns than would be available from strictly domestic common stock funds.

2. Big Capitalization
Blue-Chip Funds and Small
Capitalization Emerging
Growth Funds

Some mutual funds are structured to invest solely (or at least primarily) in nothing but the stocks of the biggest and best known companies in the United States, companies such as AT&T, IBM, Boeing, General Electric, Sears, McDonald's, Procter & Gamble, Xerox, K-Mart, General Motors, Apple Computer, Campbell Soup, General Foods, Merck, or Aetna Life. As a consequence, such funds are the least risky of domestic funds since the companies in which they invest are, for the most part, financially solid, profitable, dividend-paying enterprises, with strong franchises in their respective sectors.

On the other hand, just because those companies are so big, mature, and dominant in their fields, their opportunities for dramatic growth are limited. Campbell Soup, for instance, so dominates the soup market that its introduction of one more soup variety would barely have an effect on the company's overall revenues and earnings. Similarly, the introduction of no single new product or the penetration of no one new market would be likely to have any significant impact on the fortunes of General Electric or Procter & Gamble, which already measure their sales bases in the billions of dollars.

To be sure, over time, these companies are likely to continue to grow, their profits to increase, their dividends to rise, and their stock prices to appreciate, but any such gains would be achieved only incrementally. Their days of truly explosive growth are, for the most part, behind them.

But there are other companies today that may be on the threshold of explosive growth. They are those newer and smaller companies with much more limited financial resources and narrower product lines (sometimes, in fact, only one product) that are on the cutting edge of new technologies. Such companies today may have only limited market penetration, small revenues bases, and modest earnings (indeed, some even may be operating at losses), and they may pay only token dividends, if any, retaining most or all of their earnings to finance their future expansion and growth. But their future potential generally is much more dynamic than that of their giant counterparts. Basically, these newer and smaller companies are in economic positions similar to those that today's corporate giants were in when they were just starting out 30, 50, or more years ago.

But in addition to their potentially explosive growth, small capitalization companies have something else going for them: they tend to be less efficiently priced than their big name counterparts. This means simply that because they are small, they are less well known, and fewer securities analysts at major financial institutions follow their progress. As a result, conscientious professional investors who are willing to put in the time and effort may have a better chance of discovering attractive investment opportunities among them than among bigger and better known house-hold name stocks, before those opportunities have become generally known to the investment community.

Some mutual funds, known as *small capitalization* or *emerging growth* funds invest in companies such as these, rather than in the big capitaliza-tion, household name stocks, expecting thereby to realize higher returns than they could generate by investing in more mature companies. And, in fact, over time they have realized superior returns. Over the 25 years from 1967 through 1992, small capitalization stocks generated average annual returns of 12.4 percent compared to 10.6 percent for large capitalization stocks. And over the 50 years from 1942 through 1992, the difference was even more striking: the average annual return for small capitalization stocks was 16.3 percent compared to 12.6 percent for large capitalization issues.

But, of course, there still ain't no such thing as a free lunch, and small capitalization stocks are no exception. If the return on small capitalization stocks is likely to be higher over time than on large capitalization issues (and it is), you might guess that some trade-off would be required. And you'd be right: there is.

Although their potential returns may be higher, the risk inherent in small company stocks also is greater than the risk in big company stocks. In fact, the same characteristics that account for their higher potential returns also contribute to their greater risk.

For one thing, business risk is greater. Since they are smaller, have lim-ited finances, narrow product lines, no established franchises, and short operating histories, small capitalization companies are much more likely to fail than are mature companies. And, in fact a much higher percentage of small capitalization emerging growth companies do fail.

Additionally, market risk is greater. Small capitalization stocks are, almost tautologically, less liquid than big capitalization issues and are less efficiently priced. Hence, they are likely to be much more volatile and, over some periods of less than a generation, may underperform big capi-talization companies. In fact, despite the superior total return record achieved by small capitalization stocks over periods of 25 and 50 years, that is just what happened over the shorter periods of 5 and 10 years end-ing in 1992: during both of those periods, small capitalization stocks actu-ally underperformed big capitalization issues.

What, then, are the implications of all this for 401(k) plan investors? Simple. If you are young, just embarking upon your career, and are not very risk-averse, we believe there is a place for small capitalization or emerging growth funds in your portfolio. As you grow older and begin to approach retirement, however, you should consider reducing your expo-sure to this relatively riskier market sector.

3. Diversified
and Specialized (Single
Industry) Funds

All of the funds that we've discussed so far, whether foreign or domestic, large capitalization or small, implicitly are diversified by industry (even if not by geographic region or size). In that way, the managers of these funds seek to avoid the risk of overexposure to any one industry or economic sector because what may be bad for one industry at one time may be good for another and that through such industrial diversification they may avoid the risk of overall disaster.

For example, rising crude oil prices might be bad for the airline industry (whose fuel costs then might be expected to rise), but good for the oil producers themselves, and vice versa. By investing *both* in airlines *and* in oils, therefore, rather than in just one or the other, these funds seek to assure themselves that fluctuating oil prices would not, in and of themselves, necessarily wreak havoc with the overall value of their portfolios. If they had invested instead only in the airlines (or only in the oils), however, they might stand to lose very substantially if oil prices were unexpectedly to rise (or fall) sharply.

This kind of diversification is one of the basic principles underpinning the mutual fund industry, and investors generally have been well served by adhering to it. But what about those investors who knowingly may wish to assume the risk of concentrating their assets in just one area or another because they expect some particular sector to provide superior returns? An investor who is convinced that oil prices are going to rise, for instance, may wish to have a large portion of his assets invested in the stocks of petroleum companies and none in the stocks of airlines for that very reason, even though that would represent a riskier nondiversified strategy. An investor who thought that oil prices were likely to fall, on the other hand, might want to own lots of airline stocks and get out of the oils entirely.

In fact, there are specialized funds designed to accommodate just such investors. One such fund, for example, might invest only in chemical stocks, another only in health-care companies, a third solely in gold or precious metals issues, and a fourth in the stocks of companies involved in waste management or environmental control. Indeed, there is probably a specialized mutual fund structured to invest in just about any single industry or economic sector you might think of.

Now the question is, if one or more such specialized funds are among the choices available to you through your 401(k) plan, should you avail yourself of it? In general, we think not. For while it is true that in any given year, *some* specialized fund will outperform the broadly diversified funds, by being in the right place at the right time, it will be a *different* fund in a *different* industry that will pull off the trick each year. And over long periods of time, we believe that the broadly diversified funds will win out because no one industry or economic sector will remain in fashion forever. Mutual funds specializing in uranium stocks soared in the 1950s at the dawn of the atomic age, only to collapse when a uranium glut developed. Precious metals funds skyrocketed when gold rose to $800 and silver to $50 per ounce, only to return to earth when gold retraced to $350 and silver to $5. Energy funds boomed with the OPEC-induced quadrupling of crude oil prices and declined again when petroleum prices fell. Drug and health-care stocks had their heyday; so did high technology issues; so did the stocks of environmental companies. And all came back.

Of course, if you were astute enough to trade in and out of specialized funds successfully, always being in the right sectors at the right time, you would do better than if you just stayed in any one diversified fund. But how realistic is that? Your 401(k) plan might not even offer a whole array of specialized funds but only one or two, and even if it did, would you really have the time and knowledge to know which fund to be in when? Isn't that really what you should hire professional managers of diversified funds to do for you?

In fact, by investing in an actively managed diversified equity fund, what you really are doing is retaining professional management to make these decisions for you, decisions as to which industries and economic sectors to overweight and which to underweight as conditions change. And in the long run, we think you'll be better off doing that than trading specialized funds on your own.

4. Traditional and Socially Responsible Funds

Historically, mutual funds have considered their sole objective to be the maximization of risk-adjusted returns for their shareholders. To be sure, one fund might have sought to achieve that goal by buying intermediate-term bonds and another by investing in small capitalization stocks; one by investing in foreign securities and another by purchasing domestic issues; and one by focusing on the generation of current income while another emphasized investing for capital appreciation. But one thing they all had in common: their goal was the maximization of shareholders' financial or economic interests (within the context of their respective styles) and refused to concern themselves with issues that they deemed to be extraneous, such as the social or ethical implications of their investment activities. Indeed, many would have argued that to have done otherwise would have been violative of their fiduciary responsibilities to their shareholders.

Beginning in the early 1970s, however, a new "socially responsible investing" perspective began to emerge, with some investors and investment managers arguing that it not only was acceptable but actually was desirable that investors consider the social or ethical ramifications of their investing activities. For instance, they contended that it would be wrong to invest in a manner that supported repressive governments, so that investments in South Africa should be avoided no matter how attractive they might appear to be on strictly financial grounds. Similarly, they argued that one should not invest in companies that pollute the environment, that are guilty of racial or religious or sex discrimination in their employment practices, that manufacture "undesirable" products such as cigarettes or alcohol or gaming devices or guns, or that test their products on animals, and on and on and on.

Not all socially responsible investing advocates agreed precisely on each and every one of these issues nor on just which activities were or were not socially responsible. But a general consensus did develop, roughly along the lines of what today might be considered to be "politically correct" activities.

It wasn't long before the movement found expression within the mutual fund industry with the launching of the Pax World Fund in 1970 and the Dreyfus Third Century Fund in 1972. Over time, several other socially responsible funds, both equity and fixed income, diversified and specialized, were formed with similar goals.

Most 401(k) plans today do not include a socially responsible fund as one of their investment options. But many 403(b) plans already do, and interest in this type of investing is growing rapidly, as evidenced by the large number of new socially responsible mutual funds being formed and the increased dollar value of the assets under their management. Hence, we think it likely that within a few years, socially responsible funds may comprise a significant portion of the assets not only of 403(b) plans but of 401(k) plans as well.

It is possible that one of the mutual funds already included in your 401(k) plan is a socially responsible fund. If so, in order for you to decide whether or not to invest in it, you ought to ask yourself the following three questions:

1. If the fund were *not* a socially responsible fund, would you be considering investing in it anyway? If, for instance, the socially responsible fund in question were a small capitalization stock fund or a fund specializing in only one industry or economic sector and you are only interested in investing in a fully diversified stock fund or a fixed income fund, then this particular fund would not be appropriate for you, and the fact that it billed itself as "socially responsible" shouldn't matter.

2. Assuming that the fund does meet your general objectives (still ignoring for the moment any of its socially responsible characteristics), are the returns that it would likely generate be commensurate with what

you'd be likely to receive from a similar fund that did not present itself as socially responsible? In other words, are the returns you might expect to realize likely to be reduced, enhanced, or unaffected by the fund's overlay of social responsibility?

This is a tough question. In theory, at least, the returns generated by socially responsible funds might be expected to be lower than those produced by comparable nonsocially responsible funds. That is because a socially responsible fund will be precluded from making certain investments, even though they may be financially advantageous, for social or ethical reasons. The manager of such a fund might conclude, for example, that tobacco stocks are very undervalued and likely to generate superior risk-adjusted returns and yet he or she might be unable to invest in such stocks simply because the fund was prevented from investing in the tobacco industry on social grounds.

Socially responsible investing advocates, on the other hand, argue that the inclusion of social or ethical considerations in the investment process actually enhances returns since, over the long run, companies that are not socially responsible are likely to run into such problems as adverse legislation, low employee morale, fines and penalties, punitive taxation, and consumer boycotts. By avoiding these companies in the first place, they argue, such potential problems may be eliminated even before they come to light.

Where does the truth lie? Unfortunately, we cannot yet know for sure. Socially responsible funds, as a class, have not been around for a long enough period of time for their returns to have been measured, analyzed, and evaluated in sufficient detail that reasoned judgments might be made with certainty (nor even to a high level of statistical significance). During some periods, some socially responsible funds have, indeed, outperformed the appropriate market indices and comparable actively managed funds while in others they have underperformed them. Over long periods of time, however, it seems likely that some price (albeit quite small) may have to be paid by socially responsible investors.

3. Finally, do you actually agree with the social or ethical goals espoused by the particular fund in which you are considering investing? Perhaps the fund considers it an ethical imperative never to invest in companies that perform animal experiments, whereas you believe that under certain circumstances such experiments are necessary as a way to advance our medical knowledge and find cures for the worst diseases ravaging mankind. Or perhaps the fund won't invest in companies unless they have affirmative action hiring programs in place, whereas you oppose affirmative action because you consider it a form of reverse racism. In either of those cases, that particular fund wouldn't appear to suit your needs.

Of course you also might find yourself in total agreement with the fund's social goals and, if so, the fund might be just what you've been looking for. But make sure to find out and not automatically assume that just because the fund bills itself as being socially responsible, it must necessarily be more ethical (in terms of your own values) than one that does not.

So what should you actually do? We believe that the conservative assumption for you to make is that the returns you might realize from a socially responsible fund could fall slightly short of what you might realize from a similar fund without social constraints but that any such shortfall likely would be minimal, perhaps amounting to less than 1 percent annually. Then, if the goals of the fund are consistent with your own, if the fund meets your requirements on financial grounds, and if you're willing to pay that small financial price to implement your socially responsible convictions, you might select the fund as one of your 401(k) plan investments. But if the fund does not otherwise meet your needs, or if you're unwilling to accept any reduction in your potential returns in order to implement your social goals, or if the fund's goals are not consonant with your own, then you're probably better off investing elsewhere.

5. Actively Managed Funds and Passively Managed (or Index) Funds

In Chapter 6, we explained the differences between an actively managed fixed income fund (one whose manager seeks to select specific securities from a given universe in order to outperform the average of that universe) and a passively managed (or index) fixed income fund (one whose manager seeks to structure a diversified portfolio whose return will replicate that of a particular securities universe). That distinction is equally applicable to equity funds, and there is no need to repeat our entire discussion regarding the pros and cons of active versus passive investing at this time.

Suffice it to say that just as any fixed income fund may be managed either actively or passively, even if it is subject to very specific restrictions, so, too, may virtually any stock fund, whether it be a large capitalization fund, a small capitalization fund, or even a foreign or regional or specialized fund restricted to the purchase of stocks of only one country or geographic region or industry.

In deciding whether to invest in an actively or passively managed stock fund, you might wish to review the case for and against the two approaches in Chapter 6. What your decision finally will come down to is this: if you are willing to accept average returns in order to avoid the risk of doing worse than average (and, therefore, are willing to forego the possibility of realizing above average returns), then you might choose passively managed index funds. But if you're hoping to outperform a particular index and are willing to incur the risk that in trying to do better, you might do worse, then you might opt for actively managed funds instead.

Or, in order to hedge your bets, you might commit most of your 401(k) assets earmarked for equities to a passively managed equity index fund and only a small amount to one or more actively managed funds. In that way, you probably would realize an overall total return on your equity funds close to that of the market, even if your actively managed assets fared poorly, while retaining a chance of doing at least somewhat better should your actively managed assets perform particularly well.

6. Value Management and Growth Management Styles

The managers of different actively managed funds, whether foreign or domestic, large capitalization or small, diversified or specialized, employ a wide variety of styles, techniques, and strategies in attempting to achieve their goals. One, for instance, might rely heavily on the analysis of *technical data*, i.e., information relating to historic price and volume statistics in seeking to determine how prices might move in the future. Another might bill itself as a *sector rotator*, which means that it will overweight its positions first in one industry or economic sector and then in another, depending on where he perceives us to be in the economic cycle. Indeed, one fund manager even claimed to rely on astrological charts in reaching his decisions while another refused to invest in companies whose chief executive officers were obese!

The two most common approaches to active equity fund management, however, are "value" investing and "growth" investing. Both approaches have much to commend them as well as some limitations.

Value Investing

The fundamental beliefs underlying value investing are

- That every stock has an "intrinsic" or "fair" value, relating to the worth of the company's assets, cash flow, earning power, and dividend paying ability.

- That over time, a stock's price will gravitate around that fair or intrinsic value.

- That sometimes a stock may become temporarily undervalued in the marketplace and at other times temporarily overvalued.

That being the case, the value investor seeks to discover stocks that are temporarily undervalued and to invest in them then, reasoning that he thereby will profit handsomely when the pendulum swings in the opposite direction (as he believes it inevitably will).

In seeking companies selling below their intrinsic worth, value investors look for those trading at prices substantially below their former highs; at low multiples of earnings; at low multiples of cash flow; at deep discounts (or only small premiums above) book values; below the replacement values of their plant and equipment; below the in-ground values of their natural resources; below the market values of their real estate; and/or on high dividend yield bases.

As a consequence, the stocks in which value investors invest are seldom growth stocks, since companies that are recognized as having considerable growth potential seldom sell at bargain prices. The value investor is not put off by that, however. He reasons that *anything* (including a company with limited growth potential) will prove to be a good investment if it is purchased cheaply enough, just as anything (including a company with outstanding growth potential) will turn out to be a poor investment if it is purchased at too high a price.

Analogously, we all might agree that a new Jaguar is a higher quality car than a new Chevrolet. But if one is buying cars with the intention of reselling them at a profit, the Jaguar is not necessarily the better investment. If, for instance, the Jaguar can only be purchased for $100,000 while the Chevrolet can be bought at a "fire sale" for $5000, the Chevrolet would represent the better deal and likely would return a higher profit to the car buyer when resold.

Staying with a value approach to investing requires sound analytical skills, considerable self-confidence and willpower, and something of a contrarian nature because when a stock appears to be statistically cheap, it is not *always* because of random market fluctuations, public misperceptions, or only temporary problems; sometimes there is something genuinely wrong. And that's why sound analytical skills are imperative: the good value investor must be able to distinguish those stocks that really *are* undervalued from those that only superficially appear to be.

When there is nothing fundamentally wrong and a stock is statistically cheap, however, it generally is because the company is temporarily out of favor with the investment community. Its growth may have slowed in the most recent quarters (albeit for nonrecurring reasons). New competition may have entered the company's traditional markets, and it may be feared that the company's products are about to become obsolete or that the company could be on the verge of losing market share. Or there might be some concern that new adverse government regulations are about to take their toll.

Under such circumstances, value investors in those stocks often must accept the mockery of those who question how they could possibly be purchasing such potential "dogs" or "fallen angels." But if, as often develops, the ostensibly adverse circumstances prove to be just temporary, it is the value investor who will have the last laugh. This is where self-confidence in one's own reasoned opinion and willpower in the face of overwhelming criticism comes in.

Finally, value investors generally look for their new investment ideas among those stocks that are making new lows, not new highs, since that's where bargains are likely to be found. They tend to buy stock in companies long before those companies make the front pages of *Barron's*, *Forbes*, or *Fortune*. And that's where having something of a contrarian nature proves to be an advantage.

Well-disciplined, intelligent, professional value investors have accumulated sizable fortunes over time because their approach really does make sense. But that does not mean that it works every time or right away. Sometimes a stock may decline sharply in price because of what a value investor interprets as only a temporary business reversal, leading the investor to believe that the stock is statistically undervalued—and the investor turns out to be wrong! The business reversal may be much more serious than the investor perceived, fully justifying the stock's decline.

Or a stock may truly have been undervalued and yet continue to decline in price anyway. In other words, it may become even more undervalued before reversing direction. (Nothing, after all, guarantees that an undervalued stock will immediately rise in price to the point of being fairly valued just because you bought it. Remember that the stock doesn't know you own it!)

Growth Stock Investing

The other principal style of equity investing, very different from value investing and yet often as successful in its own right, is known as *growth investing* or *growth stock investing*. Utilizing this approach, one seeks to invest in companies that are growing much faster than the overall economy (in terms of revenues, earnings, and potential dividends), with little regard to the prices initially paid for those stocks. The growth stock investor reasons that, in the long run, it won't really matter very much how much he initially paid for these stocks—if they continue to grow as he expects. For even if they were statistically overvalued at the time of the purchase, their future earnings growth would bail him out.

When growth stock investors are correct in their stock selections, choosing companies that do grow much more rapidly than the overall economy, they can do very well indeed. Even if, for example, they buy a stock selling at a relatively high multiple of current earnings (say, 30 times, when the overall market is selling for 15 times), they still will make out well if the company's earnings continue to climb. Should the company's earnings quadruple over five years, they would double their money—even if the stock's price-earnings multiple concurrently declined from 30 times to a more normal 15. And if the company's high growth rate continued to be perceived as likely to persist, the multiple might even stay at that high 30 times; in that event, the investors would have quadrupled their money.

Of course, growth stock investors can lose, too. If earnings growth for the companies in which they invest should slow down, (and eventually they will for all companies as those companies mature, or else one company would end up owning the world!), then not only will earnings prove to be disappointing, but the stock's multiple would be likely to decline steeply too—a double whammy.

Balanced Funds

In addition to all-fixed income funds and all-equity funds, there also are hybrids, known as balanced funds, which are designed to invest both in stocks and bonds. And as is true of all-stock or all-bond funds, these balanced funds also may be foreign or domestic. They may diversify or concentrate their equity investments, limiting them, for instance, to large capitalization or small capitalization stocks or to companies in only one industry or economic sector. Similarly, they may limit their fixed income exposure to issues of only certain maturities or quality grades.

Moreover, different balanced funds may have different *overall* objectives. The manager of one, for instance, may emphasize capital appreciation potential, purchasing those stocks and bonds that it considers most likely to appreciate in value, while paying little attention to yield. Another, however, might emphasize current income, focusing his attention primarily on those issues, whether fixed income or equity, that provide the highest current yields, with capital appreciation potential a decidedly secondary objective. And yet a third may emphasize total return, without especially distinguishing between current income and capital growth potential.

Balanced funds also may differ among themselves in terms of the mix they may be required to maintain between fixed income and equity securities. It is possible, of course, that the manager of one might be allowed to invest all of his assets in bonds and then, when he believed that conditions warranted it, switch all of those assets into equities, or vice versa (although, as a practical matter, few, if any balanced fund managers ever

HOW VARIOUS INVESTMENTS STACK UP

Money Market Funds

Advantages

- Invest mostly in low-risk securities, such as U.S. treasury bills and CDs of top-rated banks.
- Generally regarded as the safest investments.
- Because securities held in these funds mature quickly, there is little risk of losing principal.
- The rate of return is almost always positive.
- Yields are pegged to short-term interest rates and will rise quickly when rates climb.

Disadvantages

- Return less than stocks and bonds over long term.
- Double-digit money-market returns of the late 1970s-early 1980s not likely to be repeated anytime soon.
- A drop in interest rates will quickly lead to lower money-market fund yields.

Fixed-Income Contracts

Advantages

- Provide a stable and relatively high rate of income.
- Rate of return usually "guaranteed" for a year and sometimes longer.
- There is little risk of losing principal.
- Yields usually higher than money-market yields.
- The issuer of the contract bears any risk associated with the securities underlying the contract.

Disadvantages

- Long-term returns lower than those from stocks.
- Afford only limited protection against inflation.
- Yields tend to lag interest rates and will increase slowly when rates rise.

Figure 7-1.

- There's a remote chance that the issuer of the contract won't be able to repay principal. That's why plan sponsors often buy contracts from a number of issuers.

Bond Funds

Advantages

- Generally provide a relatively high and stable rate of income.
- Returns from bond funds tend to fluctuate less than those from stocks over most periods of time.
- Funds can lower credit risk by limiting holdings to government bonds (the safest kind) and investment grade (high-quality) corporate bonds.
- Funds can also reduce market risk by buying bonds that mature (will repay principal) within relatively short periods of time.

Disadvantages

- Long-term returns have been inferior to those of stocks.
- The principal value of the fund itself can fluctuate significantly as interest rates change.
- Bond funds, particularly those that emphasize long-term bonds, are much more volatile than money-market investments.

Balanced Funds

Advantages

- These funds blend stocks and bonds and sometimes other investments as well. Returns, therefore, tend to be more stable than those from stock funds.
- You have the benefit of a professional money manager deciding what the allocation among the investments will be.
- Long-term returns and the level of inflation protection tend to be superior to those of bond funds and fixed income contracts.

Disadvantages

- Don't optimize stocks' full potential and are likely to provide lower long-term total returns than funds investing exclusively in stocks.

Figure 7-1. (*Continued*)

- They involve more risk than bond funds and fixed income contracts.
- Both stocks and bonds can fall out of favor at the same time.

Stock Index Funds

Advantages

- Broadly based stock index funds offer a high degree of diversification. Many of these passively managed funds attempt to replicate the movement and composition of the Standard & Poor 500 stock index, which tracks a broad group of large company stocks.
- Long-term total returns exceed those of money-market funds, fixed income investments, and balanced funds.
- Few portfolio managers consistently beat the Standard & Poor 500.

Disadvantages

- Stock prices can fluctuate significantly over short periods.
- Negative returns and loss of principal are distinct possibilities.
- Carry more risk than money-market, fixed income, and balanced choices.
- You do only as well (or poorly) as the overall stock market.

Managed Equity Funds

Advantages

- With a good portfolio manager, you can benefit from superior stock selection and performance.
- Depending on the fund's objective, returns can exceed those of a stock index fund.
- Over long periods, can also provide higher returns than money-market and bond funds, fixed income contracts, and balanced funds.

Disadvantages

- Few portfolio managers consistently beat the Standard & Poor 500.
- Returns over short term less assured than those from more conservative investments.

Figure 7-1. *(Continued)*

- You can do worse than the overall stock market.
- A successful manager could resign or retire.

Company Stock Funds

Advantages

- Can provide high long-term total return.
- Permit you to participate in your company's future.
- May include special benefits at purchase, such as discounts and company match.

Disadvantages

- Ownership of only one stock, particularly if your sole investment, leaves you essentially undiversified.
- Developments within the company or industry in which it operates could hurt the stock's price.
- It could take years to recover from a major setback.

Figure 7-1. (*Continued*)

would make such all-or-nothing bets). More often, however, balanced fund managers are restricted regarding the minimums and maximums that they may invest in each asset class.

One, for instance, might be required to maintain a minimum of 50 percent and a maximum of 80 percent of its assets in fixed income securities at all times, with the remainder to be committed to equities, whereas another might be permitted to invest as little as 25 percent or as much as 75 percent in bonds and as little as 25 percent or as much as 75 percent in stocks. What this means is that either of the two funds might be, say, 50 percent invested in bonds and 50 percent invested in stocks or 65 percent invested in bonds and 35 percent invested in stocks at any given time. But only the first could ever have as little as 20 percent of its assets committed to stocks or as much as 80 percent invested in bonds. And only the second could ever have more than 50 percent of its assets invested in stocks or less than 50 percent invested in bonds.

8

Choosing the Best 401(k) Plan Investments for You

It is one thing to understand the basic principles of investment and the differences among GICs, company stock funds, common stock funds, fixed income funds, and balanced funds, as discussed in Chapters 5 to 7. But, even knowing all that, it is quite another thing to be able to determine which of those alternatives actually may be most appropriate for you at any given time. In order for you to do that intelligently, you must also be prepared to answer the following four questions:

1. Which of your 401(k) choices make the most sense in light of your own age and personal financial circumstances?
2. Which of those alternatives are best for you in light of the quality of the managers of those asset classes?
3. Which appear to be most appropriate for you in view of current and prospective market conditions?
4. And, finally, which seem best suited to you, given your own personality and emotional or psychological risk tolerance?

In this chapter, we'll show you how to answer the first three questions. Then, in Chapter 9, we'll show you how to answer the fourth and how to tie everything together into a cohesive whole so that you might make your own asset allocation decisions most intelligently.

139

Life-Cycle Investing
and the Process of Growth

We all change over time—physically, mentally, emotionally, and psychologically. The child who can't sit still, running everywhere rather than
walking, evolves into a young adult who must schedule time in which to
exercise regularly when exercise no longer is second nature to him, only
to develop into a middle-aged occasional jogger or golfer, and finally a
sedentary couch potato whose sports involvement consists solely of
watching televised events. The teenager who unconcernedly lunches on
double cheeseburgers and milkshakes, while maintaining a lean, healthy
body, must modify his diet as he matures, lest his body betray him as
he ages.

Puppy loves in adolescence are succeeded by grand passions in early
adulthood, only to be replaced again by less passionate but, in many
ways, even deeper commitments and more intimate relationships in later
years. Tastes in food, drink, art, literature, and music all change over time.
Political radicalism evolves into liberalism, then moderation and, finally,
conservatism.

These changes are a function of many things, both endogenous and
exogenous. Endogenously, whether we like it or not, our bodies and brains
change over time, our hormonal balances are altered, our metabolisms
slow. Puberty, menses, fertility begin . . . and end. Thus, even if we wanted
to continue to live the same kind of life from cradle to grave, we would find
that we couldn't.

We couldn't remain dependent children because we would grow too
strong and too smart, we would develop sex drives, we would find ourselves seeking independence, and we would become interested in things
other than just playing games—such as love, family, community, productive work, and achievement. Nor could we remain as young adults for we
would discover that over time we would begin to lose our strength, our
stamina, our speed, and our sex drives, and that our interests again would
begin to change.

These are the inevitable endogenous changes which would occur and
over which we would have no control. Exogenously, moreover, as we
found ourselves in different situations because of these changes, the new
situations themselves would produce even greater feedback alterations.

Thus, while our changing bodies, minds, and sex drives would be the
proximate causes of our choosing to marry and raise families, once we
began to do so, the presence of the families themselves would produce
additional changes since raising children, in and of itself, would affect the
amount of time, energy, and money we would have available to do other
things. At age 26, for example, we might still have the strength, intelli-

gence, and stamina we had two years earlier when we were able to work all day and party all night, but now, with two infants in tow, we may find ourselves choosing to expend our time, energy, and money on our children rather than on dining, drinking, and dancing.

If our bodies and minds change over time and if our interests, desires, goals, and risk tolerances are very different at age 40 from what they were at age 20 and different still at age 60 from what they were at age 40, then the financial plans we develop must also evolve over time to accommodate those changes. It is the evolution of such plans over time which is what we mean by *Life-cycle investing.*

The Five Stages of Life-Cycle Investing

The financial life cycle of the typical investor may be divided into five stages: the beginning, the early years, the middle years, the preretirement period, and retirement.

Stage 1: The Beginning

Young adults, generally in their twenties, who are just starting out on their own, have some tremendous advantages as investors—and some enormous disadvantages. Both these advantages and disadvantages should enter into their financial plans.

First, let's consider the obvious disadvantages:

1. Typically, they don't have much money to invest. Unless they were fortunate enough to have a trust fund or to have inherited some wealth, it's likely that they're starting out with virtually nothing. Their net worths may even be negative because they may be saddled with college student loans to pay off.

2. Their current earnings are not likely to be very high. Chances are that they're beginning their careers in trainee or entry level positions which don't pay a lot. On limited salaries, they may be hard-pressed just to cover their day-to-day expenses, let alone set anything aside for investment.

3. So they don't have much to begin with and they don't have much cash flow. But it gets even worse. These are also the years in which they have major start-up expenses (in addition to possible college-related debt repayment): a wardrobe suitable for that first job, furniture for that first apartment, a savings account to provide for emergencies.

Few assets. Debt repayment obligations. Minimal cash flow. Significant start-up expenses. The disadvantages are obvious and it's tough to see what the advantages might be. But there *are* four advantages, and they're very real.

1. Many young adults just starting out don't have any obligations to anyone other than themselves. Chances are they're unmarried and have no children. Nor are there yet aged parents they must concern themselves about. What money they can manage to accumulate, they can spend however they choose: on clothes or books, a new bicycle or a VCR, on entertainment—or on investment. (Only too soon will they learn how quickly these days of freedom will vanish, when they marry, begin a family, buy a house, and begin considering the needs of others than themselves.)

2. The fact that they have little to invest (and, therefore, little to lose) also allows them to assume substantial risk with less concern. After all, suppose they manage to put together a small stake, invest it very aggressively, and lose it all: that would represent no great disaster since the amount they would have invested would have been so small to begin with (even if it did represent 100 percent of their investable funds).

3. Additionally, since their earning power is so low, it almost assuredly will rise over time (both as a result of inflation and as a result of their own efforts as they advance in their careers). What this means is that if they should lose all their currently investable funds, they will be able to replace all of the money they lost from their future earnings with little difficulty.

4. Finally, time is on their side. With many years of life ahead of them, they stand to benefit substantially from the magic of compounding. (That, remember, was one of the important reasons we cited for starting an investment program early; by so doing, not only does the money you initially invest earn a return, but that return earns a return, and that return on the return earns a return . . . and on and on, year in and year out.)

Table 8-1 indicates what we mean. Assume that you were paid $22,000 per year on your first job and that you received raises of 15 percent annually during your first five years on the job, 10 percent annually during the next five, and 5 percent annually thereafter. (The higher percentage raises in the earliest stages of your career reflect the fact that your increases were from a smaller base and that that was the period in which you were progressing from an entry level or trainee position to that of becoming a full-fledged productive member of your company's work force.)

Table 8-1. The Beginning and Early Years: Salary, Savings, and Investment Fund

Age	Annual salary ($)	Annual savings ($)	Annual investment return ($)	Year-end investment fund value	Months to recoup
22	22,000	0	0	0	0
23	25,300	2,530	0	2,530	1
24	29,095	2,910	253	5,692	2
25	33,459	3,346	569	9,608	3
26	38,478	3,848	961	14,416	4
27	44,250	4,425	1,442	20,283	5
28	48,675	4,867	2,028	27,179	6
29	53,542	5,354	2,718	35,251	7
30	58,897	5,890	3,525	44,665	8
31	64,786	6,479	4,467	55,611	9
32	71,265	7,126	5,561	68,298	11
33	74,828	7,483	6,830	82,611	13
34	78,569	7,857	8,261	99,133	14
35	82,498	8,250	9,913	117,296	16
36	86,623	8,662	11,730	137,688	18
37	90,954	9,095	13,769	160,552	20
38	95,502	9,550	16,055	186,158	22
39	100,277	10,028	18,616	214,801	24
40	105,291	10,529	21,480	246,810	26

Assume further that, beginning with your second year on the job, you contributed 10 percent of each year's wages to your 401(k) retirement plan and that you realized a 10 percent return on your portfolio annually. Then your investment funds would grow as indicated in the next to last column in Table 8-1.

Now suppose in any one year you were to lose your entire investment. How long would it take you to replenish your investment fund from your wages alone? The final column shows how many months it would take you to rebuild that fund to its former value if *all* of your future wages could be devoted to that purpose.

If you lost all your money in the second year of your career, you could recoup your entire loss by saving just your next one month's salary. If the total loss occurred in your fifth year, you still could replenish your fund in its entirety by saving your next four months' wages. But if a total loss occurred in the 19th year of your career, at age 40, it would take you more than two years to recover—despite the fact that by then you'd be earning more than five times as much as you had when you first started out.

What this all means is that probably at no other time in your life will you be able to afford to take as much risk as when you are just starting out.

In all likelihood, responsible to no one but yourself, with little to lose, and with a lifetime of presumably rising earnings ahead of you, even the possibility of losing 100 percent of your investable funds in one speculative venture may be contemplated with equanimity.

If you are ever going to take the chance of making it big in the securities markets, now is the time to try. Common stocks, including small capitalization growth companies and foreign equities, are reasonable investments in your beginning years.

Stage 2: The Early Years

Table 8-1 spans not just the very beginning of your career but extends into your early years (your late twenties and thirties) as well. And this is a much more difficult time.

By the time you reach your late twenties, you will have come a long way from where you were when you were just starting out. In all probability, you will have progressed in your career, having received several raises and having become much better established in your job or profession. If you were saddled with college student loans, you may have paid them off. You may have furnished your first apartment, established a savings account cash reserve for emergencies, and begun an investment program.

Even more importantly, however, you may have married or have become involved in a long-term relationship that you expect to lead to marriage. You may be planning a family and budgeting for the purchase of a house. If your partner is also employed, you may discover that even if two can't live quite as cheaply as one, you're still able to save (and invest) more money together than you could have managed separately.

Or at least you may be able to do that for a while. Once children come along, your combined income may decline if one of you stays at home, while your expenses soar with the purchase of a house, additional insurance, another car, and your children's expenses. Anticipating this, it would be appropriate for you to reconsider how the assets in your 401(k) plan and any other investment portfolios you might have are allocated.

When you were first starting out, you could afford to take the biggest risks of your life in terms of investments. But such investments would no longer be appropriate once you married, decided to raise a family, and established specific goals of home ownership and providing for your children's educations. Or at least no more than a very small fraction of your funds should remain committed to highly speculative investments.

Since you'd still be relatively young, had an appropriate cash reserve and adequate insurance to guard against emergencies, and could look forward to decades of productive earning power ahead of you, however, you still could afford to be relatively aggressive in your 401(k) plan and could emphasize investments in common stocks, including smaller capitalization emerging growth companies. To be sure, you'd be nowhere near the point of having to shift to fixed income securities or cash equivalents for safety. But having established specific goals and having assumed responsibilities to others than yourself, you no longer could afford to risk losing everything in the hopes of making a big killing. Now if you were to try and fail, it would take much longer to recoup and could seriously jeopardize not only your own life but also those of your spouse and children.

Stage 3: The Middle Years

When you reach your middle years (roughly equivalent to your forties), you'll be approximately midway through your productive working career: you will have been working for about 20 years, and in another 20 years you'll at least be contemplating entering retirement. If your children are not already in college, they're probably approaching college age. Your parents are aging and you may have to start considering whether you'll need to be of financial assistance to them.

In these circumstances, you ought to consider adjusting your 401(k) plan and other investment portfolios again, acquiring higher quality dividend-paying blue-chip stocks and some fixed income securities to provide greater balance and safety and reduce the volatility of your portfolio. But your portfolios still should remain heavily weighted in equities as an inflation hedge.

Stage 4: The Preretirement Period

A decade later (now in your fifties), your circumstances will again be very different, and it will be appropriate for you to take a fresh look at your financial situation. Your children may have graduated from college and embarked on their own careers, and your financial obligations to them may have been greatly reduced. (On the other hand, grandchildren may also be on the way and you may want to make some provision for them!) Your earnings are probably peaking and the value of your 401(k) plan and other investment portfolios (assuming you had the foresight to begin investing early) may well be worth hundreds of thousands of dollars. But you may be planning to retire in only another 10 years or so which means that you won't have a lot of time left in which to increase the value of your assets and that you couldn't afford to incur much risk of losing what you've already accumulated (since there also won't be many years left in which to recoup any losses).

Under these circumstances, you should make every effort to maximize your savings and investments and, at the same time, consider making changes in your 401(k) plan and other retirement portfolios. One thing you might do would be to increase the component of fixed income securities with staggered maturities in your accounts. Another would be to review your equity holdings, pruning your portfolio of any highly speculative investments you might have missed. But while making sure that your equity investments are concentrated in relatively high-quality issues, you shouldn't eliminate common stocks entirely: since inflation would be likely to continue, you still ought to maintain at least some equity exposure as an inflation hedge.

Stage 5: Retirement

When you finally do retire, you may not find it necessary to make any significant further modifications in your investment portfolio. In light of the changes you made in your preretirement years, your 401(k) plan and other retirement accounts already will have been very conservatively structured and heavily weighted toward fixed income securities, with some high-quality equities as an inflation hedge.

Life-Cycle Investing in Summation

In essence, the fundamental principle underlying life-cycle investing is that an investment program that might be appropriate for a single 20-year-old with responsibilities to no one other than himself or herself might not be appropriate for a 40-year-old married parent of two and that neither of those programs might be appropriate for a 62-year old contemplating retirement within three years. In sum, the younger you are, the more working years remaining to you in your career, and the fewer your responsibilities to others, the greater the investment risk that you can (and should) assume. Conversely, the older you are, the fewer the number of working years remaining to you, and the greater your responsibilities to others, the less the investment risk you ought assume.

Since equity investments provide higher potential returns but are inherently riskier than fixed income investments, this translates into a broad recommendation that younger investors emphasize common stocks in their portfolios, that middle-aged investors shift toward a mix of equities and fixed income securities, and that older investors (those who are retired or on the verge of retirement) invest primarily in fixed income securities.

Within these broad parameters, of course, even finer distinctions may be made in terms of relative risk and reward, with small capitalization stocks, for instance, generally being riskier (and providing greater potential returns) than large capitalization issues, and with short-term fixed income securities generally proving safer than long-term bonds. Depending on your age and circumstances and the number of 401(k) plan alternatives available to you, therefore, you might consider these finer distinctions in structuring your own 401(k) portfolio. With this in mind and based on your age alone, you might consider allocating your 401(k) assets in roughly the proportions shown in Table 8-2.

In Table 8-2, we proposed that investors in their thirties might consider committing all of their 401(k) assets to balanced funds. Alternatively, we proposed that they might invest one-fourth of their assets in small capitalization funds and three-fourths in large capitalization funds. Or, we allowed how they might invest one-quarter in long-term bond funds and three-quarters in balanced funds or large capitalization stock funds.

But why should one investor choose one course of action and another choose a different path? There may be many reasons. For one, their financial circumstances might vary greatly. Although they might be roughly of the same age, one might still be unmarried, relatively wealthy, and earning a considerable income in a secure job, while the other might be less affluent, be drawing a smaller income from a less secure position, and be married with two children. Obviously, under such circumstances, notwithstanding their comparable ages, the former would be in a position to incur the greater risk while the latter would be wise to opt for a more conservative investment strategy.

Here is another way to look at this: If the bulk of 40-year-old investors' retirement plan assets are in their 401(k) plans, if they intend to retire, for instance, at age 65, and if, when they do retire, there will be few if any other sources of income available to them to provide for their retirement, then these investors would be well advised to structure their 401(k) plan portfolios more conservatively than would investors of similar age who had substantial other retirement assets upon which to draw. Similarly, 55-year-old plan participants who didn't expect to begin drawing upon their 401(k) plan assets until they were 70½ (when they would legally be required to do so) could afford to be more aggressive in managing their 401(k) plan portfolio than would 55-year-old investors who expected to be drawing on their 401(k) plan assets by age 65 or even earlier.

What all of this means, of course, is that we are not simply proposing a strict life-cycle investing approach to 401(k) plan management but, rather, a *modified life-cycle approach,* i.e., one that takes account not only of plan participants' ages and the number of years remaining until their "official" retirement but also one that considers the availability of other retirement

Table 8-2. Preliminary % Allocation of 401(k) Assets to Different Asset Classes

Age	Money-market funds	GICs	Intermediate bond funds	Long-term bond funds	Total fixed income funds	Balanced funds	Small capitalization funds	Large capitalization funds	Total common stock funds
20-29	0	0	0	0	0	0-25	25-50	25-75	75-100
30-39	0	0	0	0-25	0-25	0-100	0-25	25-75	50-75
40-49	0	0	0-25	0-25	0-25	0-100	0-25	25-75	25-75
50-59	0	0-25	0-25	0-25	50-75	0-50	0	25-50	25-50
60+	25	0-25	0-25	0-25	75	0-25	0	0-25	0-25

assets upon which they might draw and the reality of just when they might actually have to begin drawing upon the assets in their 401(k) plans.

The Evaluation of Investment Managers

Within the previous framework, you might choose to modify your 401(k) plan investment portfolio based upon your perception of the differences in quality, skill, talent, or expertise of different managers of the same or different asset classes. If, for instance, you have determined that it would be appropriate for you to invest some or all of your assets in a large capitalization equity fund and you were offered the choice of investing in either of two such funds (because your 401(k) plan provided you with a very wide variety of choices), you might predicate your decision on your determination of which of the two funds had the superior management. That certainly would seem to make sense.

Of course, many plans don't offer you more than one choice in any one asset class but, even then, you might find that you have more options than you think. If, for instance, you decided that you wanted to invest about half your money in large capitalization common stocks and half in intermediate-term fixed income securities, you might discover that you could achieve that goal in two distinctly different ways.

On the one hand, you might just invest half your money in your plan's large capitalization stock fund and the other half in your plan's intermediate-term bond fund. Or you might accomplish the same objective by investing all your money in the plan's balanced fund, instead, assuming that the balanced fund historically committed about half its assets to large capitalization stocks and half to intermediate-term bonds. And, in that case, too, your decision as to which way to go might well be influenced by your judgment as to which fund or funds had the better manager or managers.

But how might you actually go about determining whether a particular fund is or is not well-managed? After all, fund managers are no different from the purveyors of any other goods: they attempt to present themselves in the best possible light, emphasizing their strengths, not their weaknesses.

The best way to determine the quality of a particular manager, therefore, is not to simply accept his own self-promotional description at face value but, rather, to do a thorough analysis of your own regarding his business and operations. Among the questions you might ask are: How long has the investment management company been in business? How large are its research, trading, portfolio management, and support staffs? Who are its principal clients? What are the education and experience levels of its key personnel? And a host of similar questions. Realistically, however, you might not be in a position to do such a thorough analysis, either because you lacked the time, or the inclination, or the experience to undertake such a laborious task. And in that event, you might choose to rely simply on your appraisal of different managers' historic performance records in reaching your decisions.

This approach (evaluating track records) is not as reliable as doing thorough analyses of investment management companies' overall businesses, operations, personnel, and so forth, since a superior historic track record does not necessarily prove that a company will do well in the future nor an inferior record that it will continue to perform badly. Over any limited period, an investment management company might simply have been lucky (or unlucky). Or it might have changed its approach over time and now be managing money in a very different fashion from that which it used when it achieved its record. Or its employee turnover might have been very high and the personnel responsible for having achieved that record might no longer be with the company. For any or all of these reasons, track records should be treated very warily. But, even recognizing that, the fact remains that these records still might be all you have to rely upon. If that is so, it is imperative that you bear four things in mind:

1. Don't rely solely on a manager's historic *absolute* returns but be sure to compare those returns to those of other managers and a market benchmark. In other words, just because a manager achieved an average annual rate of return of, for example, 12 percent over the previous five years, which might sound fine in the abstract, that doesn't mean that the manager really did well if, in fact, the market as a whole and most other managers achieved returns of 14 percent or 15 percent during the same period. Conversely, just because a particular manager realized average annual returns over a five-year period of, say, only 5 percent, which superficially might not sound like much, that doesn't necessarily mean that he managed badly—if the market as a whole and his competitors realized returns of only 2 percent or less within the same difficult investment environment.

2. When you do compare a particular manager's performance to that of other managers and to a market benchmark, be sure that the universe of managers and market index you select for comparative purposes are appropriate. In other words, don't compare the performance of a bond manager to Standard & Poor's 500 Composite Stock Price Index, which is, after all, a measure of stock, not bond, performance. And don't compare the performance of a domestic small capitalization equity fund to that of a universe of foreign stocks, or large capitalization common stock funds, or balanced funds, or fixed income funds. In other words,

make sure to compare apples to apples and oranges to oranges and not apples to oranges.

3. Try to compare *risk-adjusted,* rather than just absolute rates of return, even among managers within the same asset class. If, for instance, two small capitalization stock funds both achieved average annual rates of return of 12 percent over the past 10 years, one still might have a much better risk-adjusted rate of return than the other. If one achieved its record by realizing positive returns ranging from 8 to 16 percent in each of the last 10 years while the other endured large losses in some years that were offset by huge gains in others, then the former would have incurred much less risk overall and, all other things being equal, would be the more attractive investment.

4. Finally, the longer the track record you're relying on, the better off you are. Very short records of 6 or 12 months or even only two or three years are less likely to be indicative of an investment manager's staying power than are track records of 10 years or longer. Indeed, the longer the record you rely on, the more likely that that record will prove to be meaningful. (Of course, it is important that, in relying on a long-term record, you assure yourself that the same personnel and management styles that accounted for that record are still in place.)

Above all, however, remember that your evaluation of managers with an eye toward the selection of appropriate 401(k) plan investments should be your *second,* not your *first* consideration. *First you should determine which asset classes are most appropriate for you based on the life-cycle investing concepts discussed previously. And only then ought you consider the relative strengths of different managers.*

In other words, you shouldn't select a small capitalization equity fund just because it's well managed, if an intermediate-term bond fund is more appropriate for you. Nor should you choose a superbly managed bond fund, if what you really require is a common stock fund.

Adapting to Changing Economic and Market Conditions

In general, 401(k) investors make a serious mistake when they attempt to select their investments primarily on the basis of their perception of current or prospective economic or market conditions. Consider, for instance, young investors for whom equities really would be the most appropriate investment choice (based on their life-cycle investing considerations). If they were to commit their 401(k) assets, even "temporarily," to short-term money market instruments or GICs instead, because they perceived interest rates as being very high or common stocks as overpriced, they would run a considerable risk of missing out on the realization of much of the long-term benefits inherent in equity investing.

To be sure, it may well have been their intention to invest in GICs or money market instruments only temporarily and to recommit their assets to equities just as soon as the stock market pulled back sufficiently or interest rates declined enough to create a true stock-buying opportunity. But how could they know for sure that such a real buying opportunity had arrived? No bell goes off and no announcement to that effect is made on the floor of the New York Stock Exchange.

Moreover, stocks that may appear to be temporarily overpriced often have a notorious habit of becoming even more overpriced before their apparent market overvaluation is corrected—and by then, their underlying values may have increased substantially. Additionally, there are probably no economic series more difficult to forecast than interest rates: rates that appear high today often go higher, while those that currently seem low often continue to fall.

As a consequence, young 401(k) investors who are reluctant to plunge into what they perceive as an overpriced equities market could discover that the market simply passed them by, as one quarter drifted into the next and one year into another. While they continued to roll over their money-market instruments or GICs, awaiting an opportunity that never developed or which they failed to recognize when it did, they would have realized much lower returns than they might otherwise have achieved over an extended period by investing in the stock market.

But what about older investors who are already retired or on the verge of retirement and who, therefore, really should have the bulk of their assets in less risky or volatile fixed income securities? If anything, they would run an even bigger risk if they made a major bet on a different asset class (in this case, equities) because they thought that stock prices were low and on the verge of taking off. For if they turn out to be wrong, they will not have many years left in which to recover their losses and the fixed returns they were banking on to provide for their living expenses could be jeopardized.

What this all comes down to is that investors who attempt to move in and out of various asset classes in their 401(k) plans run a major risk of being in the wrong asset classes at the wrong time and of not being in the very asset classes that, over time, will prove most appropriate for them. What they might gain on the curves, they are very likely to lose on the straightaways.

Even with all this in mind, however, some particularly active and knowledgeable 401(k) investors still might want to make small modifications in their investment programs, based on their perceptions of current or prospective economic or market conditions and as long as they really did know what they were about and stuck to those broad asset classes that really were most appropriate for them, that would be all right.

Sophisticated investors who determined that it would be most appropriate for them to keep about half their assets in stocks and the other half in bonds, for instance, might adjust those proportions to 40 percent in stocks and 60 percent in bonds or vice versa (assuming that their particular 401(k) plans permitted such fine tuning). But an adjustment to, say, 80 percent in stocks and only 20 percent in bonds or the other way around, even if allowed, would be excessive and a mistake.

Similarly, young knowledgeable investors who wanted to have some of their assets in aggressive equities might choose between investing in a small capitalization domestic stock fund and a foreign stock fund based on their appraisal of relative financial, monetary, investment, and economic conditions, but it still would not be appropriate for them to invest in short-term bonds instead of stocks. Middle-aged investors might choose between an intermediate-term and a long-term bond fund for their assets that they decided to allocate to fixed income securities, based on their appraisal of prospective conditions in the credit markets, although investing those assets in equities instead of bonds still would be an error.

And what about 401(k) investors who are not knowledgeable or sophisticated about investment or financial affairs but who still would like the opportunity to modify their portfolio holdings based on changing market conditions? For them, those equity and fixed income and, in particular, those balanced funds that have the broadest investment latitude may be ideal, for that is just what the managers of those funds attempt to do.

The managers of fixed income funds who are not restricted as to the maturity ranges in which they must invest, for instance, will lengthen or shorten the maturities of their holdings based on their perceptions of prospective credit market conditions. Similarly, the managers of equity funds with broad mandates will overweight or underweight different industrial or economic sectors, based on their perceptions of prospective economic and stock market conditions. And the managers of balanced funds will do not only what the managers of both those equities and fixed income funds do but also will allocate their assets between fixed income and equity securities (within predetermined limits) as they deem appropriate.

9

Choosing the Best 401(k) Plan Investments for You (Continued)

In Chapter 8, we showed you how you might go about answering the following three questions in order to make intelligent asset allocation decisions in your 401(k) plan:

1. Which of your 401(k) choices make the most sense in light of your own age and personal financial circumstances?

2. Which of those alternatives are best for you in light of the quality of the managers of those asset classes?

3. Which appear to be most appropriate for you in view of current and prospective market conditions?

It now remains for us to consider one last question before showing you how to put all of this together to structure an appropriate 401(k) plan portfolio for yourself. That question is: Which 401(k) plan options are best suited for you, given your own personality and emotional or psychological risk tolerance?

The Human Element: Determining Your
Own Psychological Risk Threshold

It is all very well for you to structure your 401(k) investment portfolio on the basis of your objective determination of what the most appropriate asset mix is for you in terms of your age, marital status, financial position, job security, and life goals—i.e., all the factors that should enter into your own life-cycle investing analysis. It is even better for you to modify that portfolio in light of the relative strengths, weaknesses, and performance records of the managers of the different funds offered by your plan and better yet if you can fine-tune that portfolio by considering economic and market conditions or by delegating that responsibility to your investment managers. But none of that is enough if you find that you're very uncomfortable with what you end up with, either because your portfolio is not aggressive enough or because it's too risky for your taste.

The fact is that some individuals are very uncomfortable with risk: they would prefer to accept smaller but more assured returns than to run the risk of loss, even if incurring just a little more risk would greatly increase the probability of their realizing substantially higher returns. On the other hand, there are those who would much prefer to shoot for high returns, even if that necessitated their incurring such considerable risk that they were more likely to realize sizable losses.

You may think that you know whether you have a high or low tolerance for risk, but don't be too sure. According to Kenneth MacCrimmon, a professor at the University of British Columbia and coauthor of a study on risk-taking behavior, "almost everybody would like to see themselves as a risk-taker." But when Professor MacCrimmon compared the self-assessments of more than 500 executives in their willingness to incur risks and the risks they had actually taken, he discovered that there actually was a considerable difference.

There are also a lot of other misconceptions about our attitudes toward risk. Many believe, for instance, that we become more risk-averse as we grow older, that wealthy individuals are less risk-averse than the poor or the middle class, and that men are more prone to take risks than are women. But, in fact, none of those beliefs are necessarily true.

To help you determine your own investment risk tolerance, we have developed the following short multiple choice quiz. Although most of the questions don't relate directly to 401(k) plan investing but are intended only to elicit your general disposition toward incurring or avoiding risk, the results of the quiz should enable you to better determine just how much risk you'd be comfortable assuming in your own 401(k) investment program.

1. Which best describes your feelings about investing?

   a. "Better safe than sorry."
   b. "Moderation in all things."
   c. "Nothing ventured, nothing gained."

2. Which is most important to you as an investor?

   a. Steady income
   b. Steady income and growth
   c. Rapid price appreciation

3. You have just inherited $50,000. Within the last two months, the stock market has risen very sharply and now looks very vulnerable to a technical correction. However, the economic outlook remains strong and stocks don't appear overvalued on fundamentals. You are trying to decide whether to invest your inheritance in stocks or to put that money into a money-market fund, at least temporarily. Under which circumstances would you feel better:

   a. You decided to put the $50,000 into equities right away and ended up doubling your money in six months.
   b. You put the $50,000 into a money market fund which saved you from losing half your money, since the stocks you had been thinking of buying declined 50 percent.

4. As an employee of a small but highly profitable privately owned biotechnology company with excellent growth prospects, you have just been given an opportunity to purchase restricted stock in the company. Management hopes to bring the company public in about five years at which time you think that its shares might trade for 10 times what you'd now have to pay for them. Until then, however, you would not be able to sell any shares you purchased and the stock would pay no dividends. How much of an investment, if any, would you make?

   a. None at all
   b. No more than one month's salary
   c. Anywhere from three to six months' salary
   d. As much as possible, even if you had to borrow the equivalent of a year's salary or even more in order to do so

5. You're the big winner on a television quiz show and are given your choice of the following prizes. Which would you select?

   a. $2500 in cash
   b. A 50 percent chance to win $10,000

    c. A 20 percent chance to win $50,000

    d. A 10 percent chance to win $100,000

6. In light of your age and overall financial circumstances, you decided three months ago that it would be most appropriate to invest half the money in your 401(k) plan in common stock funds and the other half in bond funds, and that, in fact, is what you did. Since then, however, the common stock funds in which you invested dropped 20 percent. Market experts are optimistic on the economic outlook and consider the stock market decline to have been nothing more than a technical correction. What would you like to do?

    a. Shift all the money in your stock funds to bond funds in order to avoid losing more.

    b. Maintain your asset allocation as it is and wait for your stock funds to recover.

    c. Keep the money in your stock funds where it is and shift the money from your bond funds into your stock funds. If common stocks made sense before, they're a bargain now.

7. As of three months ago, approximately half the money in your 401(k) plan was invested in common stock funds while the other half was committed to bond funds, which you considered to be an appropriate asset allocation given your personal circumstances. Since then, however, the stock market has soared and the equity funds in your 401(k) plan have gone up about 20 percent, while your fixed income investments have remained essentially flat. What would you like to do now?

    a. Transfer all the money in your stock funds into your bond funds in order to lock in your gains.

    b. Maintain your asset allocation as it is.

    c. Transfer the money in your bond funds into your stock funds in order to benefit from the bull market.

8. You've lost the equivalent of a week's salary playing roulette in Las Vegas. How much more are you prepared to lose in attempting to win it back?

    a. It's a silly question. You would never have played or, if you had, you would have quit long before you lost that much.

    b. Nothing—you quit now.

    c. Another week's salary.

    d. As much more money as you can get your hands on.

9. Which of the following situations would please you most?

    a. Inheriting $50,000 from a distant rich relative.

    b. Winning $50,000 in a lottery.

   c. Realizing a $50,000 profit by trading in the options market, having risked only $3000.

   d. Who cares? $50,000 is $50,000.

10. The apartment house in which you presently live is being converted to condominiums, and you shortly will be given an opportunity to purchase your unit for $90,000. Alternatively, you will be able to sell the option to purchase the unit for $25,000. Once the condominium plan is effective, you estimate that the market value of your unit will be between $140,000 and $150,000. You also estimate that if you bought your unit, it might take you anywhere from 6 to 12 months to sell it. Meanwhile, the monthly maintenance charge on the unit will be $1000, you'll have to borrow $20,000 as a personal loan for a down payment, and you'll have to arrange for a $70,000 mortgage. Interest on the personal loan and the mortgage will amount to another $600 a month. You have decided that after the building is converted to condominium ownership, you will no longer want to live in the building. What would you do?

   a. Sell your option for $25,000 and move.

   b. Buy the unit and immediately put it up for sale in the open market. Continue to live in the apartment until it's sold, even though you'd prefer not to, in order to avoid paying the carrying costs on two apartments simultaneously.

   c. Buy the unit and put it up for sale. Move out immediately, even though that means you'll be paying the carrying costs on two apartments at the same time.

11. Your old college roommate who has become a highly regarded independent petroleum geologist is seeking investors in an exploratory oil well which he estimates could return more than 50 times its original investment if it proves successful. If the well should prove to be dry, the entire investment would be worthless. Your friend is investing in the oil well himself and has offered you the opportunity to invest on the same terms as his own. He has honestly admitted to you, however, that he estimates that the well has only one chance in five of proving successful. How much, if anything, would you invest?

   a. Nothing at all

   b. No more than one month's salary

   c. Up to three months' salary

   d. As much as six months' salary or even more

12. You have just inherited a house valued at about $150,000, free of any mortgage. The house is in a rising neighborhood and you expect it to appreciate in value over the next 10 years at a rate in excess of inflation.

However, the house is not currently in good condition and could use extensive renovations that you estimate would cost about $25,000. After such renovations, you estimate that the house would be worth $200,000 in today's market. If you were to rent the house as is, it would net you $1000 monthly; if you were to renovate it first, however, and then rent it, it would net $1500 per month. The renovations could be financed by an 8 percent mortgage on the property. What would you do?

    a. Put the house up for sale for $150,000 immediately as is.

    b. Rent the house for $1000 per month as is, with the intention of putting it up for sale in a few years after it has appreciated in value.

    c. Renovate the house and then rent it for $1500 per month, with the intention of putting it up for sale in a few years after it has appreciated in value.

    d. Renovate the house and put it up for sale immediately thereafter for $200,000.

13. Would you ever borrow money to take advantage of a good investment opportunity?

    a. Never

    b. Maybe

    c. Yes

14. How would you characterize yourself as an investor?

    a. Aggressive

    b. Moderate risk taker

    c. Conservative

15. You own a small company that manufactures computer peripheral equipment. Last year, you invented a new product that, in test marketing, has been extremely successful. Prior to your invention of this product, your company was valued at about $1 million but, if your new product pans out, you estimate that your company could be worth as much as $5 million or more. A major competitor, ABC Hardware Inc., with far greater financial resources than your own, however, has a product somewhat comparable to your own and has brought suit against you for patent infringement, seeking to force you to cease manufacturing and marketing your product and to remit to ABC any profits you may have realized on its sale. Although your lawyers think that you have a very good case and a 90 percent chance of winning, ABC is vehemently pressing their suit; should they win, you could effectively be put out of business since your other products are becoming obsolete and you would have incurred enormous nonreimbursable legal costs. ABC has offered to settle the case out of court by buying your company

from you for $1 million or by having you pay royalties to them on the sales of their product; the royalties they are asking would reduce your potential profits by an amount sufficient to lower the future value of your company to $2 million. What would you do?

a. Sell your company to them for $1 million. That would still be $1 million more than it would be worth if you lost the suit.

b. Agree to the royalty offer. You'd still own your company and it still would have a potential value of $2 million.

c. Fight them all the way. You know you didn't infringe on their patent and you're not going to submit to what you consider to be legal extortion.

In order to determine your psychological risk profile, add up your score, using the point system below for your answers:

1. (a)1 (b)2 (c)3
2. (a)1 (b)2 (c)3
3. (a)3 (b)1
4. (a)1 (b)2 (c)3 (d)5
5. (a)1 (b)2 (c)3 (d)4
6. (a)1 (b)2 (c)3
7. (a)1 (b)2 (c)4
8. (a)1 (b)2 (c)3 (d)5
9. (a)1 (b)2 (c)4 (d)1
10. (a)1 (b)2 (c)4
11. (a)1 (b)2 (c)3 (d)5
12. (a)1 (b)2 (c)4 (d)3
13. (a)1 (b)2 (c)3
14. (a)3 (b)2 (c)1
15. (a)1 (b)2 (c)5

Here's what it all means. **If you scored between 15 and 29 points**, your temperament would appear to be that of a basically conservative investor who would be most comfortable avoiding risk—even knowing that that may entail your sacrificing some potential return over time. In general, you probably would find that you would sleep better owning a portfolio weighted toward fixed income securities than one heavily concentrated in equities. Among fixed income securities, you should favor government securities and investment grade corporates rather than speculative grade issues, and your predilection should be toward issues with short- or intermediate-term, rather than long-term maturities.

On the equity side, you should emphasize large capitalization blue-chip companies, even though that means that you will forego the potentially superior returns that you might otherwise have realized by investing in smaller capitalization, emerging growth, or foreign equities.

In view of your psychological risk profile, you might consider revising your preliminary 401(k) plan asset allocation at various stages of your life (as originally suggested in Table 8-2) so that it looked more like that shown in Table 9-1 and Figure 9-1.

When a conservative investor retires, his 401(k) plan may be worth somewhat less than it otherwise would have been, had he adopted a more aggressive stance, but he will have avoided big fluctuations in the market value of his holdings over the years and almost assuredly still would have a substantial retirement nest egg.

If you scored between 30 and 43 points, you are basically a middle-of-the-road investor who is willing to incur a reasonable level of risk, provided that the risk you incur is commensurate with your potential return. You are equally comfortable owning stocks or bonds and are willing to base your asset allocation decisions largely on (1) your own financial rather than emotional requirements, (2) your judgment regarding the relative values of different asset classes at different points in time, and (3) the quality of the different investment managers who would be responsible for managing your money. You wouldn't be willing to "bet the farm" on anything, even for a potentially very high return, but neither would you

20-29   30-39   40-49   50-59   60+

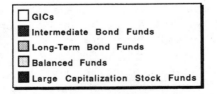

□ GICs
■ Intermediate Bond Funds
▨ Long-Term Bond Funds
▨ Balanced Funds
■ Large Capitalization Stock Funds

Figure 9-1. Evolution of a conservative 401(k) plan at different ages.

Table 9-1. Suggested % 401(k) Plan Asset Allocation for a Conservative Investor

Age	Money-Market funds	GICs	Intermediate bond funds	Long-term bond funds	Total fixed income funds	Balanced funds	Small capitalization funds	Large capitalization funds	Total common stock funds
20–29	0	0	0	0	0	25	0	75	75
30–39	0	0	0	0	0	50	0	50	50
40–49	0	0	25	0	25	25	0	50	50
50–59	0	0	25	0	25	50	0	25	25
60+	0	25	25	0	50	50	0	0	0

want to avoid sound growth opportunities either, just because a more conservative investor might deem them somewhat risky.

While you're probably more comfortable owning big capitalization household name blue-chip stocks than small capitalization, emerging growth, or foreign equities, you certainly would be willing to commit at least a small portion of your assets to those riskier asset classes too. Similarly, while you prefer government and investment grade corporate bonds of short- or intermediate-term maturities, you'd also be willing to invest in long-term bonds, or even junk bonds, in moderation.

With that psychological risk profile, you might consider revising your preliminary 401(k) plan asset allocation as shown in Table 9-2 and Figure 9-2.

Upon your retirement, you as a middle-of-the-road investor likely would discover that your 401(k) plan was worth somewhat more than it otherwise would have been worth had you adopted a more conservative investment strategy throughout your career but not quite as much as it would have been worth had you adopted a more aggressive stance. Your trade-offs would have been, however, that you would have incurred greater risk than had your conservative counterpart, albeit not nearly as much risk as had his more aggressive coworkers.

If you scored between 44 and 58 points, you are an aggressive investor who is comfortable assuming a high level of risk in seeking above average investment returns. You are much more at home with equities than with fixed income securities and you probably are happy to invest in small capitalization, emerging growth companies, and foreign securities, as well as in big capitalization blue-chip issues. Where your conservative friends perceive risks, you see opportunities.

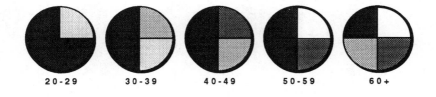

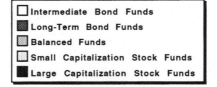

Figure 9-2. Evolution of a middle-of-the-road 401(k) plan at different ages.

Table 9-2. Suggested % 401(k) Plan Asset Allocation for a Middle-of-the-Road Investor

Age	Money-market funds	GICs	Intermediate bond funds	Long-term bond funds	Total fixed income funds	Balanced funds	Small capitalization funds	Large capitalization funds	Total common stock funds
20–29	0	0	0	0	0	0	25	75	100
30–39	0	0	0	0	0	25	25	50	75
40–49	0	0	0	25	25	25	0	50	50
50–59	0	0	25	25	50	0	0	50	50
60+	0	0	25	25	50	25	0	25	25

Among fixed income securities, you favor longer maturities and more speculative issues, rather than short- or intermediate-term government securities or investment grade corporates. Those issues are riskier, to be sure, but they also hold forth the promise of higher potential returns.

Given your psychological risk profile, you might revise your 401(k) plan asset allocation as shown in Table 9-3 and Figure 9-3.

As an aggressive investor, you probably would be able to retire with more than either your conservative or middle-of-the-road counterparts (assuming that each of you invested the same amounts at the same times throughout your careers). That is because your more speculative investments (particularly in small capitalization funds in your twenties, thirties, and forties) probably provided higher returns than did your co-workers' relatively more conservative investments.

But there would be no *guarantee* that you would end up with more than they did. The very investments that *might* have generated superior returns were also the riskiest, and they might not have worked out as you expected, causing you to fare more poorly than your counterparts.

When Should You Change the Asset Allocation in Your 401(k) Plan?

There are several circumstances under which you should consider changing your 401(k) plan's asset allocation and, not surprisingly, they relate directly to the four questions that we raised in this chapter and in Chapter 8.

First, when you enter a new stage in life, you ought take a fresh look at your investment portfolio. This is what we have been referring to as life-

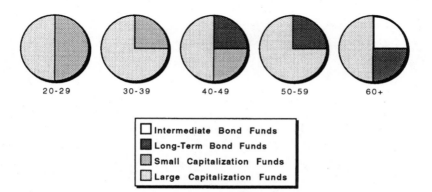

Figure 9-3. Evolution of an aggressive 401(k) plan at different ages.

Table 9-3. Suggested % 401(k) Plan Asset Allocation for an Aggressive Investor

Age	Money-market funds	GICs	Intermediate bond funds	Long-term bond funds	Total fixed income funds	Balanced funds	Small capitalization funds	Large capitalization funds	Total common stock funds
20–29	0	0	0	0	0	0	50	50	100
30–39	0	0	0	0	0	0	25	75	100
40–49	0	0	0	25	25	0	25	50	75
50–59	0	0	0	25	25	0	0	75	75
60+	0	0	25	25	50	0	0	50	50

cycle investing. The investments that suited you at age 20 won't necessarily be appropriate for you at age 40 and those that were right for you at 40 won't necessarily be best for you when you're 60. So, at the very least, you should take a fresh look at your portfolio every 10 years or so.

If reviewing your portfolio every decade is a good idea, would reviewing it every five years or every three years or even annually be an even better idea? Not necessarily. Since you are investing in your 401(k) plan for the long-term, reviewing your portfolio at very frequent intervals could result in your focusing on short-term market fluctuations to the detriment of your long-term plans. (We'll have a little more to say about that when we discuss your evaluation of managers' performance and adapting to changing market conditions below.)

On the other hand, there's nothing magical about 10-year reviews. Should your personal or financial position change significantly in just two years or five, by all means take a fresh look at your 401(k) portfolio at that time, whether or not a full 10 years have passed since your last review. If, for instance, you have gotten married or divorced or been widowed, if you have had a child or your child has just entered or graduated from college, if you have decided to return to school, if you are considering accepting an offer of early retirement, or if you have inherited a large sum of money, a review of your 401(k) plan portfolio would be in order and a reallocation of your assets should be considered.

Second, if you find that your psychological risk tolerance has changed, for whatever reason, you might want to consider modifying your asset allocation. If, for instance, you believe that you have grown more (or less) risk-averse over time, you might decide that in the future you'd be more comfortable with less (or more) equity exposure than you'd previously elected.

There is a real danger is modifying your portfolio on this basis, however. At the peak of a bull market, when stock prices have climbed for a long period of time, it is only natural that you may decide that you'd be more comfortable assuming greater risk (since, in effect, the additional risk that you might have assumed actually would not have been encountered). Conversely, near the bottom of a bear market, it is human nature to think of oneself as becoming more risk averse.

If you decide that you want to assume more risk only because risky securities performed well recently, however, or if you think that you might like to restrict your holdings to low-risk securities only because risky stocks have fared poorly for a time, and if you adjust your portfolio accordingly, you may run the biggest risk of all—that of getting whipsawed, missing out on the purchase of securities when they are cheap and owning too many stocks when they are temporarily overpriced. So don't decide that your personal risk tolerance really has changed simply because market conditions have.

Rather, if you suspect that your risk tolerance may have changed and if you find yourself tempted to restructure your portfolio accordingly, we urge you first to retake the multiple choice test we provided earlier in this chapter. If your score turns out to be substantially different from what it previously had been, only then should you consider modifying your asset allocation to reflect changes in your own risk profile.

Third, are we suggesting, then, that your 401(k) plan portfolio *never* should be changed to reflect changing market conditions? Not quite, but almost. Certainly, we recommend strongly against your changing the asset allocation of your 401(k) plan simply because you believe that the economy is on the verge of a recovery (or a recession), that the market is about to rise (or fall), that interest rates are about to climb (or decline), or on the basis of any other short-term economic, financial, or market prognostications that you might make. For one thing, economic forecasting is a hazardous game, and predictions made by even the most highly regarded professionals have proven over time to be notoriously unreliable.

Moreover, even when economic forecasts do prove to be accurate, they don't necessarily translate into parallel market moves: since the securities markets are at least somewhat efficient, even those economic developments that you might forecast correctly could prove to have been discounted already by the market. In a nutshell, what that means is that even if you should be right in forecasting an economic recovery, the stock market might still decline, whereas if you correctly predict a recession, the market might still advance.

Are there *no* circumstances, then, when you should consider restructuring your portfolio to take advantage of changing economic or market conditions? As we said, not quite: if the *actual* relative prices of stocks, bonds, and short-term money-market instruments are clearly out of whack, you might consider making small adjustments in your portfolio to take advantage of such anomalies.

For instance, if short-term interest rates should decline precipitously while long-term rates remain very high, you might consider shifting some of the assets you hold in money-market instruments into fixed income securities with somewhat longer maturities and vice versa. If price-earnings ratios on common stocks are very low while bond yields are also low, you might consider moving some of your fixed income assets into equities instead. Or if growth stocks become available at prices generally commanded only by value stocks, you might consider reallocating some of your equity funds from a value manager to a growth manager (if that option is available to you).

In all of these cases, however, note that we are suggesting that action only be taken on the basis of clearly evident *existing* market anomalies— not on your or anyone else's forecast of what *might* happen. And even then, we suggest that any portfolio restructuring you undertake be minor.

Finally, should you consider altering your asset allocation on the basis of your managers' recent performances? Again, usually not. If, for instance, one of your managers has had an outstanding 10- or 20-year track record but has underperformed his universe over the last three or six months (or even a year), that generally would *not* justify your making a change. Remember that when you first selected that manager, you presumably based your decision at least in part on the manager's long-term track record, weighing that much more heavily in your deliberations than his short-term record. If you were right to do that then (and you were), then it is equally correct that you continue to focus on the long-term now and not be sidetracked by short-term considerations.

In effect, asset management is analogous to marathon running, not sprinting, and what happens over short-term periods is seldom statistically significant. Even the best of managers will underperform his universe sometimes, and if you switch from one manager to another only on the basis of recent short-term performance, your long-term results likely will be random or worse. Rather, you should stay with those managers who succeed in outperforming their universes, on average, over extended periods, without being misled by their interim results.

There is, however, an exception to all this. If the company responsible for managing one of your investments has had an outstanding long-term record but now has underperformed the market for the last three or six months for a *clearly discernible reason,* you certainly might consider making a change on that basis. If, for instance, over the last three or six months, the company dramatically changed its investment approach or experienced considerable employee turnover (perhaps even losing the individual who, for many years, had been primarily responsible for successfully managing the fund in which you invested), and if the fund's performance suffered concurrently, of course you should consider making a change.

Even under such circumstances, however, it is important to bear in mind that while it might *look* as if you had restructured your portfolio because of adverse short-term performance, in reality, you would have restructured because of deteriorating fundamentals at the management company itself, not because of the superficial short-term performance results per se. In other words, poor interim performance results never should be considered to be sufficient reason to justify restructuring your portfolio, but they certainly should prompt you to investigate to determine whether anything deeper and more fundamental might be going on, which could justify such a change.

10

Structuring 401(k) Portfolios in Limited Plans

In the last several chapters, we provided you with some general advice as to how you might go about selecting the most appropriate investments for your own 401(k) plan. We showed you how to integrate your psychological or emotional risk constraint characteristics with financial and economic considerations (your life-cycle investing factors) in order to come up with the best possible program for you—one that not only made economic sense but one with which you'd also feel emotionally comfortable. And we suggested how you might evaluate the performance of the managers responsible for the assets in your plan, and to what extent, if any, you should allow yourself to be influenced in your 401(k) investment decisions by current or prospective economic or market conditions.

Earlier in this book, we also noted that different plans offer very different arrays of choices, with some limiting your options to no more than one or two asset classes while others offer dozens or more. And in doing all this, we dealt, of necessity, in generalities. Now it's time for us to put all of this together and provide you with much more specific recommendations relating to your age and financial circumstances, your psychological temperament, and the investment choices available to you.

Since we don't know you personally, however, and don't know the details of your specific plan, we cannot, of course, tell you precisely what you should do in allocating your particular 401(k) plan assets. But we can do the next best thing. In this chapter, we will show you how three different individuals, of different temperaments and at different stages in their lives, might best structure their own plans when confronted with very *limited* 401(k) choices. And, in Chapter 11, we'll show you how three others might structure their plans when confronted with a very *broad* array of 401(k) options.

Ideally, you may find that your own circumstances closely mirror those of one of these six hypothetical individuals and that your plan is very similar to one or the other of our two hypothetical plans. But even if that is not the case, you should be able to chart a course for yourself somewhere between two of these individuals that would be appropriate for you in your own plan.

Here's how we're going to go about this. In this chapter, we're going to assume that three different individuals—Andrew, an aggressive investor; Barbara, a moderate or middle-of-the-road investor; and Charles, a conservative investor—are all beginning work at ABC Company at about the same time, when they are all in their early twenties. We are going to assume, further, that all three will remain at ABC Company throughout their entire careers, retiring at about age 60. And we are going to assume that ABC Company's 401(k) plan provides very few options, consisting only of (1) a U.S. government money-market fund, (2) a guaranteed investment contract (GIC), (3) an actively managed balanced fund, and (4) a passively managed large capitalization stock fund. Within that context, we will suggest what Andrew, Barbara, and Charles might best do now and in the future.

In Chapter 11, we will make similar assumptions for Doris, Edward, and Frances, but with one difference: we will assume that they went to work not for ABC Company with its limited 401(k) plan choices but for XYZ Company, which offered a much more comprehensive plan. We will assume that, in addition to the options provided in ABC Company's plan, XYZ's plan also offered a small capitalization stock fund, several foreign stock funds, four bond funds (short-term investment grade, intermediate-term investment grade, long-term investment grade, and high-yield or junk), a company stock plan, actively and passively managed large capitalization stock funds, and a number of other specialized industry funds. Within that context, we will suggest what Doris, Edward and Frances might best do now and in the future.

But first, let's take a look at ABC Company and Andrew, Barbara, and Charles.

ABC Company and Its 401(k) Plan

ABC Company is a small company with fewer than 100 employees. Despite its size, however, it provides its employees with a relatively generous array of benefits, including a pension plan, a comprehensive health insurance plan, a flexible benefits plan, and a 401(k) plan. Employees are permitted to contribute up to 10 percent of their compensation to the 401(k) plan (subject to those legal maximums discussed earlier), and the company matches 50 percent of any employee contributions. The plan provides for full vesting of company contributions after five years, in 20 percent annual increments.

Employees may invest their 401(k) assets in any or all of four funds, in 25 percent increments. In other words, they may invest all of their contributions (100 percent) in any one of the four funds of their choosing; or they may invest 75 percent in any one of the funds and 25 percent in any of the others; or they may invest 50 percent in one and 50 percent in another; or they may invest 50 percent in one and 25 percent in each of two others; or they may invest 25 percent in each of the four. They are permitted to change their asset allocations quarterly.

The four funds in which they may invest are:

1. *A U.S. government money-market fund.* Among the safest, most risk-free, and most creditworthy of all funds, this fund is limited to investing only in U.S. government securities with maturities of less than one year. This means that it generally is restricted to investing in treasury bills, although it sometimes also invests in government notes or bonds when their maturity dates are less than 12 months away. The fund's average maturity usually is less than 90 days.

   The fund is actively, not passively, managed but, since there is little latitude available to the managers of such funds whose choices are quite circumscribed, the relative performances of such funds (as measured by their average annual yields) generally vary little from one to another. In fact, over the past 10 years, this particular U.S. government money-market fund has generated average annual returns that have placed it smack in the middle of the performance range for funds of this kind.

2. *A guaranteed investment (or income) contract (GIC).* The 401(k) plan has negotiated a GIC with one of the nation's most highly rated insurance companies. Over the past 10 years, the yield on the GIC has been consistently higher than the yield on the money-market fund, to the tune of anywhere from 2.5 to three percentage points (250 to 300 basis points) annually. In some individual years, the GIC even outperformed both the

balanced fund and the large capitalization stock fund, although, on average over the past decade, it has returned less than either of those funds.

3. *An actively managed balanced fund.* The balanced fund is managed by one of the nation's largest and most highly regarded mutual fund complexes. It has been in existence for over 20 years and has achieved a respectable record both for performance and consistency over that time. For the past 10 years, it has been managed by the same portfolio manager, and he is expected to remain primarily responsible for its management. The fund has generated positive returns in all but one of its 20 years and has ranked in the first or second quintile of all balanced funds in 14 of those years (it ranked in the middle quintile three times, in the fourth quintile twice, and in the fifth quintile only once).

The fund is permitted to invest in common stocks, preferred stocks, or fixed income securities but is not permitted to purchase or sell options nor to sell short. For the most part, it may only purchase the common stocks of companies that have been in business for at least five years, that have been profitable during at least three of those five years, that have market capitalizations of at least $200 million, and that are paying dividends. (A maximum of five percent of the fund's assets may be invested in the stocks of companies that do not meet those criteria.)

Fixed income securities in the fund's portfolio must be rated BBB or higher (if corporates) or be obligations of the U.S. government or one its agencies. No more than 10 percent of the fund's assets may be invested in any one industry, and no more than five percent may be invested in the securities of any one company, in order to provide the fund with adequate diversification.

A minimum of 35 percent and a maximum of 65 percent of the fund's assets must be invested in fixed income securities (including cash equivalents or money-market instruments) at all times; conversely, a minimum of 35 percent and a maximum of 65 percent must be committed to common or preferred stocks. In fact, on average over the past 10 years, the fund has committed approximately 50 percent of its assets to common stocks, 10 percent to preferred stocks, 35 percent to fixed income securities with maturities longer than one year, and five percent to money-market instruments.

The fund is actively managed both in terms of asset allocation and in terms of individual security selection. Based on the manager's perception of the relative values of different asset classes and different individual issues, the fund increases or reduces its fixed income exposure vis-à-vis equities, extends or shortens the average maturities of its fixed income holdings, overweights or underweights its equity positions in different industries, and buys or sells specific issues—notwithstanding the weighting of those individual issues, industries or asset classes in the popular market indices. In making those active decisions, management has been correct more often than not, as evidenced by the fund's superior historic performance record. In seven of the last 10 years, the actively managed equity portion of the balanced fund outperformed the passively managed stock index fund; in three years it did underperform, however.

4. *A large capitalization stock index fund.* The same mutual fund complex that actively manages the balanced fund also passively manages a large capitalization common stock index fund, the objective of which is to generate returns in line with those attained by Standard & Poor's 500 Index. The fund seeks to achieve this goal by owning the same stocks (in the same proportions) that comprise the S&P 500, with no consideration given as to whether any of those stocks may be undervalued or overvalued from an investment standpoint. Over the past 10 years, the fund has been successful in achieving its goal: its annual performance has come within one percentage point (100 basis points) of that of the S&P 500 in each of those 10 years.

As indicated above, in seven of the last 10 years, the actively managed equity portion of the balanced fund outperformed the passively managed stock index fund, although in three years it did not. Since common stocks generally outperformed fixed income securities over that decade, however, and since virtually all of the index fund's assets were committed to equities (compared to only half the assets of the balanced fund on average), the index fund still managed to outperform the balanced fund in eight of the 10 individual years and over the entire 10-year period on average.

Andrew: The Aggressive Investor

Shortly after his graduation from college at age 22, Andrew joined ABC Company in its management training program. Andrew was unmarried at the time and did not have a steady girlfriend, nor did he have any financial obligations to anyone other than himself. His parents were relatively well-to-do, and Andrew didn't think it was likely that he would be called upon to help them out financially any time soon (if ever). Indeed, he knew that he could still turn to them himself for financial aid in the event of an emergency.

Temperamentally, Andrew considered himself to be relatively aggressive. He had majored in economics in college and had been interested in the stock market ever since high school. Since his junior year in college, he had been investing for his own account, often trading in options and speculative stocks (albeit with relatively small sums of money since he didn't have much to begin with). Then, when he took our psychological test designed to measure his risk tolerance (in Chapter 9), his judgment of himself as an aggressive investor was confirmed: he scored a relatively high 52 points.

When Andrew joined ABC Company, he was delighted to learn that the company had a 401(k) plan, and he immediately determined to participate—and to contribute the maximum permitted. But he was disappointed by the investment choices the plan provided. He really would have liked to invest aggressively in options, small capitalization stocks, and foreign securities, but none of those choices were available to him. So he did the next best thing: he invested all of his 401(k) money in the common stock index fund.

In deciding how to allocate his 401(k) contributions, Andrew never even considered investing in the money-market fund or the GIC. After all, he knew that common stocks historically had generated much higher returns on average than fixed income securities (especially short-term fixed income issues), and he felt perfectly comfortable assuming the incremental risk that equity investment would entail. But before making his final decision, he did seriously consider whether he might not be better off investing in the balanced fund instead of the common stock fund.

The balanced fund did have three characteristics that Andrew found attractive:

1. Unlike the common stock index fund, it was actively, rather than passively, managed. Andrew liked that: it was consistent with his personality to strive to realize superior returns, even if that meant he'd run the risk of underperforming the market averages, rather than investing for average returns at lower risk.

2. The balanced fund's active management appeared to have paid off: in seven of the last 10 years, the actively managed equity portion of the balanced fund's portfolio had outperformed the passively managed common stock index fund.

3. The balanced fund could shift its assets back and forth between equities and fixed income securities (within limits), whereas the common stock fund could not. Although Andrew realized that equities were likely to provide higher returns than bonds over time, there were sure to be some interim periods in which bonds would outperform stocks. If the managers of the balanced fund were really good, they might be able to anticipate such developments and alter their asset allocations accordingly. The common stock fund, on the other hand, would have no choice but to remain in equities.

For those reasons, Andrew considered investing in the balanced fund instead of the common stock fund (or investing some of his money in each rather than all in one), but, in the final analysis, he opted to invest only in the common stock fund. What it came down to for him was this: Andrew really wanted to invest in common stocks (the most aggressive asset class available to him and the one most likely to generate the highest returns for him over time). And if he had invested in the balanced fund, approximately half his money would have gone into fixed income securities.

Even if the balanced fund's managers were superior stock pickers (as suggested by their equity track record), the fact remained that with only half their fund's assets committed to equities, they probably wouldn't be able to outperform even a passively managed equity index fund. At least that was the case over the last 10 years. During that period, virtually all of the common stock index fund's assets had been committed to equities (compared to only half the assets of the balanced fund on average). As a result, the common stock fund outperformed the balanced fund (overall) in eight of the 10 individual years and during the entire 10-year period on average (even if it did underperform just the equity portion of the balanced fund's portfolio).

Andrew continued to invest all of his 401(k) contributions in the common stock fund over the next eight years. Then, as he was approaching age 30 and about to be married, he decided to take a fresh look at his plan. When he took the psychological risk profile test again, he discovered that his risk tolerance had not changed: he again scored 52 points, suggesting that he still would be most comfortable with an aggressive investment stance. But, appreciating the fact that he was a little older and that he hoped to begin raising a family soon, Andrew decided to become just a bit more conservative.

Accordingly, he shifted 25 percent of his 401(k) portfolio from the common stock fund to the balanced fund. (In effect, this meant that he still would have about seven-eighths of his 401(k) assets invested in common stocks and only about one-eighth in bonds, since the balanced fund, on average, tended to maintain about half its assets in common stocks.) This was still quite an aggressive stance, and Andrew still eschewed any investment in the GIC or the money-market fund.

A decade later, Andrew reexamined his 401(k) plan. He was approaching 40 now and was a husband and father of two children, aged eight and six. To be sure, he felt no more risk-averse than he ever had, and his score on the psychological risk tolerance test confirmed his feelings: he scored 51 this time, still placing him in the aggressive range of investors. But given his age and his family responsibilities, he decided to become a little more conservative in his plan.

Table 10-1. Andrew's % Asset Allocation in ABC Company's 401(k) Plan

Age	Money-market fund	GIC	Balanced fund	Common stock fund	Total
22–29	0	0	0	100	100
30–39	0	0	25	75	100
40–49	0	0	50	50	100
50–59	0	0	75	25	100
60 and Above	0	25	50	25	100

So Andrew shifted another 25 percent of his investments from the common stock fund to the balanced fund. He still had no interest in the GIC nor the money-market fund, but he thought that, under the circumstances, some increase in his fixed income exposure at the expense of his equity holdings would be appropriate. Now, with half his assets in the common stock fund and the other half in the balanced fund, he had effectively established an asset allocation of 75 percent common stocks and 25 percent bonds.

Ten years later, Andrew's older child was just entering college while the younger, turning 16, was only two years away from college herself. Andrew, himself, was almost 50 years old and in his prime earnings years, but he hoped to retire at age 60, which meant that he only had another 10 years in which to accumulate the retirement assets he would need. And, although he didn't feel himself to be quite as much of a risk taker as he had been in his youth, he still believed that he was more aggressive by temperament than most others of his generation. In fact, he was: this time, when he took the psychological risk tolerance test, he scored 49, which was a little lower than he had scored the previous three times, but still placed him in the aggressive category of investors.

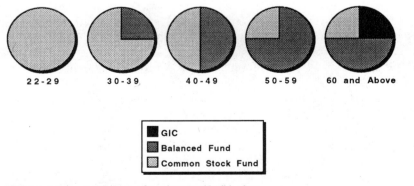

22-29   30-39   40-49   50-59   60 and Above

■ GIC
▦ Balanced Fund
☐ Common Stock Fund

Figure 10-1. Evolution of Andrew's 401(k) plan.

Within this context, Andrew decided to continue to commit the bulk of his 401(k) assets to common stocks and to become only a little more conservative. Since he still had no interest in the GIC or the money-market fund, he simply transferred another 25 percent of the assets in the common stock fund to the balanced fund, as a result of which he now had three-quarters of his 401(k) assets in the balanced fund and one-quarter in the common stock fund. Since the balanced fund continued to invest about half its assets in bonds and the other half in common stocks, this meant that Andrew effectively had committed five-eighths (62.5 percent) of his assets to common stocks and three-eighths (37.5 percent) to bonds.

Over the course of his career, Andrew's investments had done well, and he did, indeed, manage to retire at age 60. That's when he decided that the time had come for him to lock some fixed income returns into his 401(k) retirement plan. He still was relatively aggressive by temperament but he was 60 years old, not 20, and prudence dictated that his portfolio now be structured somewhat more conservatively than it had been. But he still didn't want to forego equity exposure entirely, both because he was comfortable with common stock investments and because he realized that it was stocks, not bonds or GICs, that would enable him to keep abreast of inflation.

So Andrew shifted 25 percent of his assets from the balanced fund to the GIC, thereby locking in the fixed return on the GIC, while retaining much of his equity and other fixed income exposure. His portfolio now was allocated 25 percent in GICs, 50 percent in the balanced fund, and 25 percent in the common stock fund. As a result, his total equity exposure, directly through the common stock fund and indirectly through the balanced fund, stood at 50 percent.

Table 10-1 and Figure 10-1 show how Andrew's 401(k) asset allocation had changed over the course of his career.

Barbara: The Middle-of-the-Road Investor

Barbara joined the ABC Company at about the same time that Andrew did, when she, too, was about 22 years old and upon her graduation from college. She was single and had no financial obligations to anyone other than herself. Her parents were financially independent, and she didn't have to concern herself over their welfare.

While Barbara's financial and social circumstances were similar to Andrew's, however, her temperament was quite different. When it came to investment matters, not only didn't she consider herself to be very aggressive but she readily admitted that she was neither very knowledgeable nor very interested. She had majored in English literature in college and had taken no economics courses. At ABC Company, she hoped to progress through the Advertising and Public Relations Department, rather than climb the corporate ladder through the Finance Department (as Andrew hoped to do and did).

When Barbara learned that ABC Company had a 401(k) plan, she was pleased, and, unlike Andrew, she was not at all disappointed to discover that there would be only four options available to her. Four seemed like more than enough, and she had little doubt that at least one or two of them would suit her just fine.

When Barbara took the psychological risk profile test in Chapter 9, she scored 40 points, confirming for her what she already knew: that she would be comfortable incurring a reasonable amount of risk in order to generate reasonable returns, but that she would neither be happy "shooting the moon" in order to seek very much above-average returns nor in so minimizing her risk exposure as to reduce substantially the probability of her realizing even reasonable rates of return on her investments. Then, when Barbara realized that one of her four choices would be the balanced fund, she was ready to stop right there. That seemed ideal to her for four reasons:

1. The balanced fund invested both in large capitalization common stocks (a relatively, but not unduly, risky asset class), in bonds (which were even less risky), and in money-market instruments (which were even more conservative). That mix seemed to suit her middle-of-the-road investment personality ideally.

2. While she would be able to invest in common stocks or money-market instruments outside of the balanced fund, there was no way that she could gain exposure to the intermediate- or long-term fixed income markets except indirectly by investing in the balanced fund. And there might be certain times when investing in fixed income securities would prove to be a more attractive option than investing in equities.

3. Additionally, one of the biggest attractions to her of investing in the balanced fund was that someone other than herself, someone who was experienced and professional would determine, on a continuing basis, how to allocate her assets (in stocks, bonds, or money-market instruments, and in what proportions), in response to changing market conditions. Alternatively, Barbara felt that she would have had to keep making those decisions, shifting her assets from the common stock fund to the GIC or the money-market fund or vice versa, and she really didn't feel up to that.

4. Finally, when Barbara learned that the balanced fund's track record really had been quite commendable, she was almost totally convinced that she shouldn't even consider investing in anything else.

Table 10-2. Barbara's % Asset Allocation in ABC Company's 401(k) Plan

Age	Money-market fund	GIC	Balanced fund	Common stock fund	Total
22–29	0	0	50	50	100
30–39	0	0	75	25	100
40–49	0	0	100	0	100
50–59	0	0	100	0	100
60 and Above	0	25	75	0	100

Almost, but not quite. Barbara also realized that at her young age, she could afford to commit more than half of her 401(k) plan assets to equities, which is all she would end up with on average if she were to put all of her contributions in the balanced fund. In fact, she thought that she would be comfortable committing as much as 75 percent of her contributions to equities, which she could accomplish by putting half her funds in the balanced fund and the other half in the common stock fund. So that's what she did.

Barbara married three weeks before her twenty-eighth birthday and bore a child two years later. Shortly after her daughter was born, she reviewed her financial position and decided to become a little more conservative in her 401(k) plan. So she transferred 25 percent of her assets from the common stock fund to the balanced fund. As a result, she now had three-quarters of her 401(k) assets in the balanced fund and one-quarter in the common stock fund. And, since the common stock fund was totally invested in equities while the balanced fund had half its assets in stocks and half in bonds, approximately 62.5 percent of her 401(k) assets were indirectly invested in common stocks while about 37.5 percent were in bonds.

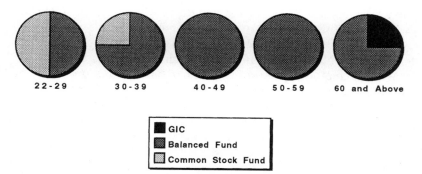

Figure 10-2. Evolution of Barbara's 401(k) plan.

A decade later, just before turning 40, Barbara was divorced and, as it turned out, she never remarried. Even had she remained married, she probably would have decided to reduce her equity exposure a little more at this time, simply because she was 10 years older, but now that she was no longer married, that was just one more reason, she felt, for her to become a little more conservative in her investments. So Barbara shifted the rest of her common stock fund holdings to the balanced fund. All of her 401(k) assets were now in the balanced fund, which meant that about half her assets were in stocks and the other half in bonds. Barbara continued to invest all of her 401(k) plan contributions in the balanced fund until she finally retired at age 60.

Then, when Barbara retired, she decided to shift 25 percent of the assets she had accumulated in her 401(k) plan from the balanced fund into the GIC. This reduced her indirect equity exposure from about 50 percent to about 37.5 percent, and it assured her of a fixed return on one-fourth of the assets in her plan.

Table 10-2 and Figure 10-2 show how Barbara's 401(k) asset allocation looked over the course of her career.

Charles: The Conservative Investor

Charles joined ABC Company at about the same time that Andrew and Barbara did, although, at 26, he was a little older than they were. He was the only one of the three who was married at the time of his employment. In fact, Charles had married almost immediately upon graduating from college four years earlier and already was the father of a two-year-old son. His second child was expected in four months.

Whether because of his family circumstances or simply because of basic differences in his underlying temperament, Charles was by far the most conservative of the three. When he took our psychological risk profile test, his score was a very low 24, which really didn't surprise him at all. He had always been cautious and risk-averse, and he could see no reason why those attitudes shouldn't be reflected in his investing proclivities as well.

In terms of his interest in economic, financial, and investment affairs, Charles was much more like Andrew than like Barbara. For one thing, he not only understood what the securities markets were all about but he enjoyed being involved in the process of selecting his own investments. So the advantage that Barbara perceived in delegating the responsibility for her asset allocation to a professional manager by investing in the balanced fund was not seen as a positive by Charles. He much preferred to choose his own investments.

In terms of *which* securities to invest in, however, Charles couldn't have been more unlike Andrew. As a result, when Charles learned that ABC Company had a 401(k) plan, he, like Andrew, was disappointed to learn that there would be only four options available. But what he would have liked to have seen were many more fixed income choices, not additional equity alternatives.

In a way, structuring a satisfactory 401(k) portfolio was more difficult for Charles than it had been for either Andrew or Barbara. On the one hand, he understood that, at his age, he really should commit a significant portion of his assets to equities (either directly through the common stock fund or indirectly through the balanced fund). But that was more easily said than done: he really couldn't ignore his emotions, and the fact remained that he was not all that comfortable in incurring the risks inherent in equity ownership.

Concomitantly, he really wanted to invest in fixed income securities that might provide lower returns than equities but that also were less volatile and less risky. But, unless he settled for the very shortest term fixed income instruments by investing in the money-market fund (which was likely to provide the very lowest return over time) or invested in GICs (which would provide him with no opportunity for capital gains), he could only invest in fixed income securities through the balanced fund (which would entail his abdicating a degree of control over the whole asset allocation process). The idea of investing in GICs (which guaranteed fixed returns and nonfluctuating market values) did appeal to him, but he feared that the returns that GICs would provide would be less than he might realize through equity investment.

So Charles compromised by committing 25 percent of his assets to the common stock fund, 50 percent to the balanced fund, and the remaining 25 percent to GICs. Since the balanced fund was likely to be 50 percent invested in equities on average, that provided him with approximately a 50 percent direct and indirect investment in common stocks (25 percent directly through the common stock fund and 25 percent indirectly through the balanced fund) and approximately an equivalent amount in fixed income (or quasi-fixed income) securities (25 percent directly in GICs and 25 percent indirectly in intermediate and long-term bonds through the balanced fund).

A few years later, in his early thirties, Charles shifted 25 percent of his assets that were in the common stock fund into the balanced fund. He knew that his overall returns might be penalized slightly as a result, but he also expected to be able to sleep more soundly—and he did. His assets now were distributed 75 percent in the balanced fund (which gave him about a 37.5 percent indirect equity exposure) and 25 percent in GICs.

Table 10-3. Charles' % Asset Allocation in ABC Company's 401(k) Plan

Age	Money-market fund	GIC	Balanced fund	Common stock fund	Total
26–32	0	25	50	25	100
33–39	0	25	75	0	100
40–49	0	50	50	0	100
50–59	0	50	50	0	100
60 and Above	25	50	25	0	100

When he turned 40, Charles reduced his equity exposure still further, by shifting another 25 percent of his assets from the balanced fund to the GIC. This now meant that half his assets were in GICs and half in the balanced fund, which left him with indirect equity exposure of approximately 25 percent. Charles maintained this asset allocation until his retirement at age 60.

When he retired, Charles reduced his equity exposure yet again by moving 25 percent of his assets in the balanced fund to the money-market fund. Now his portfolio was truly very conservatively positioned, with only 25 percent in the balanced fund, 50 percent in GICs, and 25 percent in the money-market fund. The overall volatility and risk of his portfolio now was minimal, but his potential returns also were reduced. Still, through the balanced fund, Charles did maintain about a 12.5 percent indirect equity exposure, which he hoped would provide him with some hedge against inflation.

Table 10-3 and Figure 10-3 show how Charles' 401(k) asset allocation evolved over the course of his career.

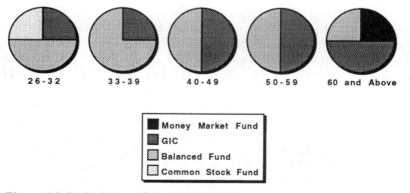

Figure 10-3. Evolution of Charles' 401(k) plan.

11
Structuring 401(k) Portfolios in Expansive Plans

XYZ Company, a huge corporation with more than 70,000 employees nationwide, provides its workers with an exceptional array of benefits, including a defined benefit pension plan, a profit-sharing plan, a comprehensive health insurance plan (including dental coverage), a flexible benefits plan, and a 401(k) plan. Employees are permitted to contribute up to 10 percent of their compensation to the 401(k) plan (subject to the legal maximums discussed earlier), and the company matches 100 percent of any employee contributions up to the first five percent. The 401(k) plan provides for immediate vesting of the company's matching contributions.

Employees may invest their 401(k) assets in any or all of four different funds, in 25 percent increments, and may select those funds from a menu consisting of 30 different choices. In other words, they may invest all of their contributions (100%) in any one of the 30 funds of their own choosing; or they may invest 75% in any one of the funds and 25% in any one of the other 29; or they may invest 50% in any one and 50% in any other; or they may invest 50% in any one and 25% in each of any two others; or they may invest 25% in each of any four of the 30. 401(k) plan participants are permitted to change their asset allocations quarterly among the 30 funds in any way they desire, but at any one time they may not be invested in any more than four of the 30 funds, because of the 25 percent stipulation.

The 30 funds in which they may invest are as follows:

1. *A company stock fund.*   This fund exists solely to invest in the common stock of XYZ Company itself. Both the company and the stock, which pays a small dividend and is listed on the New York Stock Exchange, have performed well over time.

2. *A U.S. government money-market fund.*   This is the same money-market fund as that which is included in ABC Company's 401(k) plan, described in Chapter 10.

3. *An investment grade money-market fund.*   Like the U.S. government money-market fund, this fund is limited to investing in securities with maturities of less than one year. Unlike the U.S. government money-market fund, however, it is not limited to investing only in U.S. government securities. In addition to investing in treasury bills or government notes or bonds when their maturity dates are less than 12 months away, it also may invest in investment grade corporate commercial paper, bank certificates of deposit, or corporate bonds that are due to mature within 12 months. The yield on this fund has generally been slightly higher than the yield on the U.S. government money-market fund, reflecting the fact that even the highest grade corporate securities are not as risk-free as are government securities. This fund also is actively managed and its average maturity usually is measurable in days.

4. *A short-term investment grade bond fund.*

5. *An intermediate-term investment grade bond fund.*

6. *A long-term investment grade bond fund.*   These three funds are all actively managed by the same long-established and highly regarded fixed income asset management company that manages the U.S. government money-market fund and the investment grade money-market fund. All three bond funds limit their investments solely to U.S. government securities and investment grade corporate securities. What distinguishes one from another are the maturities of portfolio holdings: the short-term fund invests in issues with maturities of more than one but less than five years; the intermediate-term fund invests in securities with maturities ranging from five to 10 years; and the long-term fund invests in bonds with maturities of longer than 10 years.

   On average, the short-term fund has yielded a little more than the investment grade money-market fund and has been slightly more volatile. The intermediate-term fund has yielded a little more and has been a little more volatile than the short-term fund. And the long-term fund has returned more than the intermediate-term fund but has been the riskiest of the three. Within their respective universes, the performance records of all three funds have been slightly above average.

7. *A guaranteed investment (or income) contract (GIC).*   XYZ Company's 401(k) plan negotiated a GIC contract with the same insurance company as did ABC Company and on comparable terms (see Chapter 10). Historic returns for the two GIC plans have been similar, and future returns are expected to be comparable.

8. *A high-yield (junk) bond fund.*   This fund is actively managed by the same fixed income asset management company that manages the money-market funds and the investment grade bond funds. Unlike those funds, however, the junk bond fund invests in corporate bonds of widely varying maturities rated *below* investment grade, i.e., those rated below BBB by Standard and Poor's. Such issues are inherently riskier than those of investment grade and, as a result, over time, a few of the securities in the junk bond fund's portfolio have gone into default. But precisely *because* these noninvestment grade issues *are* riskier than investment grade bonds, they also have yielded more than the securities held in the portfolios of the three investment grade bond funds or the money-market funds and, over time, those incremental returns have more than offset any losses resulting from defaults. On balance, what that has meant is that the junk bond fund has generated *net higher* returns than any of the money-market funds, the investment grade bond funds, or the GIC, but that those higher returns have been accompanied by greater risk, volatility, and variability in rates of return.

9. *An international stock fund.*
10. *A global stock fund.*
11. *A Far Eastern stock fund.*
12. *A Southeastern Asian stock fund.*
13. *A Western European stock fund.*
14. *An Eastern European stock fund.*
15. *A Latin American stock fund.*   XYZ Company's 401(k) plan also offers an array of foreign funds managed by a well-known international investment management company with extensive resources around the world. These funds are all equity funds, they are all actively managed, and each focuses on a different geographic area.

Five of the funds focus on areas that have been of particular investment interest in recent years: the Far East, Southeast Asia, Western Europe, Eastern Europe, and Latin America. A sixth, the international stock fund, invests in equities anywhere in the world outside the United States. And a seventh, the global stock fund, invests anywhere in the world, both within and outside the United States.

All of these foreign funds have had relatively short histories—at least relative to those of the domestic stock and bond funds included in XYZ Company's 401(k) plan. While most of the domestic funds in the plan have been in existence for 30 or 40 years (or even longer), only the international stock fund and the global stock fund (among the foreign funds) have existed for even as long as 20 years. The Western European stock fund has been in existence for 15 years, the Far Eastern stock fund for 10, and the Southeast Asian stock fund for seven, while both the Eastern European and the Latin American stock funds were only introduced within the last two years (as investor enthusiasm over the potential benefits of NAFTA and the collapse of the Communist bloc generated a clamor for investment vehicles designed to capitalize on those opportunities).

During their relatively short histories, the international, global, Western European, Far Eastern, and Southeast Asian stock funds all outperformed the average of U.S. stock funds. These superior performances (denominated in U.S. dollars) resulted from a decline in the value of the U.S. dollar and the more rapid growth of foreign economies relative to our own. The records of the Eastern European and Latin American stock funds were both too short to be meaningful.

16. *A large capitalization U.S. stock index fund.*
17. *An actively managed U.S. balanced fund.*
18. *An actively managed large capitalization U.S. stock fund.*
19. *An actively managed small capitalization U.S. stock fund.*
20–29. *A series of specialized industry funds.* Just as XYZ Company's 401(k) plan offered an array of fixed income funds, all managed by the same established fixed income money management group, and just as it provided a broad selection of foreign equity funds managed by another group with extensive international experience, so, too, it has offered a number of domestic equity and balanced funds all managed by the same highly qualified U.S. investment management company.

The company that manages these funds is the same mutual fund complex that actively manages the balanced fund and passively manages the large capitalization common stock index fund, which are included in ABC Company's 401(k) plan. And, in fact, both of those funds are among the 30 funds that are offered by XYZ Company's 401(k) plan too. (Both of those funds were described in Chapter 10.)

In addition, this management company runs several other equity funds in which XYZ Company's 401(k) plan participants are permitted to invest. These include an actively managed large capitalization fund, which invests primarily in long-established, financially solid, listed, dividend-paying companies with market capitalizations in excess of $500 million, and an actively managed small capitalization fund, which focuses primarily on newer, less well-established, emerging growth companies. Both funds have been in existence for more than 30 years, and both have achieved enviable performance records within their respective universes. Not surprisingly, the small capitalization fund has generated the higher overall average annual rate of return of the two—and has been the riskier and more volatile investment.

XYZ Company's 401(k) plan participants also may invest in any of 10 different specialized equity funds. Each of these 10 funds concentrates its investments in the stocks of a different industry or economic sector, including:

Energy

Computers and high technology

Banking, insurance, and finance

Public utilities

Media and telecommunications

Gold

Drugs, health care, and biotechnology

Pollution control

Consumer sector

Capital goods

All of these funds have had very erratic records: in some years one or another among them has been a top performer, only to sink to the bottom of the investment barrel in a subsequent period, as different investment sectors have moved in and out of fashion.

30. *A socially responsible U.S. equity fund.* Finally, plan participants may invest in an actively managed and broadly diversified stock fund that bills itself as being socially responsible because its management not only considers economic, investment, and financial factors in deciding what to buy or sell but also considers the potential social or ethical consequences of its investment decisions. For example, notwithstanding the possible economic appeal of the following industries at particular times, the fund never will invest in the stocks of companies in the tobacco, alcohol, or gaming industries nor in those that manufacture armaments, because it considers all such activities to be antisocial. Similarly, in reaching its investment decisions, the fund's management concerns itself as much with a company's social record on issues as diverse as animal testing, environmental pollution, and affirmative action, as it does with the company's financial record (including its return on investment, profit margins, and dividend policy).

Over time, the performance record of the socially responsible fund has not been quite as good as the records that were achieved by the other diversified but not necessarily socially responsible equity funds available through XYZ Company's 401(k) plan, i.e., the large and small capitalization U.S. stock funds and the U.S. stock index fund, perhaps because of its self-imposed restriction limiting its opportunities pool. But the performance shortfall has been small (amounting to less than one percent annually relative to the index fund), and many of XYZ Company's employees have considered that to be a reasonable price to pay in seeking to achieve their social as well as their financial goals.

Doris: Another Aggressive Investor

Doris was very much like Andrew in background and temperament. Just as Andrew joined ABC Company as a management trainee shortly after his graduation from college at age 22, so, too, Doris joined XYZ Company in a similar capacity at about the same age. Like Andrew, Doris also was unmarried at the time and did not have any financial obligations to anyone other than herself.

Doris also considered herself to be an aggressive investor. She had majored in economics in college; she had been interested in the stock market ever since high school; and since her junior year in college, she had been investing for her own account. Her score on the psychological risk tolerance test was identical to Andrew's: a relatively high 52 points.

Indeed, had Doris joined ABC Company as Andrew did, rather than XYZ Company, she probably would have constructed a 401(k) plan for herself much like his. She, too, would have been disappointed by the investment choices ABC Company's plan provided, preferring to invest more aggressively in small capitalization stocks or foreign securities (which were not available as choices in ABC Company's plan). So she probably also would have had to settle for the next best thing: the common stock index fund.

As things turned out, however, Doris was more fortunate than Andrew and didn't have to settle for a stock index fund by default. Although ABC Company's plan provided participants with only four choices, XYZ Company's plan offered 30, so that she was able to structure a portfolio much more to her liking.

Doris quickly decided that she didn't want to invest in GICs, money-market funds, or bond funds, whether investment grade or high yield. Recognizing (as Andrew had) that common stocks historically had generated much higher returns on average than had fixed income securities and feeling perfectly comfortable in assuming the incremental risk that equity investment entailed, she determined to invest solely in equities, at least at the beginning.

Doris also decided that she *didn't* want to invest in a *passively* managed fund because she thought that any active manager worth his salt should be able to outperform an arbitrary index—or at least should try to! And she decided that she didn't want to invest in a balanced fund either (because of its fixed income component). But that still left her with the following 21 different equity funds from which to choose:

1. *A company stock fund*

2. *An international stock fund*

3. *A global stock fund*

4. *A Far Eastern stock fund*

5. *A Southeastern Asian stock fund*

6. *A Western European stock fund*

7. *An Eastern European stock fund*

8. *A Latin American stock fund*

9. *An actively managed large capitalization U.S. stock fund*

10. *An actively managed small capitalization U.S. stock fund*

11. *A specialized industry fund (energy)*

12. *A specialized industry fund (computers and high technology)*

13. *A specialized industry fund (banking, insurance, and finance)*

14. *A specialized industry fund (public utilities)*

15. *A specialized industry fund (media and telecommunications)*

16. *A specialized industry fund (gold)*

17. *A specialized industry fund (drugs, health care, and biotechnology)*

18. *A specialized industry fund (pollution control)*

19. *A specialized industry fund (the consumer sector)*

20. *A specialized industry fund (capital goods)*

21. *A socially responsible U.S. equity fund*

Since Doris believed firmly in the advantages of diversification, she decided that, if at all possible, she would invest in more than one of the equity funds and, ideally, in as many as four. Two of the funds appeared to be obvious choices: the large capitalization U.S. stock fund and the small capitalization U.S. stock fund. Both were actively managed, both had good track records, and they balanced each other nicely by covering different market subsectors. Doris elected to invest one-fourth of the assets in her 401(k) plan in each.

Next Doris decided to commit one-fourth of her assets to foreign securities in order to realize the advantages of international geographic diversification, but she still had to select from among seven different foreign funds. At first, she was tempted to choose the Latin American fund (since she thought that the passage of NAFTA would result in a big increase in trade between the United States and Mexico) or the Eastern European fund (since so many American investors appeared to be flocking to that newly emerging market because of the collapse of the Communist bloc) or the Southeastern Asia fund (because she believed that the resumption of trade relations between the United States and Vietnam augured well for the economy of that nation, and the economies of the other Southeastern countries had been among the most rapidly growing in the world in recent years). On the other hand, those were also probably the riskiest of the foreign funds so she mused that perhaps she'd be better off with the Western European or Far Eastern fund, after all, since the governments and economies of the countries in those regions were so much more stable.

Finally, however, Doris decided that if it was important for her to diversify her portfolio of U.S. stocks, it was just as important for her to diversify internationally, which suggested that she'd be best off investing in either the international fund or the global fund. Both of those funds, after all, could invest in any or all of the five different geographic regions she had considered, and she would gain the benefit of much broader diversification.

The major difference between the international fund and the global fund was that although both could invest anywhere in the world outside the United States, only the global fund could also invest in the United States. Doris decided that if she wanted one-fourth of her assets to be committed to foreign securities (and she did), she'd be better off with the international fund, which wouldn't dilute that exposure by investing in any U.S. stocks. So she invested another one-fourth of her 401(k) assets in the international fund.

That still left Doris with one-fourth of her 401(k) assets unallocated, and her choices for investing that portion came down to the company stock fund, one of the specialized industry funds, or the socially responsible fund. Now Doris decided to take something of a flyer: she chose to put the final portion of her 401(k) assets into the company stock fund.

Doris realized, of course, that investing in the company stock fund wasn't the most prudent thing she could do because it meant that 25 percent of her assets would be linked to the fortunes of her own company. But she felt that she had achieved very broad equity diversification, both domestically and internationally, with the bulk of her assets, and she really believed that XYZ Company was a solid well-positioned company with stellar potential. She also looked forward to a long career with XYZ Company and wanted to make the emotional, as well as financial, commitment that equity ownership in the company would entail; this was a convenient way to accomplish that.

Over the next eight years, Doris continued to allocate one-fourth of her 401(k) contributions to each of these four funds: the actively managed large capitalization U.S. stock fund, the actively managed small capitalization U.S. stock fund, the international stock fund, and the company stock fund. Concurrently, she advanced rapidly up the corporate ladder: she became one of the company's youngest vice presidents and received a number of stock options; she also purchased stock in the company in the open market so that by the time she turned 30, she had established a significant position for herself in XYZ Company common stock.

At that time, she took a fresh look at her 401(k) plan and took the psychological risk profile test again. Her risk tolerance had not changed (she again scored 52 points), but, realizing that she was growing older and expecting to marry soon, she decided to become just a bit more conservative.

Accordingly, Doris shifted the 25 percent of the assets in her 401(k) portfolio that were in the company stock fund to the actively managed U.S. balanced fund. She still maintained a big position in XYZ Company's stock in her personal portfolio, and she expected to be receiving an additional grant of options soon, so that eliminating her company stock holdings from her 401(k) plan caused her no emotional distress and couldn't be construed as any loss of confidence in her employer. It was strictly prudent financial planning to further diversify her holdings at this time.

Since the balanced fund, on average, tended to maintain about half its assets in common stocks, this change meant that Doris still would have about seven-eighths of her 401(k) assets invested in common stocks (domestic and foreign) and about one-eighth in bonds. This remained a relatively aggressive stance.

As it turned out, 10 years passed and Doris decided not to marry after all; she was so involved in her career that she didn't think there also was room in her life for the major commitment that marriage would entail. And so, approaching 40, Doris reexamined her 401(k) plan and her attitude toward risk. She continued to score high in terms of her psychological risk profile but, given her age, she decided to become a little more conservative in her plan.

Basically, what Doris wanted to do was to decrease her equity exposure to 75 percent from 87.5 percent and increase her fixed income exposure from 12.5 percent to 25 percent, and there were several different ways by which she might accomplish that. For one, she could simply do as Andrew had done and shift another quarter of her common stock fund holdings to the balanced fund; that would leave her with 50 percent in common stock funds and 50 percent in the balanced fund and, since the balanced fund was about 50 percent invested in fixed income securities on average, that would accomplish her goal.

If she were to do that, however, Doris would have to eliminate one entire equity class (large capitalization U.S. equities, small capitalization U.S. equities, or foreign stocks) from her 401(k) portfolio, and she really didn't want to do that. So Doris adopted a different approach.

What she did was to shift her 25 percent position in the balanced fund to the long-term bond fund. That provided her with the 25 percent fixed income exposure she sought while allowing her to retain the equity exposure she desired in three different equity classes.

A decade later, Doris turned 50. Like Andrew, Doris also hoped to retire at age 60, which meant that she only had 10 more years in which to accumulate the retirement assets she'd need. This time, when Doris took the psychological risk tolerance exam, she scored 50, which was only a little lower than she had scored in the past and still left her in the aggressive category of investors.

Doris determined to become only a little more conservative, increasing her fixed income exposure from one-quarter to three-eighths and reducing her equity exposure from three-quarters to five-eighths. But at the same time, she wanted to retain positions in large capitalization, small capitalization, and foreign stocks. Here's how she did it.

First, Doris shifted the 25 percent of her holdings in the large capitalization stock fund to the balanced fund. By so doing, she increased her direct and indirect fixed income exposure to 37.5 percent: since about half of the balanced fund's assets were in bonds, her 25 percent position in that fund gave her another 12.5 percent exposure to bonds on top of the 25 percent exposure to bonds that she retained through the long-term bond fund.

By doing this, however, Doris reduced her exposure to large capitalization U.S. stocks from 25 percent to about 12.5 percent (most of the equities in the balanced fund were large capitalization stocks), and she really preferred having a little more exposure to domestic large capitalization stocks, even if that meant having a little less exposure to foreign stocks. So the next thing Doris did was to shift her position in the international stock fund (which owned no U.S. securities) to the global stock fund (which invested about one-fourth of its assets in large capitalization U.S. stocks and about three-fourths in foreign stocks). That provided her with an asset distribution that looked like this: bonds, 37.5 percent; large capitalization U.S. stocks, 18.75 percent; small capitalization U.S. stocks, 25 percent; and foreign stocks, 18.75 percent.

Doris did manage to retire at age 60, and when she did, she decided to increase her fixed income exposure to 50 percent and to reduce her equity exposure proportionately. She couldn't do that and still retain substantial exposure in all of the equities classes she owned so something had to give: she decided to forego some (but not all) of her exposure in large capital-

Table 11-1. Doris' % Asset Allocation in XYZ Company's 401(k) Plan

Age	Intermediate-term bond fund	Long-term bond fund	Balanced fund	Company stock fund	International stock fund	Global stock fund	Large capitalization stock fund	Small capitalization stock fund	Total
22–29	0	0	0	25	25	0	25	25	100
30–39	0	0	25	0	25	0	25	25	100
40–49	0	25	0	0	25	0	25	25	100
50–59	0	25	25	0	0	25	0	25	100
60 and Above	25	25	0	0	0	25	0	25	100

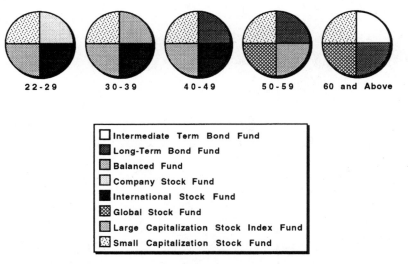

Figure 11-1. Evolution of Doris' 401(k) plan.

ization stocks (in part because she owned a large portfolio of such stocks outside of her 401(k) plan).

Accordingly, Doris shifted her holdings in the balanced fund to the intermediate-term bond fund. Now her asset distribution looked like this: long-term bonds, 25 percent; intermediate-term bonds, 25 percent; large capitalization U.S. stocks, 6.25 percent (one-quarter of her holdings in the global fund); small capitalization U.S. stocks, 25 percent; and foreign stocks, 18.75 percent (three-quarters of her holdings in the global fund).

Table 11-1 and Figure 11-1 show how Doris' 401(k) asset allocation had evolved during her career.

Edward: Another Middle-of-the-Road Investor

Edward joined XYZ Company at about the same time that Doris did—as a 22-year old recent college graduate. And like Doris (as well as Andrew and Barbara, for that matter), Edward also was single and had no large financial obligations to anyone other than himself.

Edward and Barbara had been friends at college, and his personality was much more like hers than like Andrew's or Doris'. He was neither knowledgeable, nor, indeed, even particularly interested in financial matters and by no stretch of the imagination would he have considered himself to be an aggressive investor. When he took our psychological risk pro-file test, his score was 40 (just as Barbara's had been), confirming that he would be comfortable incurring a reasonable amount of risk in order to generate reasonable returns, but that he would not be willing to assume above-average risk even in the hope of achieving above-average returns. Nor would he settle for below-average returns, even if that meant that he'd be able to further reduce his risk.

You may recall that when Barbara learned that ABC Company had a 401(k) plan, she (unlike Andrew) was not at all disappointed to learn that there would be only four options available to her. She assumed that four choices would be more than enough and, in fact, she had no difficulty structuring a satisfactory 401(k) portfolio from just those four options.

Now when Edward learned that XYZ Company's 401(k) plan offered 30 different options, he was overwhelmed, momentarily actually envying Barbara because her plan was so simple. In fact, Edward's initial thought was to do just what Barbara had done in her plan, investing all of his 401(k) assets in the balanced fund and a large capitalization stock fund until it came time to retire and ignoring all the other options available to him. On second thought, however, he decided that as long as he was being given additional choices, he might as well see what they were.

Once he did that, Edward decided that he wouldn't just invest all his 401(k) money in the balanced fund and a large capitalization stock fund after all. Rather, he would establish a diversified portfolio of stock and bond funds that he would modify over time as he grew older and his cir-cumstances changed.

Here's how Edward decided which funds to invest in. First, he deter-mined to invest only in well-diversified investment vehicles, which meant that of the 30 choices he was given, he immediately eliminated 17: the company stock fund; the GIC; the 5 regional foreign stock funds; and the 10 specialized U.S. equity funds. But that still left him with 13 funds from which to select no more than four. •

Next, Edward decided to commit about 75 percent of his 401(k) assets to equities and about 25 percent to fixed income securities. Since he was seek-ing maximum diversification, he determined to select three equity funds and one fixed income fund (which automatically eliminated the balanced fund).

On the equity side, these are the six funds he was left to choose from: the international stock fund, the global stock fund, the large capitalization U.S. stock index fund, the actively managed large capitalization U.S. stock fund, the actively managed small capitalization U.S. stock fund, and the socially responsible U.S. equity fund. From among these, he considered it most prudent to choose a large capitalization stock fund, a small capital-ization stock fund, and a foreign stock fund, which, surprisingly, was just what Doris had done.

Since he was less aggressive than Doris, however, he chose to invest in the large capitalization U.S. stock *index* fund rather than the actively managed large capitalization U.S. stock fund. And he picked the global stock fund rather than the international stock fund. It was likely, he thought, that the index fund would prove to be less risky than an actively managed fund investing in the same class of securities and he was more comfortable with a little greater exposure to U.S. equities and a little less to foreign stocks. In order to invest in small capitalization stocks, however, he was forced to select the same investment vehicle that Doris had: the actively managed small capitalization U.S. stock fund; it was the only small capitalization fund available to him.

Edward had considered investing in the socially responsible U.S. equity fund because he shared most of its social values, and if his 401(k) plan had allowed him to invest in five different funds instead of four, he probably would have. But it didn't, so something had to give and, when push came to shove, he decided to forego the socially responsible equity fund in his plan. (Shortly thereafter, he did include that fund in his personal portfolio outside his 401(k) plan, however).

When it came time to select a fixed income fund, Edward quickly eliminated the U.S. government money-market fund, the investment grade money-market fund, and the short-term investment grade bond fund from consideration as being unduly conservative 401(k) plan investments for a man of his age, even allowing for his middle-of-the-road investment temperament. He eliminated the high-yield (junk) bond fund for the opposite reason: he deemed it to be too risky. That just left the intermediate-term investment grade bond fund and the long-term investment grade bond fund. He finally decided on the somewhat riskier long-term investment grade bond fund as being the more desirable of the two at this early stage in his life.

Over the next eight years, Edward continued to allocate one-fourth of his 401(k) contributions to each of the four funds: the large capitalization U.S. stock index fund, the small capitalization U.S. stock fund, the global stock fund, and the long-term bond fund. Then, around age 30, he decided that the time had come to review his financial and psychological profile. Apparently, his risk tolerance had not changed (he again scored 40 points on our risk tolerance test), but there was no way around the fact that he was older and he was planning to marry soon. So Edward decided to restructure his 401(k) plan a little more conservatively, increasing his fixed income exposure to about 37.5 percent from 25 percent and reducing his equity exposure from 75 percent to about 62.5 percent.

He accomplished this by shifting the 25 percent of the assets in his 401(k) portfolio that were in the large capitalization U.S. stock index fund to the actively managed U.S. balanced fund. Since the balanced fund, on average, maintained about half its assets in common stocks, this change meant that Edward still would have about five-eighths of his 401(k) assets invested in common stocks (domestic and foreign) and about three-eighths in bonds.

A decade later, Edward again reassessed his 401(k) plan and his attitude toward risk. He was 40 years old now and married (although he and his wife had decided not to have any children). He continued to score in the middle range (around 40) on our psychological risk profile test, but, given his age, he decided that it was time to become yet a little more conservative in his 401(k) plan.

This time, Edward decided to decrease his equity exposure to 50 percent from 62.5 percent, thereby increasing his fixed income exposure to the same level, and to shorten the average maturities on his fixed income investments. He did this by switching his holdings in the balanced fund to the intermediate-term bond fund. That left him with 25 percent in the long-term bond fund, 25 percent in the intermediate-term bond fund, 25 percent in the small capitalization U.S. stock fund, and 25 percent in the global stock fund. Since the global stock fund was about 75 percent invested in foreign securities and 25 percent in U.S. large capitalization equities, this meant that Edward's direct and indirect equity exposure included 25 percent in small capitalization U.S. stocks, approximately 18.75 percent in foreign stocks, and about 6.25 percent in large capitalization U.S. stocks.

Ten years later, Edward turned 50 and, like all of the others we've met so far who entered the workforce at about the same time that he did, he also hoped to retire at age 60. That left him just 10 more years in which to accumulate the additional retirement assets he'd need.

So Edward decided that it was time to review his 401(k) plan retirement portfolio again and to reconsider his risk tolerance. When he took our psychological risk tolerance test, however, he found that he still had a basically middle-of-the-road investment temperament. And, after reviewing his portfolio in the context of his present and prospective financial position, he decided to make just one change: he shifted 25 percent of his assets from the global stock fund back to the large capitalization U.S. stock index fund. This had no effect on his debt-equity mix—he remained 50 percent in fixed income securities and 50 percent in common stocks—but it increased his exposure to large capitalization U.S. equities to 25 percent from about 6.25 percent, while totally eliminating his foreign stock exposure.

Shortly after age 60, Edward did retire, and when he did, he decided to make just one final change in the asset allocation of his 401(k) plan: he transferred 25 percent of his assets from the small capitalization stock fund to the balanced fund. By so doing, he increased his fixed income

Table 11-2. Edward's % Asset Allocation in XYZ Company's 401(k) Plan

Age	Intermediate-term bond fund	Long-term bond fund	Balanced fund	Global stock fund	Large capitalization stock fund	Small capitalization stock fund	Total
22–29	0	25	0	25	25	25	100
30–39	0	25	25	25	0	25	100
40–49	25	25	0	25	0	25	100
50–59	25	25	0	0	25	25	100
60 and Above	25	25	25	0	25	0	100

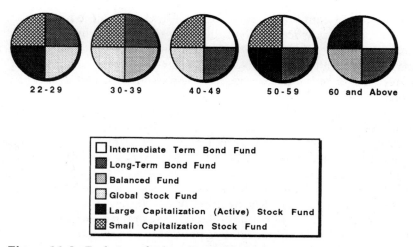

☐ Intermediate Term Bond Fund
■ Long-Term Bond Fund
▨ Balanced Fund
☐ Global Stock Fund
■ Large Capitalization (Active) Stock Fund
▨ Small Capitalization Stock Fund

Figure 11-2. Evolution of Edward's 401(k) plan.

exposure from 50 percent to about 62.5 percent and reduced his equity exposure from 50 percent to approximately 37.5 percent.

Table 11-2 and Figure 11-2 show how Edward's 401(k) asset allocation developed over a period of more than 40 years.

Frances: Another Conservative Investor

Frances joined XYZ Company when she was 25. She had graduated from college three years earlier but had gone on to earn her MBA and then spent a year abroad. Now she was engaged to be married and embarking on her career. It was an exciting time.

In financial temperament, she was most like Charles: conservative, cautious, and risk-averse. When they took our psychological risk profile test, their scores were almost the same: he scored a very low 24, and she scored 25.

Frances was very interested in economic, financial, and investment matters. Like Andrew, Charles, and Doris (but not Barbara or Edward), she not only understood what finance was all about but enjoyed selecting her own investments. As a result, Frances was much more pleased with XYZ Company's 401(k) plan with its 30 different choices than Charles had been with ABC Company's 401(k) plan that offered only four different investment options.

Frances had to confront the same internal conflict in structuring her 401(k) portfolio as Charles had faced. While she realized that, at her age, she really should commit the bulk of her 401(k) assets to equities, that wasn't so easy: in practice, she had difficulty setting her emotions aside and really wasn't comfortable investing in equities at all.

What Frances really wanted to do was to invest in fixed income securities, which might provide lower returns than equities but which also are less volatile and less risky. Here she was in a better position than Charles. As you may recall, in order to invest in fixed income securities, he had only three choices: a money-market fund (which was likely to provide very low returns over time), GICs (which would provide him with no opportunity for capital gains), and the balanced fund (which provided an indirect exposure to fixed income securities but also necessitated his abdicating some control over the asset allocation process). Frances, on the other hand, would be able to invest in GICs, in either of two different money-market funds, in a high-yield (junk) bond fund, or in any of three different investment grade fixed income funds holding bonds of varying maturities.

Frances bit the bullet and decided, at the outset, to commit half her 401(k) assets to equities and the other half to fixed income securities. She determined to bypass the balanced fund, at least initially, because she wanted to be as responsible for her own asset allocation as possible, rather that delegating it to a fund manager. She also decided that she would seek maximum diversification by investing in four different funds, rather than just one, two, or three.

The next thing that Frances did was to select two from among the seven fixed income funds available to her. That proved not to be a difficult decision at all: she quickly eliminated the two money-market funds from consideration because, although they were the least risky investments, it was for that very reason that their returns were likely to be much too low. She eliminated the high-yield (junk) bond fund because she considered it to be too risky, and she decided against the GIC for several reasons, including the facts that it provided minimal diversification and it probably would produce less of a return than she could realize from one or more of the bond funds.

That left the three investment grade bond funds, which differed among themselves only in terms of the average maturities of their holdings. Of these, Frances quickly decided to forego the short-term bond fund, which was likely to provide the lowest returns of the three. Thus, she determined to invest 25 percent of her 401(k) money in the intermediate-term bond fund and another 25 percent in the long-term bond fund.

Next, Frances had to select two equity funds, and that didn't turn out to be a difficult task either. She quickly decided to invest 25 percent of her 401(k) assets in the passively managed large capitalization U.S. stock index fund, which she thought was probably the most conservative and least risky of the equity choices available to her.

Finally, she committed 25 percent of her 401(k) money to the small capitalization U.S. stock fund. This was her most difficult decision: she was torn between this fund and either the global or international stock fund, which Frances thought also had a lot to recommend them. All three funds had good historic performance records, all would provide a good counterbalance to the large capitalization U.S. stock index fund, and all, she had to admit, were somewhat riskier investments than she was comfortable with. In the final analysis, she opted for the small capitalization U.S. stock fund because she thought she'd be more nervous over the political and currency risks inherent in either of the two foreign funds than she would be over the business risk intrinsic to the small capitalization domestic fund.

By the time she reached her early thirties, Frances was married, and she and her husband had adopted two children. That's when she decided to transfer the 25 percent of her assets that were in the small capitalization stock fund into the balanced fund.

This was also a relatively easy decision. Admittedly, Frances didn't like having to delegate any of the asset allocation decision-making process (between stocks and bonds) to a fund manager as she was forced to do by investing in the balanced fund. And she did believe that the overall returns of the balanced fund might be lower over time than the returns she otherwise would have realized on the small capitalization stock fund. But she never really was that comfortable incurring the higher risk inherent in the small capitalization stock fund, and she was eager to reduce her equity exposure and increase her fixed income exposure at this stage of life. So she made the change.

Her assets now were distributed 25 percent in the long-term bond fund, 25 percent in the intermediate-term bond fund, 25 percent in the balanced fund, and 25 percent in the large capitalization U.S. stock index fund. This meant that approximately 62.5 percent of her assets were invested in bonds and about 37.5 percent in stocks.

When she turned 40, Frances reduced her equity exposure still further, by shifting another 25 percent of her assets from the large capitalization U.S. stock index fund to the balanced fund. This meant that 25 percent of her assets now were in the long-term bond fund, 25 percent were in the intermediate-term bond fund, and 50 percent were in the balanced fund. And since half of the balanced fund's assets were in fixed income securities and the other half in equities, this meant that three-quarters of her assets were in bonds and one quarter were in common stocks. Frances maintained this asset mix until her retirement at age 60.

Sadly, shortly before Frances hoped to retire, her husband passed away. This was a major emotional blow to her and prompted her to delay her retirement for a few years—not for financial reasons but in order to maintain greater structure in her life.

Table 11-3. Frances' % Asset Allocation in XYZ Company's 401(k) Plan

Age	GICs	Intermediate-term bond fund	Long-term bond fund	Balanced fund	Large capitalization index fund	Small capitalization stock fund	Total
22–29	0	25	25	0	25	25	100
30–39	0	25	25	25	25	0	100
40–49	0	25	25	50	0	0	100
50–59	0	25	25	50	0	0	100
60 and Above	25	25	25	25	0	0	100

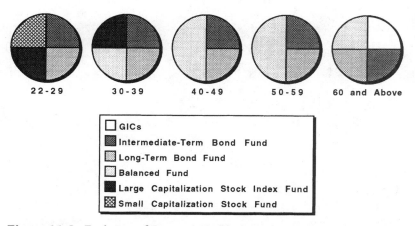

Figure 11-3. Evolution of Frances' 401(k) plan.

When Frances finally did retire, she reduced her equity exposure for the final time by moving 25 percent of her assets in the balanced fund to the GIC contract. Now her portfolio was very conservatively positioned, with 25 percent in GICs, 25 percent in the long-term bond fund, 25 percent in the intermediate-term bond fund, and 25 percent in the balanced fund. Frances had succeeded in reducing the overall volatility of her portfolio, but she also had paid a steep price by reducing her potential returns as well. Still, through the balanced fund, Frances maintained about a 12.5 percent indirect equity exposure as a continuing inflation hedge.

Table 11-3 and Figure 11-3 show how Frances' 401(k) asset allocation looked over the course of her business career.

A Final Note

All of our six hypothetical plan participants retired at or around age 60. Of course, if you expect to retire at a significantly later age than they did, say at age 70, you could afford to be more aggressive in your own 401(k) plan management than could your otherwise closest counterpart (in terms of age, type of plan, or psychological makeup). And the same thing would be true if you had very ample retirement resources available to you outside of your 401(k) plan upon which you might draw before having to dip into the assets in your 401(k) plan. If, for example, you expect to have accumulated a large taxable investment portfolio by the time you retire or if you anticipate selling your home for a very large sum when you retire, you might plan to draw upon those assets before turning to your 401(k) plan, which would allow you to manage your 401(k) portfolio more aggressively for a longer period of time than otherwise might have been the case.

12

Taking Money Out of Your 401(k) Plan

Rollovers, Hardships, Borrowing, and Retirement

Eventually, of course, the time will come when you will want to withdraw some or all of your money from your 401(k) plan (or when you may be required by law to do so). This may occur because you are changing jobs and don't want to leave your 401(k) assets with your former employer (or are not permitted to do so). It might happen in the less likely circumstances that your company's plan is terminated without a successor defined contribution plan being established or in the event of the merger or sale of your company. It may result from your having been confronted by a sudden emergency and finding it necessary to make a hardship withdrawal from your plan.

It may happen because you would like to borrow against the assets in your plan for some worthwhile purpose, even in the absence of a full-fledged emergency. And it may happen if you die or become disabled before attaining retirement age.

But those are all special circumstances. What is much more likely is that it will occur when you reach retirement age (commonly 59½ or later). And even if you still don't want to take any money out of your account then, you will be required to do so by law when you reach the age of 70½.

Since we already have discussed many of those special situations earlier in this book, we won't spend a lot of additional time on them here before turning to the all-important matter of what you should (and, in some cases, must) do when you reach retirement age. But we would like to review just a couple of points we made previously about rollovers, hardship withdrawals, and borrowing since it is important that you understand the potential financial ramifications (particularly the tax implications) of premature withdrawals from your plan prior to retirement.

Changing Jobs and Qualified Plan Rollovers

If you change jobs before retirement and before age 59½ and if you are not permitted to leave your 401(k) plan with your former employer (or choose not to), you will be offered a distribution from the plan that you might be able to roll over into your next employer's 401(k) plan (if he offers one). Or you could roll it over into your own IRA, whether or not your new employer has a 401(k) plan. In either case, however, the transfer will impose no immediate or additional tax liability upon you—provided it is handled correctly.

Alternatively, you could use the funds you received for current consumption or for some other purpose, including investments, but in that event, you would suffer a major tax liability. For starters, you would have to pay a 20 percent withholding tax on those funds as soon as you received them. Thus, if you expected to receive, say, $100,000, you'd only be given a check for $80,000; the remaining $20,000 would be withheld for federal taxes.

Subsequently, you would have to pay ordinary income taxes on the entire $100,000 just as if it all were earned in the year you received it. Depending on your tax bracket that year, that could amount to more or less than the $20,000 that initially had been withheld, but, more often than not, it would amount to more. And, to make matters even worse, you would have to pay a 10 percent penalty tax on top of all that for having made a premature withdrawal from your plan.

There are, however, two important exceptions to this. First, should you leave your company when you are 55 years of age or older, you may take the money in your corporate retirement plans, including your 401(k) plan, with you without incurring a penalty. And that would be the case whether you were fired or quit and whether or not you then took another job. Of course, you would still have to pay income taxes (which would not be eligible for five-year forward averaging) on the money you withdrew, but the 10 percent penalty tax on premature withdrawals would not apply.

Note that this option would not be available to you just because you chose early retirement at, say, age 52 or 54; qualifying for early retirement at your company would not automatically qualify you for this exemption for which you must be employed at age 55. Note, too, that this exemption is only applicable to tax-qualified retirement plans, such as 401(k)s, not IRAs.

The other way in which you could take money out of your 401(k) plan early without having to pay a penalty would be to "annuitize" or arrange to receive substantially equal payments from the plan based on your life expectancy. You could use this method at any age, and it would be applicable both to qualified retirement plans such as 401(k)s, Keoghs, and IRAs. If you took this opportunity, you would have to take substantially equal payments from your plan for five years or until you reached age 59½, whichever came later; at that time, you could reduce or stop payments if you wished, until age 70½, when minimum distributions again would be required.

If you should "annuitize" in this fashion, you would be permitted to calculate the amount of your withdrawals in any of three ways:

1. You could calculate the size of your withdrawals solely on the basis of your life expectancy.
2. You could include a reasonable interest rate on the money as well as basing your calculations on your life expectancy.
3. You could rely on an annuity table.

In any of these three methods, however, the amounts you would be permitted to withdraw would likely be small, especially if you were relatively young when first arranging to annuitize. But the price you would be paying would be large: you would be depleting the assets in your plan and foregoing the benefits of continued long-term tax-deferred compounding. As a result, you would take very little from your plan in your early years but still would have much less available to you upon retirement when you might really need it. *Our bottom line advice: don't annuitize; leave your retirement funds alone when you are young if you possibly can afford to do so.*

Getting back to the situation in which you're changing jobs, the chances are that you'll decide to roll the funds from your old employer's plan into your new employer's plan or into your own IRA. We highly recommend this strategy, largely because such transfers are nontaxable transactions, enabling you to keep your assets intact and to retain the tax-deferred status of those funds.

If your new employer's plan accepts such transfers and offers options that you consider attractive and especially if you intend to participate in your new employer's plan through continuing payroll deductions, then the simplest and most sensible thing for you to do would be to roll your old plan into the new plan. On the other hand, if your new employer does not have a qualified 401(k) plan, or if his plan does not accept rollovers, or if you would not be comfortable with the investment choices that that plan offered, then you might opt to establish your own rollover IRA instead.

The advantage of doing that would be that you then would have literally thousands of different bank and mutual fund plans to choose from and, with a little effort on your part, you should be able to structure a plan for yourself that truly met your needs. Moreover, you might even be able to transfer the assets in your 401(k) plan to a rollover IRA invested in the very same funds as those in which you were invested in your former employer's 401(k) plan in the first place since some 401(k) plans offer as options mutual funds that also accept investments from rollover IRAs and taxable accounts.

Indeed, some funds, which ordinarily carry sales charges but which waive those charges for their 401(k) plan investors, also waive those charges for rollovers from the 401(k) plans that they manage. So if you have been satisfied with your 401(k) plan investments all along but now intend to transfer those assets into a rollover IRA, the first thing you might investigate is whether you could roll over your 401(k) assets to an IRA that would remain invested in the same funds you presently own.

Once the time comes for you to make a rollover from a former employer's 401(k) plan, however, there are two very important things for you to remember. First, be sure to arrange to have your 401(k) assets sent from your old plan to the new through a direct trustee-to-trustee transfer, rather than taking possession of the funds yourself, even temporarily, since that is the only way you will be able to avoid the 20 percent withholding tax. You should do this by requesting the trustee of your new plan, whether that be your new employer or the bank, brokerage house, or mutual fund company that you have selected to manage your IRA rollover, to notify the trustee of your old plan. The trustee of your new plan will provide you with forms to fill out and forward to the trustee of your former plan in order to facilitate the transfer.

If you don't do that but, instead, request a lump sum distribution from the trustee of your old plan, 20 percent of your funds will be withheld—even if you inform the trustee that you intend to deposit the distribution immediately in your new plan—just as if your intention had not been to roll over your funds at all. It's not that the trustee of your old plan would be trying to give you a hard time: it's just that that's the law.

Suppose, for instance, that you had $100,000 in your old 401(k) plan. If you requested a lump sum distribution, that plan's administrator would have to withhold $20,000, so that you'd only get $80,000. If you immediately deposited the $80,000 in a rollover IRA, you wouldn't have to pay taxes on the $80,000 that year, but you would have to pay taxes (including a 10 percent penalty) on the $20,000 that was withheld since that $20,000 portion would be regarded as income by the IRS. In addition, you would have to pay a 10% penalty, since the withdrawal would have represented a premature withdrawal.

Under these circumstances, the only way to avoid those taxes would be for you to come up with *another* $20,000 from somewhere and deposit that, together with the $80,000 you received, in an IRA rollover within 60 days. In that way, you'd avoid any tax liability on the entire $100,000 rollover that year; the $20,000 that was withheld would represent a credit against the rest of your tax liability, if any. But, in effect, this means that you would have made a tax-free loan of $20,000 to the federal government and that you would have had to come up with another $20,000 from someplace. Think how much better off you would have been if you simply had arranged for a direct trustee-to-trustee transfer in the first place.

Second, a distribution from a 401(k) plan may be rolled over into any IRA that you might previously have established to receive your annual IRA contributions, or it may be rolled over into a brand new IRA (known as a conduit IRA) that you might establish specifically for that purpose. If you already have an IRA, it might seem simpler for you just to avail yourself of the vehicle that already exists, rather than having to go to the trouble of setting up a new IRA and, indeed, it would be. Nonetheless, *establishing a new IRA for this purpose is worth the effort and we recommend that you do it.*

Here's why. When distributions from a 401(k) plan are made to a plan participant upon his retirement, they may be eligible for advantageous tax treatment (including possible five- or 10-years forward income averaging or partial capital gains treatment.) Distributions from IRAs, on the other hand, are taxed as ordinary income when made, with no special tax-reducing rules such as forward averaging. Hence it might well be in your interest to make a secondary transfer of your rolled over 401(k) funds from an IRA to another 401(k) plan in the future, should the opportunity to do so present itself. But you only will be permitted to do that from a *conduit* IRA: any monies rolled over from a 401(k) plan into an existing IRA could *not* subsequently be rolled into a second 401(k) plan.

Another Look at Hardship Withdrawals and Borrowing

We have previously discussed hardship withdrawals at some length and won't go over all that again at this time in any great detail. Remember that the tax implications of making a hardship withdrawal from a 401(k) plan before age 59½ are the same as those of making a premature withdrawal upon leaving your job: you would have to pay ordinary income taxes on the value of the assets you withdrew in the year in which you withdrew them, just as if they all had been earned in that one year—plus a 10 percent penalty tax. Simply because you remained employed and designated the withdrawal as having been made for hardship purposes wouldn't change any of that.

Earlier in this book, we also discussed the fact that, under certain circumstances, you might be able to have access to at least a portion of the assets in your 401(k) plan before age 59½ by borrowing as much as 50 percent of your vested interest in the plan up to a maximum of $50,000 (subject to a number of restrictions). Again, we won't review all of what we've already said, but we would remind you of the tax ramifications of such borrowing.

On the positive side, no taxes would be withheld when you borrowed, and you would not have to pay any ordinary income taxes nor penalty taxes when making the loan. On the negative side, however, although the interest you would have to pay on such loans would not be tax-deductible when paid, that interest would accrue in your own account and, when you eventually did withdraw funds at retirement, you'd have to pay taxes on those interest earnings.

Moreover, if a loan from your 401(k) plan made for any purpose *other* than the purchase of a primary residence was not repaid within five years, the loan would be treated as a taxable distribution and you'd become liable to pay both ordinary and penalty taxes on it just as if you had not made a loan but an outright withdrawal. Finally, if you should leave your job before repaying the loan, it is possible, depending on how your plan was written, that the loan would become immediately repayable in its entirety; in the event that you then were unable immediately to repay it (or chose not to), the loan would be converted into a premature withdrawal, and you would become subject to the taxes and penalties on such withdrawals.

When It's Time to Retire

The withdrawal situations we've discussed so far—rollovers, hardship withdrawals, and borrowing—are important, to be sure, but they won't apply to everyone. If you spend your entire working career with just one employer, for instance, the issue of your rolling over your 401(k) plan into an IRA or into another employer's plan when changing jobs simply won't arise. Similarly, if you're fortunate, you may never have to turn to your plan for a hardship withdrawal. And, if you follow our advice, you'll certainly attempt to avoid "annuitizing" or borrowing from your plan, lest your ultimate retirement benefits be severely diminished.

Eventually, however, the time will come for you to consider withdrawing at least some, if not all, of the money in your 401(k) plan—whether or not you may have rolled over any or all of those funds, made a hardship withdrawal, or borrowed against the equity in your plan in the past. And that time will come when you reach the age of 59½ or are considering retirement. After all, isn't this why you saved and invested that money during so many of your working years? Wasn't it your intention all along to draw upon these funds to supplement a reduced level of earnings in your latter working years should you decide to work only part-time even before retiring or as a replacement for your lost earnings when you finally completely retire?

Four major issues must now be addressed:

1. When *may* you take money out of your 401(k) plan? When *should* you take your money out? And when *must* you take your money out?

2. When you do take money out of your plan, should you take it out all at once in a single lump sum distribution? If so, what should you then do

with it? And what would be the tax consequences of following this course of action?

3. Alternatively, should you elect to receive distributions from your 401(k) plan in installments over a period of years? If so, how would you determine the timing and amounts of those distributions. And what would be the tax consequences of withdrawing your money in *that* fashion?

4. Finally, if there's anything left in your plan when you die, what will happen to it?

Let's consider these issues in order:

When 401(k) Distributions Begin

Once you reach age 59½ or retire, your decision as to when to begin taking money out of your 401(k) plan will depend on three variables:

Your own financial requirements

What the law will *allow*

What the law will *require*

First let's consider the situation in which you reach age 59½ but continue in your regular job. At this time, the law will *permit* you to start withdrawing funds from your 401(k) plan, but you will not be *required* to do so. If you should withdraw some or all of your funds, you would have to pay ordinary income taxes on the amounts withdrawn, but you wouldn't have to pay a 10 percent penalty since withdrawals made subsequent to age 59½ are not premature, whether or not you've retired.

In this situation, then, your decision as to whether or not to withdraw funds from your 401(k) plan would simply be a function of your financial requirements, and since we postulated that you remained employed at your regular job, the chances are that there would be no reason for you to begin making withdrawals yet (barring some catastrophe). And that would be all to the good: *the longer you could avoid making withdrawals, the longer your funds would continue to compound in value on a tax-deferred basis, and the more money likely would be available to you down the road when you really might need it.*

Now let's consider a similar, but not quite identical, situation. Assume that you have reached age 59½ and continue to work, but only on a part-time basis. You've decided, perhaps, that you'd still like to remain gainfully employed, but only for two or three days a week, and you intend to devote the rest of your time to travel, or hobbies, or continuing education—all of the things you always wanted to do when you were younger but couldn't afford because of your greater family responsibilities in those earlier years.

Again, the law would allow you to withdraw funds from your 401(k) plan but would not require it. And again, your decision as to whether or not to draw upon your 401(k) plan funds would depend on your financial requirements. In this situation, however, since your income has been reduced because you're working part-time rather than full-time, you might consider making some withdrawals from your 401(k) plan in order to supplement those reduced earnings.

Of course, even in this situation, if you could get along without making such withdrawals, so much the better. If your income from part-time employment, your other investments, or any other sources available to you were sufficient to enable you to continue to live comfortably without drawing on the funds in your 401(k) plan, you'd still be better off leaving those funds alone to continue to compound in value on a tax-deferred basis.

Now suppose that you *have* retired, whether before or after you reach the age of 59½. Again the law would *permit* you, but not *require* you, to withdraw money from your 401(k) plan. And so again, your decision would depend solely upon your financial requirements: if you found that you needed to draw upon the funds in your 401(k) plan to live comfortably in your retirement years, well, by all means do so: that's what they're there for. But if you don't really need them yet, because you're fortunate in having sufficient other sources of income, then you ought not to touch them.

The bottom line is that it is best to delay withdrawing money from your 401(k) plan for as long as possible, allowing the funds you accumulated during your working years to continue to grow in value on a tax-deferred basis for as long as possible. Ideally, you will be able to do that for several years beyond reaching the age of 59½ (either because you continue working part-time or full-time or because you will have access to other sources of income) or even beyond the onset of your retirement (because of those alternative income sources). But if your circumstances should change and you find that you must begin drawing on the funds in your 401(k) plan, there is nothing to prevent you from doing so when you are older, say at 62, 65, or 69, rather than 59½ or when your retirement actually began.

When you reach age 70½, however, you *must* at least begin receiving distributions from your 401(k) plan, even if you have not retired and are still working full-time and even if you don't feel that you need such distributions to live on. That is what the law requires and if you don't do it, you'll be hit with a 50 percent penalty tax on the amount that *should* have been distributed to you.

Lump Sum Distributions

In general, it is *not* advisable for you to take all your money out of your 401(k) plan immediately upon retirement or upon attaining the age of 59½ if you can avoid doing so. These funds are intended to last you through many years of retirement, and the longer you can leave them in your plan, even after you've retired and stopped making additional contributions, the longer they will continue to compound in value for you on a tax-deferred basis. If you take all your funds out at once, however, and don't make any other rollover tax deferral arrangement, you'll be hit with an immediate tax liability and lose the future benefit of tax-deferred compounding.

There are three circumstances, however, in which you might want to consider receiving a lump sum distribution from your 401(k) plan upon retirement:

1. You might be required by your former employer to take the assets in your 401(k) plan with you, even though you might have preferred to leave them where they were. In such a situation, in which you don't really want the funds yet but are forced to take them, you would be best off transferring the entire distribution into a rollover IRA through a direct trustee-to-trustee transfer, thereby incurring no immediate tax liability and avoiding withholding taxes.

2. Even if you are not required by your employer to do so, you might prefer to transfer all your assets from your 401(k) plan when you retire in order to reinvest them differently in a similarly tax-advantaged rollover IRA providing you with other investment choices. Again, it would be important that you arrange for a direct trustee-to-trustee transfer in order to avoid withholding taxes. (In either of these cases, however, if you are past the age of 70½, you only would be permitted to roll over your distribution to the extent it exceeded your minimum required distribution.)

3. Finally, if you have an immediate need for a substantial sum of money, in order to pay for major medical expenses or to purchase a new home or to start a new business, for instance, and you have no other place to get it, you might consider tapping the assets in your 401(k) plan at that time, despite the adverse tax consequences of doing so. In that case, however, since you would not be rolling over your funds into another tax-advantaged account, you could be hit with a hefty tax bill.

In this instance, several different options may be available to you to minimize that tax liability and the method you choose could make a very big difference in the total amount of the liability you incur. Since the best method for you to use in calculating your own liability will depend on your age, other income, other deductions, exemptions, and so forth, there is no single best method that we can now recommend to all readers. And for that reason, you would be well-advised to discuss your particular financial circumstances with your accountant or tax adviser *before* making any decision regarding the receipt of your 401(k) distributions, so that he might assist you in minimizing any tax liability.

In general, however, these are the tax options that would be available to you, should you elect to receive a lump sum distribution from your 401(k) plan and not roll it over into another tax-advantaged plan:

1. You could simply report the entire distribution as ordinary income and pay taxes on it on the basis of your tax rate in the year you receive it. (To the extent that you might previously have made *after-tax* contributions to your plan, however, no taxes would be payable on the portion of the distribution that you would receive that was attributable to such *after-tax* contributions since taxes already would effectively have been paid on them.)

2. If you attained age 59½ and participated in your plan for at least five years, a lump sum distribution could qualify for *five-year forward averaging,* at the rates in effect at the time of the distribution. In all likelihood, that would reduce your effective tax rate.

3. If you participated in your plan before 1973 and were born before January 1, 1936, the amount you accumulated through post-1973 participation might qualify for such *five-year forward averaging* while the amount attributable to pre-1974 plan participation might qualify as a *long-term capital gain* taxable at the flat 20 percent rate in effect in 1986.

4. Alternatively, if you were born before January 1, 1936, you might elect *10-year* forward averaging at the ordinary income tax rates in effect in 1986 and the flat 20 percent tax rate then in effect on *capital gains.*

5. Finally, you could elect to roll over a partial distribution from your 401(k) plan, if the amount you chose to roll over represented at least 50 percent of the balance of your account, was not part of a series of periodic payments, and was due to your death, separation from service, or disability. If you do that, however, the amount that you did *not* roll over would *not* be eligible for forward averaging but would be taxed as ordinary income in the year it was received.

Minimum Required Distributions

Instead of taking a lump sum distribution from your 401(k) plan, however, you could arrange to accept smaller annual distributions over a period of years, and, *for most people, this makes the most sense.* After all, it is unlikely that you will need all the money in your 401(k) plan at once just because you turned 59½ or 70½ or some age in between or because you fully or partially retired. More likely, you will just want to take some money from your plan in regular installments on which to live (or to supplement whatever other funds you might have), while allowing the rest of the money in your plan to continue to grow on a tax-deferred basis until such time as you might really need it. And even if you transfer your 401(k) assets into a rollover IRA, as discussed above, you still could do the same thing, i.e., receive installment distributions from the rollover IRA over a period of years, permitting the bulk of your assets to continue to compound on a tax-deferred basis.

There are two different ways in which you might arrange to receive distributions from your 401(k) plan (or IRA rollover account):

1. The Term Certain Method

Under this method, the value of the assets in your 401(k) plan at the time you begin taking your money out would be divided by your life expectancy (or the combined life expectancy of you and your spouse or other designated beneficiary) in order to calculate your required minimum distribution benefit. (Note, however, that if your designated beneficiary were someone *other* than your spouse and that beneficiary were more than 10 years younger than you, your required minimum distribution benefit would have to be calculated as if that beneficiary were in fact exactly 10 years younger than you were.)

In the first year, you would receive a distribution from the plan equivalent to that required minimum distribution benefit. For example, if you began taking money out of your plan at age 70 (when your wife was 67), you and she would have a joint life expectancy of 22 years. That means that if the value of the assets in your plan were, for example, $1 million, you would receive a distribution of $45,454 in the first year (or ½₂ of $1 million).

That would leave you with $954,546 in your plan so if the plan appreciated by, say, seven percent in the next year, its value a year later, when it came time for you to receive your next distribution, would be $1,021,364. Then you'd have to take out ½₁ of that amount (or $48,636), leaving you with $972,728. And if the plan appreciated by seven percent in the following year, it would then be worth $1,040,819, at which time you'd have to take out ½₀ of the balance or $52,041. And so on over the next 20 years.

If either you or your wife were to die before the end of the original 22 years period, however, payments to the survivor would continue at the same rate until the funds were exhausted at the end of the full 22 years. And if both you and your spouse died before all the funds were paid out (say, in the fifth year), the money remaining would be paid to your estate over whatever number of years remained (in this instance, 17 years), allowing the assets in your plan to continue to grow on a tax-deferred basis for the benefit of your beneficiaries.

2. The Recalculation Method

Alternatively, you could recalculate your life expectancy (or the combined life expectancies of you and your spouse) annually and receive distributions based on those recalculations. To use the example above (a $1 million plan, a 70-year-old plan participant, and a 67-year-old spouse), the first year's payment would be the same $45,454 under the recalculation method as under the term certain method, that is, ½ of their combined life expectancies of 22 years. A year later, however, the combined life expectancies of the two would be 21.2, not 21 years, since life expectancies decline annually by less than a full year, so the minimum amount that they could withdraw would be $48,177 rather than $48,636. And that would mean that, assuming the same seven percent growth rate, there would be $1,041,309 in the plan at the end of the second year rather than $1,040,819.

The major benefit of using the recalculation method, rather than the term certain method, is that smaller amounts would be distributed in the early years. Thus, payments would be stretched out over a longer period in the event that one or both spouses were to live considerably longer than expected. But there are two big problems in using the recalculation method too.

First, when one spouse dies, the life expectancy of the surviving spouse alone becomes the basis on which future distributions are determined, resulting in a sudden big increase in the annual amount that must be withdrawn. And second, when the surviving spouse also dies, all of the assets remaining in the plan go to the estate and are immediately taxable in their entirety.

For these reasons, the term certain method is generally considered preferable to the recalculation method and is probably the method for you to select when the time comes for you to make that decision. But be sure to discuss this with your accountant or tax adviser before making your final decision.

Moreover, when the time for you to make this decision does come, it is imperative that you actually *do* make a decision, informing your plan's administrator in writing before your distributions begin as to just what you want him to do: to transfer your funds to a rollover IRA through a direct trustee-to-trustee transfer; to send you a check representing a single lump sum distribution; to send you minimum distributions calculated on the basis of the term certain method; or to provide you with minimum distributions based on the recalculation method. The reason it is so important that you inform the plan administrator of your choice is that, in the absence of any such instructions from you, he will automatically use the recalculation method when he begins sending checks to you prior to April 1 of the year in which you turn 70½.

It is also imperative that when you reach the age of 70½, you at least *begin* to take minimum distributions from your 401(k) plan, whether calculated by the term certain or the recalculation method. And it is necessary that you do that even if you still are employed and do not really require the additional income. For under the law, if you don't, you'll be hit with a truly confiscatory tax of 50 percent on the minimum amounts that legally *should* have been distributed.

You also should attempt to avoid withdrawing any more than $150,000 in any one year. That is because amounts withdrawn in excess of $150,000 in a single year are subject to an additional tax of 15 percent.

The Ultimate Disposition of Your 401(k) Account

Finally, if there's anything left in your plan when you (or both you and your spouse) die, what will happen to it? When you die, or when your surviving spouse dies, whatever is left in your 401(k) plan will become part of your estate to be left to your beneficiaries. But how they will receive and be taxed on that portion of their inheritance will depend on the manner in which you had been receiving your own distributions all along.

If you took all the funds out of your plan at once and paid taxes on them at that time (whether as ordinary income or capital gains and whether or not you availed yourself of the tax law's income averaging provisions), any funds that might be left when you die would simply be a part of your overall estate and would be subject to the same estate tax provisions as those that would be in effect at the time and applicable to the rest of your estate. If you transferred the assets in your 401(k) plan to a rollover IRA, anything left in the IRA upon your death also would immediately become part of your estate. Similarly, if you had been receiving distributions from a 401(k) plan under the recalculation method, when you or your surviving spouse die, anything remaining in that plan would be immediately taxable as part of your estate.

On the other hand, if you had been receiving distributions from a 401(k) plan under the term certain method, anything remaining in the plan upon your death (or upon the death of your surviving spouse) would be paid to your estate over whatever number of years remained under this calculation method. That would allow the remaining assets in your 401(k) plan to continue to grow on a tax-deferred basis, even after your death, for the benefit of your beneficiaries.

If you had not yet begun receiving distributions from your plan at the time of your death, however, your beneficiaries could receive distributions from your plan in one of the following three ways:

1. They could accept a lump sum distribution of the entire amount that would immediately be taxable when received and, in all likelihood, would move them up into a higher tax bracket.

2. They could make withdrawals over a period of five years, which could reduce their immediate tax liability.

3. They could make minimum withdrawals based on their own life expectancies, which could reduce their tax liability even further and allow the funds they inherit to continue to compound in value on a tax-deferred basis for many additional years.

The method to be employed would depend not only on your beneficiaries' preferences but also on the terms of your plan and the law. Your plan may have specified which method would apply to distributions in which case, that would be it. Or your plan might have permitted you or your beneficiaries to elect the method of distribution, in which case the choice would be yours (or theirs).

If your plan did not specify the method of distribution, however, or if no election were made, the law provides that distributions would have to be made over a period of five years, unless the beneficiary were your spouse. If the beneficiary were your spouse, distributions would be made over the period of his or her own life expectancy.

Because of the complexity of the beneficiary distribution rules, it generally will be in your interest (and in the interest of your desired beneficiary) for you to be sure to specify who you want that beneficiary to be and the method of distribution (if your plan permits that). Moreover, it would be advisable for you to review your designation of a plan beneficiary from time to time in order to be sure that the beneficiary whom you originally designated is still the individual whom you desire to inherit the assets in your 401(k) plan. Divorce, remarriage, the death of a spouse, or the birth or death of siblings, children, or grandchildren could justify your changing your beneficiary at some time after you originally enrolled in your plan.

You also should at least consider the desirability of naming a very young individual, for example, a grandchild, rather than a spouse or sibling, as the beneficiary of your 401(k) plan in order to capitalize on the rule that would permit that beneficiary, under certain circumstances, to receive distributions over a period of time equivalent to his own life expectancy. By naming a child, therefore, rather than an adult, you would be providing for the bulk of the assets in your 401(k) plan to continue to compound in value on a tax-free basis over a considerably longer number of years.

Whether or not this would make sense for you, however, would depend on your own financial position and the availability of other assets to provide for your spouse or other dependents. And in making that determination, the wisest thing for you to do probably should be to consult a personal financial adviser who can assist you on the very complex issue of beneficiary distributions within the light of your own circumstances.

Because of the complexity of the subject and the importance of the tax and financial implications, we strongly recommend that you obtain professional estate planning advice before you finalize your decisions.

Your 401(k) Plan:
A Summary

This summary is intended to offer you a quick overview of the important aspects of investing in a 401(k) plan.

Why Is It Important to Plan
Now for My Retirement?

The cost of living probably will be higher when you retire than it is today, by an amount dependent upon the number of years until your retirement and the rate of inflation during those years. A primary goal in investing for retirement is to accumulate sufficient assets so that you can maintain your standard of living after you stop working even in the face of an increase in the cost of living. The earlier you start a retirement plan, the more dramatically your assets can grow in value through the power of compounding (see Table 3–1).

What Retirement Plans Are
Available to Me?

This book is primarily about 401(k) plans, but there are a number of other types of tax-advantaged retirement plans of which to be aware. If you're eligible, you can establish one or more of these funds to supplement future retirement income from Social Security, pension funds, and other sources. SEP IRAs and Keoghs are plans available only to the self-employed and to employees of relatively small companies. Generally speaking, all of these types of plans offer expanded benefits compared with a regular IRA.

What's So Great About a 401(k)?

A 401(k) plan is tax-advantaged in two ways. First, your contributions to a 401(k) come out of your wages on a pretax basis [unlike IRA contributions, which under current tax law are deductible only by those with income below certain levels and/or those not covered by a pension or 401(k)]. In addition, any investment gains in your 401(k) account will accrue on a tax-deferred basis (this is also true for IRAs). In short, you pay no taxes until you make a withdrawal. These tax advantages may enable you to build a much larger nest egg than you could with a taxable retirement plan (see Table 4-1).

A 401(k) is a *defined-contribution* plan, as opposed to a *defined-benefit* plan. In other words, contributions are made within certain parameters, but there is no upside limit to the potential value of your eventual 401(k) withdrawals. Of course, this means that there is no downside limit either.

In contrast, most pension plans are typically defined-benefit plans, meaning that payments from such plans to their beneficiaries are set at predetermined levels, whereas contributions into such plans are not. The bottom line is this: The "nominal" value of the payments which you will receive is much more assured in a defined-benefit plan than in a defined-contribution plan. But the "real" value—i.e., the value adjusted for inflation—is much more certain in a defined-contribution plan than in a defined-benefit plan.

How Does "Matching" Work?

Matching is another attractive feature of many 401(k) plans. If your plan offers matching, your employer will make contributions to your 401(k). In some cases, an employer offers to match an employee's 401(k) contributions by 100 percent—doubling the amount of money going into the employee's 401(k) for a given period. Most plans, however, offer lower matching.

Often, matching programs are tied into vesting schedules designed to encourage employees to stay with the company. If you leave the company before you are fully vested, you will forfeit some or all of the contributions the company has made to your 401(k). Under current law, employees (other than those covered by multiemployer plans under collective bargaining agreements) must become fully vested in their 401(k) plans by the time they've been with the company for seven years (with gradual increases in vesting along the way) or after a maximum of five years of employment (if there is no partial vesting before that).

How Much Can I Invest?

The Internal Revenue Service sets a dollar limit on annual 401(k) contributions per employee. This ceiling is adjusted upward every year based on cost of living increases. For 1994, the maximum annual 401(k) contribution you could make was $9240. (By comparison, IRA contributions are presently limited to $2000 per year, or $2250 if a spousal IRA is included, and these amounts are not adjusted annually.) In 1994, the IRS limit on your total contributions to defined-contribution plans (including employer and employee contributions to 401(k)s) was the lesser of $30,000, or 20 percent of your gross income before retirement plan contributions. Other legal limits on contributions are designed to prevent companies from giving a substantially greater percentage of benefits to higher-paid workers than to lower-paid workers.

In addition, companies themselves can establish maximum contribution levels (as long as they do not exceed the legal limits). Your company will tell you what percentage of your gross income can be deducted from your paycheck and contributed to your 401(k) plan.

How Much Should I Invest?

If your current financial situation permits it, you should contribute the maximum amount allowed by your company's plan. The cardinal rules of investing for your future retirement are to start as early as possible and to invest as much as possible each year. This maximizes the impact of the "magic of compounding."

How Should I Invest the Assets in My 401(k)?

You can choose how to distribute your assets among the different investment alternatives offered by your company's 401(k) plan. Generally speaking, your choices will fall within two primary categories: equities (stocks) and fixed-income securities (government bonds, corporate bonds, and other fixed-rate investments). Over the short term, the risk of price fluctuations is generally higher with stocks. Over long-term periods, however, equity investments have historically outperformed fixed-income investments—and by a significant amount. (See Figure 4-2.)

Therefore, you would be wise to emphasize equity holdings in your 401(k) plan if you are still a long way from retirement. In such situations, there still would be plenty of time for you to recoup any interim losses.

As you move closer to retirement, you may want to reduce your exposure to equities and increase the portion of your assets that is allocated to fixed-income alternatives. Even when you're near retirement, however, you should retain some high-quality equity investments to hedge against inflation, but at this phase your top priority should be to protect your principal. This is known as the life-cycle approach to investing.

In addition to your time horizon, you should also keep in mind any personal circumstances (marital status, dependents, job security, etc.) that would influence your investment decisions. You should also periodically review your financial situation over the course of your life—particularly at times of such major events as marriage, purchase of a home, birth of a child, your children's education, a death in the family, and retirement—and make appropriate changes in your asset allocations.

It is important, however, not to make too frequent changes in your holdings based on your assessment of the outlook for your investment alternatives. You are more likely to achieve investment success by taking a long-term view, rather than trying to play short-term swings in the markets.

Appropriate asset allocation levels are different for each individual. Chapters 10 and 11 illustrate the development of life-cycle asset allocation models for a few hypothetical investors with varying personal profiles. Although your situation is unlikely to match any of these exactly, these examples should help you in understanding the life-cycle process of asset allocation and in developing asset allocation models most suitable for yourself.

How Much Risk Is Right for Me?

In personalizing your 401(k) portfolio, you should also consider your tolerance for risk. There are a number of kinds of risk in the investment world. Business or credit risk is the risk that the company (or government entity) in which you are investing may run into trouble, in the worst extreme leading it to default on its fixed-income securities and/or the rendering of its equity securities worthless. You must also contend with market risk (gyrations in the financial markets), liquidity risk (the ease with which assets can be bought or sold on relatively short notice), and reinvestment rate risk (the possibility that the returns available in the market when your fixed-income securities reach maturity and the money must be reinvested may be lower than those you're presently receiving).

Generally, the higher the potential rewards you seek, the greater the risk you will have to assume. But while some investors thrive on aggressive investment strategies, others lose sleep. The short quiz we offer in Chapter 9 might help you determine your comfort zone. When making asset allocation decisions regarding your 401(k), be sure to take into consideration your own psychological threshold for risk.

How Can I Guard Against Risk?

Whatever your overall investment strategy, diversification is one of your strongest weapons against risk. Basically, the idea is to avoid putting all your eggs into one basket. In your 401(k) plan you can diversify holdings among asset classes, within asset classes, and over time.

Diversification among asset classes could lessen your exposure to certain types of market risk. Although you should give top billing to equities in your younger years, some diversification among asset classes could lessen your exposure to a decline in the stock market.

Diversification within asset classes lessens your exposure to the business risk or credit risk associated with a particular company or security. Most 401(k) plans automatically offer you this feature, by letting you invest in professionally run mutual or commingled funds, whereby you would own a portion of a broadly diversified portfolio. These funds own a large group of stocks and/or fixed-income securities, so their overall performance will be less affected by a loss in any one particular security.

Among your equity alternatives, you may have a chance to buy stock in your own company, but, for diversification reasons, you probably should not invest much if anything at all in your own company's stock. There is one exception to this prudent rule: In some cases, your employer might offer matching only on this option, and not on any of your other 401(k) investment choices. If that's the case, purchasing company shares might make some sense.

Finally, because you are making regular contributions of a fixed dollar amount over time, your 401(k) plan allows you to "diversify" over time. This concept is known as dollar-cost averaging. In simple terms, when mutual fund or company stock prices per share are high, you'll get fewer shares for your contribution dollars; when prices per share are low, you'll get a greater number of shares for that same dollar amount. Thus, since more shares are purchased when prices are lower, this approach automatically will lower your average cost per share over time.

What If I Need to Take Money Out of My 401(k) Plan?

The rules governing distributions are complicated. This summary will cover just the basics, so please see Chapters 2 and 12 of the text for further details. Considering the changeable and complex nature of the tax laws, it's also advisable for you to get help from a tax expert when planning for your 401(k) distributions.

Having said all that, under most circumstances, it's best to avoid taking any money out of your 401(k) plan before retirement. One obvious reason is that lump-sum withdrawals made prior to the age of 59½ are subject not only to ordinary income taxes, but also to a 10 percent penalty tax. This is true even if you make a lump-sum "hardship" withdrawal before that age to cover necessary housing, medical, or education costs. Under current tax law, the only exception to this is if you are employed at age 55 but subsequently leave your job for any reason at age 55 or older. Under these conditions, you could take all the money in your 401(k) plan and the 10 percent penalty tax would not apply.

The only other way you could take early distributions from your 401(k) plan without having to pay a tax penalty would be to "annuitize" rather than make a lump-sum withdrawal. You can use this method at any age to receive substantially equal annual payments from the plan based on your life expectancy (as discussed further below) or on certain other annuity schedules. The amounts you would receive would be relatively small, however, and you would be depleting the assets in your plan and undermining the power of compounding. Our advice, then, is to leave your retirement accounts alone for as long as you can possibly afford to do so.

How About Loans?

If you feel you must gain access to your funds before retirement for some worthwhile purpose, the best approach might be to take out a loan on your 401(k). Under certain circumstances, you can borrow as much as 50 percent of your vested interest in the plan, up to a maximum of $50,000. No taxes would be withheld when you borrowed, and no income tax or penalty tax would be applied. In addition, the loan would likely bear a competitive or perhaps even a below-market interest rate. In effect, you would be making interest payments to yourself, and these payments would accrue in your 401(k) account with taxes deferred until withdrawal.

Be forewarned, however, that a 401(k) loan made for any purpose other than the purchase of a primary residence must be repaid within five years. Otherwise, the loan would be treated as a taxable distribution, subject to income taxes and the 10 percent penalty. In addition, should you leave your job before the five years are up, the loan might be repayable immediately in its entirety. If you were unable to repay the loan, the early withdrawal taxes and penalties would apply.

What's a Rollover?

If you change jobs, you might have the option of leaving your 401(k) with your prior employer. You might also have the option of rolling it over into another 401(k) plan, if your new employer has one. Whether or not these options exist, you can roll your 401(k) into an IRA account. Even if you already have an IRA, it's preferable to establish a new "conduit IRA" specifically for the rollover in order to maintain your eligibility for possible preferential tax treatment after retirement. In addition, you can move your 401(k) to a rollover IRA when you retire. Your employer may require you to take your 401(k) at this time, or you may simply want more flexibility in running your investments.

Be sure to arrange a trustee-to-trustee transfer of the assets directly into the new 401(k) or IRA account. If you take possession of the funds yourself, even temporarily, the 20 percent withholding tax and premature withdrawal penalty (if applicable) will be imposed automatically. If handled properly, however, a rollover occurs with no adverse tax consequences to you. The assets in your fund will retain their full tax-deferred status.

When Will I Begin Receiving Distributions?

At the age of $59\frac{1}{2}$, whether you are retired from work or not, you become eligible to begin taking distributions from your 401(k) plan without incurring any tax penalty, although distributions would be subject to income taxes. If you are still working, you will pay taxes on these distributions at your ordinary tax rate. Distributions made upon retirement, however, may be eligible for advantageous tax treatment, including possible five- or ten-year forward income averaging and/or partial capital gains treatment.

Therefore, if you are still working, you should postpone taking distributions, and continue to make contributions as long as possible. But be aware that you can postpone distributions only until the age of $70\frac{1}{2}$. If you don't begin receiving distributions at age 70½, you'll pay a 50 percent penalty tax on the amount that should have been distributed to you. Another tax consideration to be aware of is that amounts withdrawn in excess of $150,000 in a single year are subject to an additional tax of 15 percent. For most people, instead of taking a lump-sum distribution at retirement, it makes sense to accept smaller annual distributions over a period of years.

How Will My Annual Distributions Be Calculated?

Minimum required distributions from your 401(k) or rollover IRA are based on your life expectancy (or the combined life expectancies of you and your spouse or other beneficiary) which, in turn, is determined by your age(s) at the time distributions begin. They can be calculated in one of two ways. Under the Term Certain method, the assets in your 401(k) are divided by the number of years of your life expectancy or the joint life expectancy of you and your spouse (or other beneficiary). Each year the original calculation of life expectancy is reduced by one year, and the new value of assets is divided by that amount. Asset distributions would continue to be calculated this way after the deaths of you (or you and your spouse), which is generally an advantageous feature for estate planning purposes.

Under the Recalculation Method, life expectancy is recalculated each year, which has the effect of decreasing the size of distributions in the early years. Under this method, however, when one spouse dies, the life expectancy of the surviving spouse alone becomes the basis for calculation, which may result in a sudden big increase in annual distributions. Moreover, when both spouses die, all assets go immediately to the estate and are immediately taxable in their entirety. For these reasons, the Term Certain method is usually preferable to the Recalculation Method. But be sure to discuss this complex issue with a professional tax adviser before making your decision.

Glossary

Accrued Benefit: A benefit that an employee has earned through participation in a retirement plan. In a 401(k) plan, this is the value of the participant's account at a given time. The participant may not have an absolute nonforfeitable right to this benefit, however. (See **Vested Benefit**.)

Active Management: Investment management with the goal of selecting specific securities from a given universe in an attempt to outperform the average of that universe. (See **Passive Management**.)

Agencies: See **Government Securities**.

Asset Allocation: The apportionment of funds in a 401(k) plan or other investment portfolio among different asset classes, for example, 25 percent in common stock funds, 35 percent in long-term bond funds, 25 percent in GICs, and 15 percent in money-market instruments.

Asset Classes: Classifications of investments that make up a portfolio, most commonly stocks, bonds, and short-term reserves.

Business Risk: The chance that a company in which you invested (whether by purchasing its stocks or its bonds) will fare poorly, lose competitive position, or even go bankrupt, causing you to lose some or even all of your original investment.

Capital Gain (Loss): An increase (decrease) in the market or principal value of a fund's securities. Among mutual funds this is reflected in the net asset value of its shares. Among individual stocks, such as IBM, this is reflected in the value of its stock.

Cash Equivalents: See **Money-Market Instruments**.

Cash Or Deferred Arrangement: See **CODA**.

CODA: Acronym for Cash Or Deferred Arrangement means that an eligible employee has the right to decide whether he wants his employer to contribute a specific amount to a retirement plan on his behalf or to pay him an equivalent amount in cash.

Commingled Account: An account in which the investment funds of individual investors are pooled, with each investor owning a share of the account proportionate to his or her contribution. A mutual fund is one type of commingled account.

Common Stocks (or Equities): Shares in a company evidencing proportional ownership of that corporation.

Conduit (or Rollover) IRA: An individual retirement account established to accept a rollover from a qualified retirement plan. Funds in a conduit IRA subsequently may be rolled into another qualified retirement plan.

Credit Rating: Several rating agencies, including Standard & Poor's, Moody's Investors Service, and Fitch Investors Service evaluate the investment or credit risk of specific fixed income securities, assigning ratings to those issues reflecting their own opinions of the creditworthiness of corporate obligors with respect to their specific obligation. In the case of Standard & Poor's, these assessments are based on a number of considerations including: (1) the likelihood of default as evidenced by the capacity and willingness of the obligor to make timely payment of interest and principal in accordance with the terms of the obligation; (2) the nature and provisions of the obligation; and (3) the protection afforded by and relative position of the obligation in the event of bankruptcy, reorganization, or other arrangement under the laws of bankruptcy and other laws affecting creditors' rights. Based on these considerations, Standard & Poor's rates corporate debt issues from AAA to C.

Credit Risk: The chance that the company in which you invested might default on its obligations to pay interest and repay principal when due.

Currency Risk: The chance that foreign securities, denominated in foreign currencies, could decline in value in terms of U.S. dollars if the dollar should rise in value against those other currencies.

Defined Benefit Plan: Traditional retirement plan that promises an employee-participant specific fixed future benefits determined according to a formula that usually depends on the employee's earnings, years of employment by the company, or both. Contributions are not preestablished since the amounts that will have to be contributed will vary depending on the returns realized on investments. Risk is borne by employers, not employees: if investment returns are too low to fund the payment of predetermined benefits, employers have to ante up the difference through higher plan contributions.

Defined Contribution Plan: A retirement plan in which the amount of contributions, but not of benefits, is preestablished, with the ultimate amount of benefits depending on both the amounts contributed and the rate of return realized on the plan's assets. To that extent, the risk of a defined contribution benefit plan is borne by the employee, not the employer: if investment returns are poor, or too little has been contributed, the employee's ultimate benefits will be low, and the employee will have no recourse to his or her employer who, in turn, will have no obligation to supplement those benefits. Includes 401(k) plans, 403(b)s, Keoghs, and SEPs.

Diversification: A strategy for spreading assets among many different securities to reduce the risks inherent in investing in only one or a small number of securities.

Efficient Market: A market in which all information that could affect the price of a security is, in fact, known by all market participants simultaneously, and any new information that could bear upon the value of a security is instantaneously disseminated to all, with the result that market prices always reflect determinable values.

Elective Contributions: Voluntary employee contributions to a 401(k) plan generated from deferred pretax income.

Equities: See **Common Stocks**.

Financial Planning: (1) The consideration and evaluation of the financial consequences of alternative economic choices and the rearrangement of your financial affairs in light of those considerations. (2) The design of an investment program for the purpose of achieving one or more specific financial goals, such as the creation of a college fund for children or grandchildren, the purchase of a home, or the establishment of a retirement nest egg.

Foreign (or International) Fund: A mutual fund that invests *only* in foreign securities (differs from a global fund which invests *both* in U.S. and foreign securities).

Forfeitable Benefits: In a 401(k) plan, an employer's matching contributions may be subject to a vesting schedule, in which case a plan participant might forfeit some or all of those matching grants if he were to leave his job within less than 10 years. (See **Nonforfeitable Benefits**.)

401(k) Plan: A cash or deferred arrangement (see **CODA**), named after the section of the Internal Revenue Service Code that authorized it, whereby a covered employee may elect to defer income by making pretax contributions to a qualified defined contribution retirement plan.

403(b) Plan: A qualified defined contribution retirement plan, named after the section of the Internal Revenue Service Code that authorized it, which is similar to a 401(k) plan but is available only to employees of schools, churches, and certain other tax-exempt organizations.

Fundamental Analysis: The analysis of corporations' economic and financial conditions, including their earning power, asset values, competitive positions, and managements in order to form reasoned judgments regarding the relative investment attraction of those companies' securities.

GIC: See **Guaranteed Investment (or Income) Contract**.

Global Fund: A mutual fund that invests *both* in U.S. and foreign securities (differs from a foreign fund or international fund which invests *only* in foreign securities).

Government Obligations (or Treasuries): U.S. government debt instruments, including treasury bonds, bills, notes, and savings bonds that the Government has pledged to repay. These are the safest, most risk-free, and most creditworthy of all fixed income securities since they are backed by the full faith and credit of the U.S. government which, if necessary, could always simply print money to pay principal and interest.

Government Securities (or Agencies): The debt issues of federal agencies, such as Federal National Mortgage Association, Student Loan Marketing Association, Resolution Funding Corporation, and the Federal Land Banks which are *not* backed by the full faith and credit of the U.S. government (although most people believe that the government still would always recognize a moral, even if not legal, obligation not to allow agencies to default).

Growth Stock Investing: An approach to equity investing that entails investing in the stocks of companies that are growing much faster that the overall economy (in terms of revenues, earnings, and potential dividends), with less regard to the prices initially paid for those stocks. The growth stock investor's rationale is that, in the long run, it won't matter how much he initially paid for those stocks—if they continue to grow as he expects—since, even if they were initially statistically overvalued, their future earnings growth would bail him out.

Guaranteed Investment (or Income) Contract (GIC): A contract between an insurance company and a corporate profit sharing or pension plan (such as a 401(k) plan) whereby the plan invests a sum of money with the insurance company for a specified period of time and the insurance company, in turn, pays interest on the loan at a fixed rate over the life of the contract.

Hardship Withdrawal: A premature in-service withdrawal from a 401(k) plan predicated upon a plan participant's immediate and heavy financial need that may only be satisfied by means of the withdrawal.

High-Yield Bond Fund: A mutual fund that invests in high yield bonds. Also known as a Junk Bond Fund. (See **Yield.**)

High-Yield Bonds: See **Junk Bonds**.

Highly Compensated Employees: The law limits the extent to which the percentage of elective contributions to a 401(k) plan made on behalf of highly compensated employees may exceed the percentage of elective contributions made on behalf of nonhighly compensated employees. For this purpose, highly compensated was defined in 1994 as those earning $66,000 or more annually and nonhighly compensated as those earning less than $66,000. The amount will be higher in future years since it is indexed to the inflation rate.

Index Fund: A mutual fund or other portfolio that is passively managed in an attempt at replicating the performance results of a preselected securities index. (See **Active Management** and **Passive Management**.)

Individual Retirement Account (IRA): A personal tax-deferred retirement plan that may be established by anyone under the age of 70½ who receives compensation, or by anyone, of whatever age, seeking to defer taxes by rolling over eligible distributions from a qualified retirement plan.

Inflation (or Purchasing Power) Risk: The chance that the overall price level will rise so steeply over time that, even if your investments appreciate in nominal terms, they may not appreciate in real terms, i.e., the funds you receive upon selling an investment will have less real purchasing power than the funds you originally invested, even though the nominal amount may be the same or greater.

Interest: The cost of borrowing money, usually expressed as a rate per year, in which instance it is referred to as an annual interest rate.

International Fund: See **Foreign Fund**.

Investment Grade: Bonds whose credit quality, and ability to pay interest and principal, as determined by Standard & Poor's, range from AAA to BBB–.

Investment Letter Stock: See **Restricted Stock**.

IRA: See **Individual Retirement Account**.

Junk Bond Fund: A mutual fund that invests in junk bonds. Also known as a High-Yield Bond Fund.

Junk Bonds: High-yield bonds issued by companies without long records of sales and earnings or by companies of questionable creditworthiness and rated below BBB– by Standard & Poor's. A popular means of financing takeovers and leveraged buyouts.

Keogh Plan: A qualified retirement plan maintained for the benefit of employees of unincorporated businesses or for self-employed individuals. (See **Qualified Plan**.)

Letter Stock: See **Restricted Stock**.

Life-Cycle Investing: The modification of an individual's investment portfolio over time to reflect his changing circumstances. In short, the younger an investor is, the more working years remaining in his career, and the fewer his responsibilities to others than himself, the greater the investment risk that he should assume; conversely, the older he is, the fewer the number of working years remaining to him, and the greater his responsibilities to others than himself, the less the investment risk he ought assume.

Lump Sum Distribution: Distribution from a 401(k) plan that includes the entire balance credited to an employee's account and that is made on account of the employee's death, separation from service, disability, or attainment of age 59½.

Market Risk: The chance that the value of an investment will decline to a level below its current market price.

Matching Grants: Additional employer contributions to a 401(k) plan for the benefit of plan participants, usually proportional to employees' own elective contributions.

Minimum Required Distribution: Minimum distribution from a 401(k) plan or other retirement plan that must be made to a plan participant upon his attaining age 70½.

Money-Market Funds: Mutual funds whose investments are limited to money-market instruments or other securities with average maturities usually measurable in days.

Money-Market Instruments: Commercial paper, certificates of deposit, treasury bills, and other fixed income securities with maturities of less than one year. Also known as Cash Equivalents.

Net Asset Value (NAV): The worth of a mutual fund's assets, including securities, cash and accrued earnings, after deducting liabilities, divided by the number of shares currently outstanding. NAV is expressed as the value of a single share in the fund.

Nonforfeitable Benefits: 401(k) plan benefits that belong to a plan participant in their entirety and that cannot be taken back by his employer under any circumstances. These include elective contributions, after-tax voluntary contributions by an employee, vested employer matching contributions, and the earnings generated by any of those contributions. (See **Forfeitable Benefits**.)

Nonhighly Compensated Employees: See **Highly Compensated Employees**.

Passive Management: Investment management that seeks to structure a diversified portfolio whose return will replicate, or at least approximate, the average return generated by a preselected securities universe. (See **Active Management**.)

Premature Withdrawal: A withdrawal from a 401(k) plan made before attaining the age of 59½.

Price-Earnings Ratio or Price Earnings Multiple (P/E): The price of a share of stock divided by earnings per share. A high ratio may be indicative of an overpriced stock and/or one with superior earnings growth potential; a low multiple may be indicative of an underpriced stock and/or one with below average growth potential.

Principal: The face amount of a fixed income investment. Also the basic amount of an investment, exclusive of earnings.

Purchasing Power Risk: See **Inflation Risk**.

Qualified Plan: A retirement plan that receives special tax treatment because it has met certain requirements of the Internal Revenue Code: in essence, contributions to a qualified plan are tax-deductible by employers when made, but employees may defer paying taxes on those contributions until they actually are received by them in the form of benefits. Earnings on qualified funds also accumulate on a tax-deferred basis.

Real Return: The return on an investment adjusted for inflation.

Recalculation Method: Method for determining the amounts of minimum required annual distributions from a 401(k) plan by recalculating the life expectancies of the plan participant or the participant and his beneficiary annually.

Regional Fund: A mutual fund that invests in the securities of just one country, such as Japan or Germany, or of just one geographical region, such as Southeast Asia, the Pacific Rim, Latin America, or Europe.

Reinvestment Risk: The chance that interest rates may decline, so that funds that become available upon the maturation of high-yield (based on cost) fixed income securities could not be rolled into new bonds at equivalently attractive rates.

Restricted Stock: Stock which is not registered with the SEC so that it cannot be sold in the public market. Also known as Letter Stock or Investment Letter Stock.

Retirement Plan: (1) An overall plan intended to provide for all aspects of one's retirement, including medical care, travel, residence, and budgeting. (2) Any financial plan specifically designed to provide funds to cover expenses in one's retirement years. (3) (Legal) A plan maintained by an employer or employee organization (such as a union) or both that is designed to provide employees with retirement income and that allows employees to defer receipt of income until the end of their employment or even later.

Rollover: A tax-free transfer of assets from one retirement plan to another, such as from one 401(k) plan to another or from a 401(k) plan to an IRA.

Rollover IRA: See **Conduit IRA**.

Sector Rotation: The management of a securities portfolio by overweighting positions first in one industry or economic sector and then in another, in an attempt at capitalizing on fluctuations in the economic cycle.

SEP: See **Simplified Employee Pension Plan**.

Simplified Employee Pension Plan (SEP): An individual retirement account (IRA) established by an employer for an employee.

Socially Responsible Investing: An investment program that considers ethical, political, social, and environmental factors in addition to purely financial concerns.

Speculative Grades: Bonds whose investment grades as determined by Standard & Poor's range from BB+ to C.

Spousal IRA: An individual retirement account established for the non-working spouse of an employee who qualifies for an IRA.

Stand-Alone Plan: A 401(k) plan that only permits elective contributions by employees with no matching grants made by the employer nor additional voluntary after-tax contributions permitted by employees.

Tax-Advantaged: Investments that are either tax-deferred or tax-exempt.

Tax-Deferred: A tax-deferred plan (such as a 401(k), 403(b), IRA, Keogh, or SEP) is one in which any taxes you might owe are postponed until the future. When you earn income from tax-deferred savings or investments, you may postpone taxes on that income until some future date. In addition, any taxes you might otherwise have had to pay on pre-tax contributions to a retirement savings plan and employers' matching grants to that plan also would be deferred to the future.

Tax-Exempt: Since exempt means excuse, if income is tax-exempt, you are excused from paying taxes on it forever. In other words, that income would be tax-free (which means the same thing as tax-exempt). Depending on its source (usually municipal bonds or U.S. treasury obligations), tax-exempt income might only be exempt from federal taxes; or it might just be exempt from state and local taxes; or it might be exempt from federal, state, and local taxes.

Tax-Free: See **Tax-Exempt**.

Technical Analysis: The analysis of individual securities or entire securities markets on the basis of historic price patterns and volume statistics on the assumption that such historic data could be indicative of future price trends. (See **Fundamental Analysis**.)

Term Certain Method: Method for determining the amounts of minimum required annual distributions from a 401(k) plan by calculating the life expectancies of the plan participant or the participant and his beneficiary when distributions first begin and basing all future distributions on that initial determination.

Total Return: Dividends, interest, or other income received from an investment plus or minus capital appreciation or depreciation.

Treasury Bills: Short-term U.S. government debt securities with maturities of less than one year.

Treasury Bonds: Long-term U.S. government debt instruments with maturities of 10 years or longer.

Treasury Notes: Intermediate-term U.S. government debt instruments with maturities of one to 10 years.

Treasury Securities: See **Government Obligations**.

Value Investing: The basic beliefs underlying value investing are (1) that every stock has an intrinsic value, relating to the worth of a company's assets, cash flow, earning power, and dividend-paying ability; (2) that over time, a stock's price will gravitate around that intrinsic value; (3) that sometimes a stock may become temporarily undervalued in the marketplace and at other times temporarily overvalued relative to that intrinsic value; and that (4) a value investor can profit by discovering stocks that are temporarily undervalued and investing in them, retaining his positions until their intrinsic values are again recognized in the marketplace. Specifically, value investors look for stocks trading at prices substantially below their former highs; at low multiples of earnings; at low multiples of cash flow; at discounts from book values; below the replacement values of their plant and equipment; below the in-ground values of their natural resources; below the market values of their real estate; and/or on high-dividend yield bases.

Vested Benefit: All elective contributions to a 401(k) plan as well as the accrued benefit in a retirement plan that has become nonforfeitable under the plan's vesting schedule.

Yield: The return on an investment. Annual dividend per share of stock divided by the price of the stock. Annual interest paid on a bond divided by the price of the bond.

Further Reading

Stock Investing

Dunnan, Nancy: *Dun & Bradstreet Guide to Your Investments,* HarperCollins, 1994.
Engel, Louis, and Henry R. Hecht: *How to Buy Stocks,* Little, Brown, 1994.
Graham, Benjamin: *The Intelligent Investor,* HarperCollins, 1986.
Little, Jeffrey B., and Lucien Rhodes: *Understanding Wall Street,* McGraw-Hill, 1991.
Lynch, Peter: *One Up on Wall Street,* Viking Penguin, 1990.
Miller, Alan J.: *Socially Responsible Investing,* New York Institute of Finance/Simon & Schuster, 1991.

Bond Investing

Thau, Annette: *The Bond Book,* Probus, 1992.
Thomsett, Michael: *Getting Started in Bonds,* Wiley, 1991.

Mutual Funds

Bogle, John C.: *Bogle on Mutual Funds,* Dell, 1994.
Laderman, Jeffrey M.: *Business Week's Guide to Mutual Funds,* McGraw-Hill, 1994.
Vujovich, Dian: *Straight Talk About Mutual Funds,* McGraw-Hill, 1992.

Financial Planning/ Retirement Planning

Hallman, G. Victor, and Jerry S. Rosenbloom: *Personal Financial Planning,* McGraw-Hill, 1993.
Kehrer, Daniel: *Kiplinger's 12 Steps to a Worry-Free Retirement,* Kiplinger Books, 1993.
Lerner, Joel: *Financial Planning for the Utterly Confused,* McGraw-Hill, 1994.
Quinn, Jane Bryant: *Making the Most of Your Money,* Simon & Schuster, 1991.

Index

About the Author

Alan J. Miller has had 30 years experience at several leading New York Stock Exchange firms, including positions as Research Director, Chief Investment Strategist, and Director of Investment Management. In addition, he has served as President and Portfolio Manager of two mutual funds, Managing Editor of a national investment advisory service, and Head of the Pension Plan Investment Advisory Division of a nation-wide actuarial firm. He has taught financial courses at Columbia University Graduate School of Business, Adelphi University College, and the New York Institute of Finance. He is the author of *Socially Responsible Investing: How to Invest With Your Conscience.* A Chartered Financial Analyst, he recently returned from a consulting assignment in Jakarta, Indonesia, jointly sponsored by the Indonesian Ministry of Finance and the Jakarta Stock Exchange.